Information First

Information First

Integrating Knowledge and Information Architecture for Business Advantage

Roger Evernden and Elaine Evernden

ELSEVIER
BUTTERWORTH
HEINEMANN

AMSTERDAM   BOSTON   HEIDELBERG   LONDON   NEW YORK   OXFORD
PARIS   SAN DIEGO   SAN FRANCISCO   SINGAPORE   SYDNEY   TOKYO

Elsevier Butterworth-Heinemann
Linacre House, Jordan Hill, Oxford OX2 8DP
200 Wheeler Road, Burlington MA 01803

First published 2003

British Library Cataloguing in Publication Data
A catalogue record for this book is available from the British Library

Library of Congress Cataloguing in Publication Data
A catalogue record for this book is available from the Library of Congress

ISBN 0 7506 5858 4

For information on all Butterworth-Heinemann
publications visit our website at www.bh.com

Typeset by Replika Press Pvt Ltd, India
Printed and bound in Great Britain by Biddles Ltd *www.biddles.co.uk*

Contents

Foreword

I think that the most important issue today for organizations of almost any size is the knowledge in the organization and the organization's ability to deal effectively with that knowledge. The message of the importance of knowledge and information has been preached more and more frequently for a couple of decades – but little is actually being accomplished in most cases.

Consider how those who stand above the marketplace have got there and you will find these twins, organizational knowledge and intelligence, as key in most cases. WalMart, for example, is in a business with no unique invention nor patent to account for its growth. Just intelligence at the organizational level.

Information technology has provided the possibility for a quantum leap in organizational intelligence but the design principles for this have not been made explicit or clear enough to be implemented. The Everndens have provided a theory, a framework and examples to help bring this immense field together and, most important, make it operational.

They provide a unique focus on language as a central element in design and operation of an information system. Few before them have observed the key importance of language in an information system.

Meaningful change in the area is not easy. Change of this importance, of this impact, of this potential magnitude on the profitability and viability of an enterprise requires effort and time. The book provides a tool to reduce the pain and effort and increase the speed of results from your efforts in increasing your organizational intelligence.

Mike McMaster

Preface

Information is seriously undervalued and underused as a corporate resource. The pressures of global competition and a growing dependence on information technology mean that the effective use of information is more important now than it has ever been. This book is a fundamental guide for unleashing information potential, by combining the discipline of information architecture with the power of knowledge management, to drive organizational changes.

Most organizations have made huge investments in information technology, but few have yet made a strong commitment to information as a corporate resource. Because of the growth in computing power and the benefits it offers, most organizations have overlooked the need to cultivate and nurture the resource that computers sustain – information. It is as important as the human, financial and physical assets of the industrial age.

Consider this parallel with music. Think of the many factors that allow a great musician to perform, such as talent, command of an instrument, familiarity with the music and creativity. All of these are based on a deep understanding of music – notes, melodies, harmonies, key signatures, scales, and all the other elements that make up musical theory. Like music, information is a medium – you need to understand it in order to use it well. Musical theory has been explored and documented for centuries, and there are plenty of books to help you get started and become a proficient musician, but it is impossible to find a practical guide that shows you how to become proficient in architecting corporate information. This book fills that gap, providing a practical mix of how-to-do-its and explanations.

Ineffective techniques for managing information cost companies millions every day. The information we have is frequently not what we want. The information we want is not always what we need. The information we need may not be available (adapted from Murphy's Laws of Misinformation). The need to structure and manage information has been growing steadily over the last 50 years. *Well-structured information is one of the most powerful tools that an organization has.*

Don't just sit there – do something!

In many organizations today we hear the following comments and complaints regarding the need to see the big picture:

- We make a clear business case for action, but no-one will make the commitment. It's all talk and meetings, there's never any action.
- There are pockets of people working on this everywhere, but no coordination between us. We don't have a clear direction. Investments in infrastructure are quite random.
- Our information systems and processes were and still are designed as standalone silos or stovepipes.
- We simply don't know how much unnecessary duplication exists. We're so big we can't keep track of all the resources that are wasted or go under-utilized.
- Everything is so complex now – a global business using vast quantities of data.
- Technology is developed and implemented without adequate business involvement.

If you can identify with any of these statements, then this book is for you. Working on projects around the world, the people we meet are all trying to address these same six problems with architecting information for organizational change:

- **Inert** – there is insufficient organizational commitment, resulting in serious under-utilization of information and unsuccessful or failed projects.
- **Uncertain** – undefined requirements are making it impossible to show whether information is successfully used or not.
- **Unsystematic** – a dearth of simple, coherent, practical tools and architectural discipline to manage information.
- **Unrealistic** – trying to do too much, too soon, or get in too deep too quickly. The most common examples of this are starting with information technology before there is a good understanding of information and how it is being used, or using detailed blueprints and plans before having a clear high-level map of the whole terrain.
- **Unproductive** – not being sure how to use information once it is available.

- **Out-of-date** – lack of an intelligible feedback process to keep everything up-to-date.

Writing a book is a daunting prospect. When we started planning this book there were so many things that we wanted to say and a vast library of notes, case studies and experiences that we wanted to include. It was difficult to know where to start, or how to proceed. By outlining the contents and preparing a proposal for our editor, our thoughts gradually took shape and became clearer. We worked hard to create the big picture before we did too much work on the details. The process was not a simple flow from high-level plan to the finished volume; there were many drafts, iterations and re-writes along the way. Interestingly, the process is not dissimilar to the one that we describe in this book. There are well-established techniques for planning and writing a book that help an author toggle between the big picture and its achievement. Surprisingly, the equivalent techniques for getting a clear picture of the corporate information resource and making the most effective use of information are not always so obvious.

Each of the comments above reflects a problem in the way in which information is used to effect organizational changes. What is missing is a clear overarching framework or structure that provides the big picture, encourages coordination and collaboration, and helps direct initiatives and change. Just as a writer paints a picture on paper with words and descriptions, the big picture that is missing is one created with information. This information picture affords a better means for sharing information and knowledge, which helps to explain and justify what is required, inform decisions and actions, and use information effectively.

Lack of *the big picture* is probably the most expensive problem facing organizations today.

Organizations try to create a big picture in three ways. One organization puts its faith in information technology, purchasing one solution after another for data mining, data warehousing, customer relationship management, or enterprise integration. Each technology is designed to gain control by making it easier to view and manipulate certain types of information as a whole. A data warehouse might unite all transactional information for analysis as a single unit, while another system unit allows access to all customer information. Another organization recognizes the ability of individuals to grasp and understand organizational complexity through their personal experience and knowledge. Knowledge management programmes foster communities of practice and knowledge networks to build a fuzzy big picture, where the complete organizational portrait is a combination of personal opinions or viewpoints. Curiously, these two approaches for creating the big picture are nearly always seen as opposites, with organizations seeing themselves as technology-based or knowledge-based.

The third way to create a big picture is through a healthy balance of technology and knowledge. The bridge between the two is information architecture. Architecting organizational changes shows how to unleash the energy in combining the discipline of information architecture, with the power of knowledge management, to fashion a nimble and adaptable enterprise. It is a comprehensive approach for managing the complete information spectrum, from the information technology perspective to the knowledge management standpoint, which shows how to increase the synergy between technology and knowledge for business advantage, through information architecture.

Figure 1.1 Seeing the big picture

The resulting toolkit:

- Uses *information* to manage changes
- Effects *changes* to information structures
- Expands *the use of* information and knowledge.

Information is the keystone

Architecting information applies to all types of organizational change. It is essential for tracking and keeping control of large-scale changes, but almost anything you do will be able to use and benefit from this approach. It is not only for people who are changing the whole organization. The techniques work just as well with smaller organizations and minor changes as they do with huge multinationals and mammoth transformations!

Our mission statement

When we started writing the book we wrote a mission statement to explain how the book helps you.

Our mission is to show how:

- To manage organizational change by combining the discipline of architecture with the power of knowledge
- To create a clear picture of an organization and the way it works, by mapping the information and knowledge resource, showing where change is required and providing a plan to achieve it
- To create a more knowledgeable working environment by making processes more intelligent, and providing an informed, efficient customer service
- To streamline decision-making and action-taking by eliminating frustration and confusion, and using information in new and original ways
- To build an effective and dynamic information architecture that is genuinely useful to people from all roles
- To support an information-based culture by maintaining the right infrastructures and constantly improving the use of the information resource.

Information is a key resource for all organizations. As a consequence, this book will help you or your company achieve corporate goals such as reducing costs, improving profits, gaining better customer satisfaction and loyalty, and having happier and more comfortable staff and customers.

Acknowledgements

We are, of course, indebted to the many people who directly or indirectly helped us to write this book. There are many people whose thoughts and discussions have shaped our ideas – to all our family, friends and colleagues who have helped and encouraged us along the way – thank you.

Because of the strategic or proprietary nature of many architecture initiatives, we have not named the specific companies involved in each case study. We would like to make the following acknowledgements: Barclays Bank plc, BP plc, POSC (Petrotechnical Open Software Corporation), IBM Financial Services Solutions Centre and Tesco plc.

Above all others, I could not have written this book without the love and support of my wife, Elaine Evernden. She is passionate about life, but has sacrificed time that she could have spent drawing, painting, cycling, walking and living to help me write, revise and rewrite (many, many times). Words cannot say thank you enough, but without you this book would not exist.

Thanks also to Adrian Campbell, Ian Bowring and Chuck Bowen, and to Dan Day for his graphic designs.

Architecting organizational changes

> We have first raised a dust and then complain we cannot see.
> **Bishop Berkeley**

> Quick fixes don't fix big problems.
> **Ronald Reagan**

> All that is not a true change will disappear.
> **George Sand**

Information architecture is a term that is applied to the structure and organization of information, and it is therefore a key part of managing corporate information. Information architecture embraces a rich tapestry of techniques, drawn from disciplines as diverse as information science, artificial intelligence, linguistics, library management, management theory, knowledge management, programming, information engineering and object-oriented methodologies.

Information architecture is a foundation discipline describing the theory, principles, guidelines, standards, conventions and factors for managing information as a resource. It produces drawings, charts, plans, documents, designs, blueprints and templates, helping everyone make efficient, effective, productive and innovative use of all types of information.

This definition highlights the important characteristics of architecture:

- **Information is a resource**. If it is not treated as an asset, by nurturing it and teaching people how to use it successfully, then it will be under-utilized and wasted.

- **Information architecture helps everyone**. Information as a resource is everyone's responsibility, not just the preserve of technology departments. It provides practical tools, improving efficiency, effectiveness and productivity and supporting organizational strategy, innovation, creativity and flexibility.
- **It applies to all types of information**. Information architecture does not only apply to the design and navigation of websites, nor is it purely for the development of information technology or software. It covers basic skills that are essential for all information users, and it is a universal discipline that applies to the uses of information in general.
- **Architecture is a necessary foundation**, whether we like it or not. It is not optional, but a necessity. The more seriously information is seen as a resource, the more you need to make the architectural foundation explicit. It is especially useful for understanding the more complex information structures found in managing large organizations, running business operations, or developing technology support.
- **It is a discipline**. Architecture is based on theory and ideas, and to become a skilled practitioner requires devotion, experience and training. It takes time and effort to be good at information architecture, just as it takes years of practice to be able to play the piano.

We use the following phrases as general terms throughout this book:

- Information item refers to any piece of information – whether it is small or large, and regardless of how it is stored or presented. A date of birth, a document, or a customer record, are all information items.
- Information structure refers to information that is formally organized or arranged. Information does not have to be stored in a computer system in order to have structure. Information organized in a filing cabinet, data stored in a database, and messages displayed on a telephone screen are all examples of information structures.

Architecting change: why is it important to you and your organization?

In 1988, Gerard Egan opened his book on *Change Agent Skills* by asking 'Would it be useful to have a relatively simple and straightforward shared model, framework, or template that can be used by everyone within your enterprise to assess how things are going, to facilitate their work, and to design new projects?' (Egan, 1988a). He says that when he asked this question of the people who manage corporations, businesses, institutions and agencies they inevitably answer yes.

The most expensive challenge facing modern organizations is the lack of a big picture that shows:

- How to simplify or reduce the complex and costly infrastructure required to run and manage a global corporation.
- How to achieve the enormous potential for economies of scope, scale and experience from architecting information.
- How to take advantage of unique competitive factors created by using information and knowledge.
- How to exploit vast quantities of data, information and knowledge.
- How to maximize use of information technology.

The solution is to architect changes by using information as an instrument of change, and by making the information architecture more flexible and adaptive so that it is better able to handle unforeseen and unpredictable futures. Shared understanding is essential for effective changes. Experiences in change management show that the best way to handle on-going change is through a holistic approach that addresses all of the relevant factors in a cohesive way. Numerous organizations and thinkers have developed comprehensive frameworks for understanding complex organizational issues. Today, the stress and speed of renovation and renewal are such that a shared paradigm for change is more important than it has ever been. Many of these templates for change were pre-defined solutions intended to fit any enterprise – large or small, whether for profit or not. Just as organizations are struggling to maintain a unique identity in a ubiquitous global market and tailoring their products and services to the 'market-of-one', so they are moving away from mass-market frameworks for change towards more customized approaches.

To create a bespoke change framework is straightforward, but requires a bit of thought. Instead of using a pre-defined structure, the organization starts from first principles to create a framework that meets its exact needs. At the core of the bespoke model of change is an information architecture, which offers a holistic tool for managing information about changes. It sounds so simple, but organizations looking for a 'quick' solution are likely to ignore this critical first step by trying to run before they can walk. These organizations purchase or develop technology-based information systems before they fully understand the information needs of its users, or concentrate on knowledge creation without a formal structure for capturing personal knowledge as a corporate information asset. A technology- or knowledge-led organization is missing out on the leverage that comes from using a shared information architecture to control and manage the information resource. The three approaches are quite dissimilar: the technology approach is like expecting to become rich by buying a 'piggy bank'; the knowledge approach is like encouraging individuals to become wealthy by saving their money; and the information architecture approach is like leveraging the money saved in the piggy bank through a sound corporate investment strategy. Invest in both architecture and technology; technology alone cannot provide the optimum return from information. Architecture is the human side of information management, bringing best practice expertise and knowledge.

The shape, function and use of a building are determined by its architecture. In a similar way, information architecture provides simple shared structures that are used by everyone in the organization to investigate and assess how things are going, to improve use of information, and to plan, monitor and implement change programmes and projects. Without this it is difficult to coordinate efforts and fully leverage the use of information.

Architecting change is a holistic, systemic, big picture approach! It is *holistic* in the sense that it covers information about everything, including infrastructure, information, process, knowledge, organization design, skills, and resources. This is an ambitious claim, but it is the information that is united, rather than the things described by the information. Later we will describe the idea of an information map to chart a complete picture of the organizational landscape. The approach is *systemic* because it describes the links, dependencies, trade-offs and synergies between each component part, which is made possible through the rigour of the architecture. Much manager, employee and customer frustration occurs because it is difficult to deal with a company 'as a whole'. While architecting changes does not guarantee to remove this frustration, it does make it much easier to see the big picture.

There is an oft-repeated story of two blind men who are confronted with an elephant for the first time. Having led very sheltered lives, they know nothing about elephants and proceed by feeling their way around the beast, from trunk to tail, trying to build a mental image of this strange creature through a combination of touch and comparing thoughts. Their task would be much easier if they started with a mental list of the components that make a 'complete' elephant picture. The dilemma is the same for an organization trying to understand its information resource without the benefit of an architecture providing checklists and structure to its efforts. Imagine building the pyramids or running the space programme without an overall picture of the end results before work got started. This is not to say that someone knew exactly what the final picture looked like, as you never know the final picture, but there needs to be a strong sense of how the component parts fit together as a whole – which is the advantage that architecting brings.

Architecting information: the big picture is an information picture

The architecting approach is based on the fact that:

- Every *action* we take
- And every *decision* we make
- Requires and uses *information*.

Information is the glue that binds everything together. When organizations architect change they are working with *information about* change. It is the information that populates the architectural framework, not the objects or concepts that are described by information. An organization that wants to move into a new market gathers *information about* customer requirements within that market and *information about* the competitors it will face in the market; it may build scenarios of what that market is like in the future (more information), and describe the new products and features that it needs to develop (yes – more information). Because every action we take and every decision we make requires and uses information, the big picture is a portrait in information.

It is important to realize that architecture is pervasive: it is always present like gravity or water, whether you are aware of it or not. It is quite obvious that when basic principles of architecture are flaunted and buildings are constructed without a strong foundation they become dangerous and collapse. Architectural principles are embodied in a building, whether an architect was directly involved in its construction or not. A builder, reusing a standard design, ensures that each component of the building conforms to standards and designs that are tried and tested.

Just as architecture is the intellectual foundation for every building, information architecture is implicit in every information-based project or activity. Without some form of structure information would not exist (in-formation). Every information system, whether it is computerized or organic, is based on architectural theory even if it is tacit and unrecognized. When principles are abused or ignored the system fails in the same way as a poorly constructed building, and information becomes confusing and useless. For example, it is a good principle to make it easy for a user to look-up jargon and unfamiliar terminology that helps make sense of figures, and it is good practice to provide a 'sell by' date to show when information is no longer valid so that decisions are not made on statistics that are out-of-date.

Information architecture is not optional, but an essential and unavoidable part of an organization's infrastructure. It is the application of architecture that turns data into information, and without applying the eight factors (see Chapter 2) to some degree to data, there would be no information. The only thing that is optional is the degree to which an organization chooses to *manage formally* their information architecture. An organization can either take a proactive approach by developing new skills, expertise, experience and capability in architecture, or it can choose to make do, in a random and *ad hoc* way, without these skills.

All too often architecture is seen as a project, but a project can only hope to *change* the architecture or the processes for managing it, while the architecture is present whether there any projects or not. Information architecture should have a budget of its own, and not rely on receiving a percentage of the budget from other projects. Demonstrating that some architectural structures are limiting and restrictive while others are flexible and liberating can raise awareness of architecture as something necessary and pervasive. Objectives for projects and initiatives to develop the architecture should be defined in terms of improvements in the use of information or in terms of developing new skills and competence in using architecture.

While some architectural theory is common sense that is applied intuitively, such as arranging a set of files alphabetically, there is still a lot that can be learned. The real issue is whether you need to develop this capability and skill or whether you can 'make do' with intuitive knowledge of how to structure information. What happens to an organization that does not have a formal information architecture? Leaving the design of information to chance results in an *ad hoc* collection of information – some structures are good, but many are ineffective and inconsistencies, problems and difficulties abound. The more that an economy is dependent on the processing and exchange of information, the more architecture is necessary, providing additional rigour and discipline to processes, reducing costs and making the use of information more effective.

Furthermore, it is not widely understood that an implicit architectural framework guides even uncoordinated change. Architecture is therefore relevant for all types of change, and although not always apparent it can be quickly identified by examining the eight factors described in this book. In many situations inappropriate information architectures work against changes. The right framework becomes explicit through the process of architecting information, and once explicit it can easily be tailored to match needs. Making the architecture explicit is the source of a greater understanding of information design, which results in more robust and useful information structures, and better organization skill in using and handling information. The artifacts and deliverables from a growing range of architectures will be coordinated through the process of architecting. Increasingly it will be difficult to survive with an *ad hoc* approach as more organizations build capability and skills in architecting information and change and, as no true information architecture is ever the same as that in another organization, information architecture helps distinguish you from your competitors.

At this point you may be thinking, 'This sounds OK in theory but surely it is a mammoth undertaking in practice: you've told me to do things on a grand scale, but how do I get the funds, train people and encourage them to work together around an architectural framework?' Bear in mind that the hidden costs of an unplanned, impromptu information architecture are always far greater than a well thought out enterprise-wide approach. Obviously greater effort is required, and it will be necessary to build a team of people with the right skills – some of which are quite specialized. Architecting information and change is a process, and as with many journeys the hardest part is making a start, and the capability for architecting changes will grow and evolve the more that it is applied. The following chapters outline the eight factors that are critical for effective information management and demonstrate how these are used in typical organizational situations.

Do you see information as a distinct resource

People are the original resource. As we evolved, we became more aware of physical resources, which we started to manage by growing crops, herding animals and taking advantage of mineral and natural resources. As barter systems gave way to more complex economies, financial systems developed and money became the third resource. Over the last two or three hundred years, intellectual assets have increasingly been valued, and with the emergence of more sophisticated information systems, information has become the fourth resource.

Information is often treated as if it were as free as the air that we breathe and it comes as a shock if we have to pay for it, or if someone gets proprietorial and refuses to give us information that we ask for. When planning the budget for a project we expect to include people, equipment and accommodation costs. In stark contrast, the costs of acquiring, storing, distributing or using information are often hidden, buried within other expenses, and so we are unaware of the cost of each piece of information. The costs of updating project information at a monthly team meeting get absorbed in the administrative expenses of the project, and even the huge costs of information technology are regarded as a separate budget item that is not generally connected with the cost of information. Information is left to deteriorate over time, making information content progressively harder to maintain and understand. Much information, such as that produced for reports and meetings, has a single purpose in that it is used once and then thrown away. Some information has a limited 'shelf-life' but is not removed or destroyed, and records become inaccurate and thus useless, so out-of-date information is stored needlessly. Not managing information as a resource is expensive in terms of wasted effort and missed opportunities.

Along with the financial and human resources, information is being recognized as a vital asset that should be managed effectively by establishing a special team responsible for information in the same way that there are groups responsible for financial accounting and personnel. People should be trained in the use of information, so that they know how to take advantage of it and use it effectively.

What is the attitude of your organization towards information as a distinct resource? If it is regarded as an important asset, then information architecture should be a key part of the strategy, but if it is not treated as a valuable resource, then there are opportunities to get a better return from it. Either way, information is generally under-valued and under-utilized, leaving plenty of openings for improving its use. Information is important for survival for all organizations, so the real question is, how well does your organization look after the information resource?

Information is critical for organizational survival

These days both commercial companies and non-profit organizations use information intensively. Almost every industry sector – from finance, banking and insurance, through retail and wholesale, to travel and transportation, manufacturing, media, government and the public service, not to mention healthcare, pharmaceutical, biotechnology, education, telecommunications and the utilities – has an increasing reliance on quality information for both survival and success. Each of these industries collects and uses vast quantities of data.

As a quick check, think about information technology investments over the last 5 years. These will almost certainly include data warehousing, data mining, business intelligence, customer relationship management, e-commerce, enterprise application integration, knowledge management or corporate intranet or extranet technologies. These technologies all use information on a grand scale.

Customers expect easy access to information about products and services, opening times, locations, items in stock, and a fast response to queries – which means that information is important for survival. If they also expect information to be easy to understand and well presented, then it is a critical resource and, as organizations increase their dependence on information, information architecture becomes a must.

How well does your organization look after the information resource?

Ten statements designed to provoke discussion about the use of information as a corporate resource are given below. We have used these statements as a diagnostic in training and seminars, but also to initiate discussion with senior executives, gaining recognition that information architecture requires full management commitment and support.

In Appendix A we have provided a simple version of this diagnostic for you to assess your organization's use of information as a distinct resource, and to analyse the potential benefits of information architecture. It can be used to gain a general awareness of the value and importance of information as a corporate resource, which is particularly important in gaining the commitment of executive sponsors and supporters. The size, complexity and diversity of modern organizations mean that enterprise architecture is unique in each case. The discussions prompted by this diagnostic are therefore really important for ensuring that the architecture you develop is the right one. If there is an architecture programme already in place then this diagnostic will help review it and focus future investments.

1. There is a clear and distinct vision of information as a
corporate resource

You could be in one of the rare organizations that really do have a vision
for the information resource. A lot of organizations 'talk the talk', but
very few 'walk the walk'. Some organizations have invested heavily in
knowledge management, and if you work for one of these you might
argue that they have a strong vision for the use of corporate knowledge.

What does it mean to have a distinct vision? To agree fully with this
statement your organization would have to satisfy the following criteria:

- There would need to be recognition that managing information is a
  totally different responsibility from managing information technology.
  This would be visible as a separate organization unit that is responsible
  for information and knowledge (see the next statement).
- There would also be a significant budget allocated to information
  architecture and to training in the effective use of information.
- Customers would find it easy to get information that they wanted
  about products and services. If they needed to contact someone it
  would be easy to find out whom they should talk to and they would
  get a quick and accurate response to their questions.
- Whenever it was necessary to provide information to the organization
  it would be done with the minimum of effort and fuss.
- Everyone in the organization would have some idea of what was going
  to be done to make information even more productive. When it was
  appropriate they would also be actively involved in this process.

2. There is an organization unit responsible for information and
knowledge that is distinct from the information technology function

Many of the corporations that we work with have an information technology
department that has a fairly high profile in the organization structure
chart, with the senior executive of this unit reporting directly to the
board of directors. In some organizations there is a knowledge management
function, which may have a fairly high profile, although not always at
the same level as technology.

- If information is being taken seriously as a key corporate resource,
  then it is important that there is a separate team or group responsible
  for it. This is partly because there is still a very high proportion of
  information that is *not* stored in a corporate database or intranet.
  Estimates vary, but if we include anything that is stored manually on
  paper and in filing cabinets along with everything that comes from an
  external source, then 50–80% of the information required to run a
  large corporation is not under the direct control of the information
  technology department.
- Another reason for keeping information management as a distinct

function is that, as with the human resource and training functions, it is a specialized discipline that supports the whole enterprise. The skills required to get the most effective use from information are not the same as technology skills. For example, information skills include the ability to avoid decision-making traps, experience in graphic and information design, or knowledge of the information architecture techniques described in this book.

3. There is a well-defined strategy and action plan for improving the effectiveness of information use across the organization

Evidence of a comprehensive and dynamic information strategy includes projects to increase steadily the quality of information (and once again, this is independent from any technology-based projects), implementation plans for populating or updating an information map and an enterprise-wide training programme in basic and advanced techniques for maximizing the use of information.

Most organizations define an information technology strategy, but here we are talking about action plans for improving information content and increasing the organizational capability for using it. To be strategic, these plans must be directly related to business or management goals and objectives, such as becoming more customer-focused or reducing costs. For example, an organization that wanted to improve customer service asked their customers what *information* they could provide that would be of help or value, and whether they could present information in a better format. In addition, they gave customers the option to review information that they held on them, with a view to correcting or updating it.

Within an organization this means that it should be easy to get all the information you need to carry out your work. For example, if you are responsible for cost cutting, is it possible quickly and easily to perform 'what if' analysis of different scenarios to see the likely impact of making changes to suppliers, reducing staff, closing branches or rationalizing product lines? Another indication of a commitment to improving information quality is the availability of training in the use of information, such as instruction in management ratios or cost accounting techniques to help staff engaged in cost reduction.

4. Information that is vital and necessary to make key decisions is always readily and easily available

Answers to this one vary enormously depending on the role and types of decisions that are made.

If it is perceived that the needed information is always readily and easily available, then the following questions will determine whether there is room for improvement or not:

- Is there a better way of presenting information?
- Is there additional information that should be available?
- If the results of decisions have a wide-scale or long-term impact on the company, would it be useful to know of better decision-making techniques or business models that make estimates and predictions more dependable?
- How do users know which information is vital and necessary?
- Is there a simple way of examining alternative decision-making processes that use different information, and then comparing the results with the approaches used now?

If there is disagreement with this statement, then there is an obvious mismatch between the decisions that are taken and the information that is available to make them! The information categories will help to identify what information is needed, while mental models show alternative ways for analysing it and taking steps to improve its availability.

5. All information is available in a consistent and integrated format

Unless all information comes from one well-integrated source, it is unlikely that it is in a consistent format. Among the many inconsistencies are different definitions of key items, variations between calculations, incompleteness, inaccuracies, odd size samples, or the use of contrary measurements. Trying to eliminate or reduce these inconsistencies is an on-going task, and every time we introduce a new piece of information or use a new information source, the integration process must start over again.

A well-architected information map makes this task a lot easier by providing the big picture or integrating framework, covering a wide range of different types of information and the relationships between them. Mechanisms for reconciling differences are defined in the architecture itself, through a system of defined and assigned responsibilities.

Of course, there is always the possibility that different business units and departments want information in alternative formats, and there are many reasons why it is necessary to present the same information in different formats and styles. Again, information architecture puts mechanisms in place separating information content from its presentation, while responsibilities provide an effective way to control the 'necessary redundancy' and to balance these different needs by asking users to accept and share accountability for the information resource.

6. Management believes that there is considerable value to be gained from the organization's use of information

What do we mean by 'value' and how do we demonstrate a management 'belief' in this value? To some extent the answer to this statement is going to be based on feelings and opinion.

Management's beliefs are reflected in the use of information in one or more of the following ways:

- Information is a key and integral part of the products and services to customers.
- Information flows are assessed for the value that is added at each stage in a chain.
- Everyone in the organization has full access to any information that is relevant to his or her work.
- The return from information is actively measured and monitored.
- Projects are in place to establish and enhance an architecture for managing information.
- Staff are regularly trained in the effective and innovative use of information.

7. Information management is seen as the responsibility of business people as well as the information technology functions

It is unfortunate that the word information is included in the phrase 'information technology', because people so often assume that to be involved in *information* means that you are a computer specialist of some sort or another. It is not surprising, therefore, that information management is seen as the prerogative of the technology department, whereas responsibility for information should be much broader, and to some extent rests with everyone in the organization. Much information is never stored or manipulated using technology, and it is the people who *use* information who really understand the business models that are used to analyse and interpret information.

Information will never be as productive as it could be unless there is proactive input from business users. If the main responsibility for information rests with the information technology departments, then the various types of responsibility described in this book will help shift some of these duties back to the relevant business and management areas.

8. Information has a key role in all business processes

This statement questions two related topics – the proportion of business processes that are dependent on information quality and the importance of the decisions and actions within those processes.

Agreeing with this statement suggests that a majority of business processes have information-critical tasks, while disagreement may indicate that many routine business activities do not depend on a lot of information, or that decisions and actions are based on a small number of variable factors without too many alternatives and options.

If competitors start using information more effectively – by using new types of information, analysing it differently, or using it in innovative ways – then you may be forced into doing the same. The opportunity to do much *more* with information is enormous because most players are not using it to anywhere near its full potential. When one of the existing players in a market changes the way they use information or when a market entrant brings along new ideas, it can cause a major threat, because most organizations do not have very flexible information structures, so adapting them to fit new patterns of use can be costly and time consuming.

Information can almost certainly play a much greater role in your business processes than it does now. Some players proactively create changes through innovation and productivity enhancements, while others react to changes that their competitors force upon them, but either way, it is highly likely that information will assume even more importance for business processes in the near future.

9. Financial approval is readily available for investment in the information infrastructure of the organization (as opposed to technology investments)

The value of information and the benefits for improving its use are not well understood, so unless there is a strong role for technology or a project has the backing and support of the technology department, there is a high probability that information related projects would be turned down. Examples of initiatives that seek investment in the *information* infrastructure, as opposed to *technology*, include:

- Training a team in the use of graphs and charts to represent statistical data and to identify trends and patterns.
- Establishing support procedures so that any member of staff can ask questions about the availability and use of information in their job.
- Implementing a formal procedure for allocating, rewarding and, where necessary, enforcing responsibilities for corporate information at all levels.
- Standardizing on the definitions and use of key indicators at senior levels so as to leverage value at every step in the decision value chain.
- Providing easy access to business and management theory and practice on the corporate intranet so that each person has the opportunity to learn how to use information more effectively.

Justifying technology projects is easier in a number of ways – it is a capital investment with tangible deliverables; technology vendors spend vast sums of money educating users in the benefit and value of their products and often helping to develop the business case; and there is a well-established technology department with a vested interest in continuing its existence and political position in the organization structure.

Techniques for measuring information value chains and the return from information can be used, whether technology is involved or not, to demonstrate the benefits of using information effectively and gaining financial approval for architecting organizational changes.

10. Information is used to support innovation and creativity in product and service development, business processes, and customer support

In many organizations information is not really seen as a resource at all, but just part of the background. If it was not there then people would not be able to do their work, but it is seen as a service in the same way that we expect water to come out when we turn on a tap; water is not seen as a creative tool for developing new products or services!

When information is used to support innovation and creativity then people in the organization are asking:

- What information could we provide as part of a product or service that would make it distinctive in the marketplace or make it more useful or valuable to our customers?
- How can business processes be restructured around the flow of decisions, rather than looking at the flow of actions?
- How can information improve customer support and enhance the customer experience?

When information is used effectively it becomes one of the key, if not *the* key, organizational resources of the information age. Information architecture is critical for using that resource in more productive ways, by supporting innovation and creativity in product and service development, enhancing and improving business processes, and adding value and benefits to customer interactions.

The information architecture age

There is universal agreement, from writers and business people to academics and technologists, that this is the information age. The emerging information economy puts information in the limelight. Economies are based around the trade in a commodity between sellers and buyers. In the information economy the commodity is value-added information, sellers are information providers, buyers are information users, and trade is the processing and exchange of information. Dealing in information without information architecture is like keeping track of finances and transactions without an accounting structure. A poor accounting structure, like a weak architecture, makes the job much harder. This urgent need for architecture is recognized as a government requisite, such as the Clinger-Cohen Act of 1996 in the USA (Executive Order 13011, Federal Information Technology, established the Chief Information Officers (CIO) Council as the principal forum for improving practices in the design, modernization, use, sharing, and performance of Federal information resources. The Clinger-Cohen Act of 1996 assigned the CIOs with the responsibility to develop information technology architectures. The Office of Management and Budget (OMB) M-97-02, Funding Information Systems Investments, October 1996, requires that Agency investments in major information systems be consistent with the information technology architectures).

The information age can be distinguished from an industrial or agricultural economy by certain characteristics and trends. If any of these trends affects your organization then you need information architecture, and the more these trends affect you, the more information architecture will help.

- **Information quantity**: the most obvious characteristic of the information age is the increase in the quantity of information that is available. This affects us personally as well as having huge implications from an organizational perspective. Dealing with the sheer volume of information is both exciting and daunting. It is one of the major challenges faced by information architecture.
- **Diversity of sources**: linked to information volume is use of a wider diversity of information sources. Organizations are no longer restricted to internal data sources. A vast amount of data can be accessed on the Internet, while subscription services provide both database and multimedia materials. An architectural framework makes it easier to access information as if it came from a single, fully integrated source by providing a map of the total information resource.
- **Information-based products**: more products or services are based on information, or are in large-part dependent on information. Distributing *information about* special offers fuels retail price wars. Mortgage loans and mobile phone tariffs are sold to customers through detailed *information about* the terms, conditions and facilities. This has a big impact in the way in which companies market themselves and sell their goods. Information must be architected into components that are designed for reuse.
- **Information speed**: information hits us at a faster rate than ever before. The information resource is not a passive ocean that we dip into when we choose; it is a raging river that incessantly flows towards us. We receive information all the time whether we want it or not – via e-mails, television, junk mail, newspaper and magazine articles, meetings and discussions . . . Architecture provides techniques for handling this torrent of information.
- **Dependence on technology**: there is relatively higher spending on computers and communications equipment than industrial, manufacturing or agricultural equipment. Embedded computer chips are found in home and office equipment and in complex systems such as transport and health. This growth of equipment means a steady

expansion of computing power and communications capacity. A conglomeration of software provides different ways to process and manipulate information. Technology provides a capacity for processing information, but it is architecture that helps us to decide what information we need to process.

- **Knowledge workers**: a higher percentage of workers are using their brains more than their hands. Many workers take work home and use formal work-at-home arrangements such as telecommuting. There is a decreasing number of secretaries, as executives and managers work directly on computers. Architectural techniques increase information productivity.

- **Information quality**: as with all resources, information is more valuable and useful the higher its quality. The quality of information includes the properties of accuracy, precision, credibility, currency, pertinence, precision, relevance, reliability, simplicity and validity. Information quality tends to deteriorate over time. One of my clients points out that the information on a loan application form is most likely to be accurate and up-to-date at the time the form is completed; after that, opportunities for updating the database are rare. It is difficult to maintain information quality without a comprehensive architecture that embeds these characteristics in a management framework.

The consequence of these trends is that there are new information-related costs, risks, threats and opportunities. The value of information has increased, so it is subject to risks and threats that did not previously exist.

Information technology is the key enabler for the information economy, becoming one of the major organizational costs. Without such technology it would be much harder to trade with information. While computers and telecommunications technology are good at storing and distributing information in a wide range of forms and media, they cannot provide their maximum benefit without a parallel investment in human skills and knowledge. Information provides the link between technology and knowledge, and architecture provides the organizational means for building a bridge between the two to maximize the value of, and moderate risks and threats to, information. It is dangerous to base the emerging economy on technology or knowledge without simultaneously increasing expertise in information architecture.

Information is complex. We sometimes forget that as human beings we are constantly receiving and interpreting vast quantities of information, and many of our personal information management tasks are instinctive, happening largely in our subconscious. From birth we steadily acquire expertise in grammar and language that we use to structure our thoughts, express our ideas and communicate with others. The human brain is the most complex structure on this planet, extracting patterns, meaning and sense from the mass of information around us, and giving us an enormous individual capacity to handle information through the manipulation of human language and symbols. We internalize grammatical rules and vocabulary that allow us to generate an infinite number of grammatically correct sentences (Chomsky's theory of transformational grammar). We do not need to be programmed, nor are we required to follow organizational procedures or other constraints that limit the ways in which we can handle information.

In comparison to this, the mechanisms we use to handle corporate communications and manage corporate information are extremely primitive. As soon as we try to automate or formalize the handling of information by an organization – whether we do this using computers, policy guidelines, filing cabinets, e-mail, or software that imposes pre-defined style templates to our presentations – we have exposed ourselves to 'information gridlock'. To make 'a machine as competent in a language as a human being, it would be necessary to write a separate rule for every conceivable grammatical sentence in the language, and a grammarian would die long before that task could be completed' (Campbell, 1982, p. 128). It is the complexity of organizational information that is at the root of many ingrained problems, such as the high maintenance costs of legacy applications and databases and the difficulty in getting a complete overview of all of a customer's agreements and relationships with an organization.

When is architecting appropriate?

An explicit approach for architecting information is most necessary when organizations are large and complex, change is constant and far-reaching, there is huge potential for economies of scale and scope, and a high degree of coordination and collaboration is necessary. Information architecture handles a diverse range of information management problems that face organizations today and is vital when there is some combination of the following characteristics:

- **When there are huge quantities of complex information**. Information architecture provides an overview of the information resource which can be used to simplify information structures, coordinate effort and reduce costs by dividing the complexity into sensible and manageable chunks.
- **When the business environment is unforeseen or unpredictable**. Information architecture can be used to create information designs that are highly flexible and adaptive, able to handle growth and change, and are responsive to changing needs. It is particularly important that information remains flexible even when technology platforms are rigid.
- **When you need accurate and reliable information**. Conformance with architectural principles creates strong information structures that are stable and enduring, easier to understand and use and more reliable.

Simpler designs make it easier to integrate software components into a single coordinated information system.

- **When your products and services are information-based**. Information architecture improves the quality of information-based goods and helps identify opportunities for innovative new services by defining a formal map that shows how information creates value in the marketplace.
- **When the majority of your staff works with information on a daily basis**. Information architecture increases knowledge worker productivity and reduces information-processing costs, helping people do more with less information.
- **When you need to share information along a supply chain**. Architecture provides a framework for sharing information and working in cooperation with other companies across organization boundaries.
- **When there is constant and large-scale change**. Long-range planning is often too rigid and inflexible to satisfy the needs of managers responding to a challenging world. Information architecture supplements change management by providing simple mechanisms for controlling and keeping track of information about change.
- **When your information needs are constantly changing**. Information architecture provides stable but adaptive information structures that meet the needs of a diverse user population and their shifting requirements.

Dealing with unforeseen or unpredictable futures

When industry is heavily regulated, products and services are very similar from one organization to the next, procedures and tasks are routine and competition is limited, information architecture remains stable over a long period of time and architectural changes take place in a slow, evolutionary and generally predictable manner. In these situations, most organizations are automating routine tasks for better efficiency, so architectures are aimed at meeting specific and predictable information needs.

Unfortunately, most information needs are not that predictable, and if anything they are becoming more turbulent and changeable. In today's aggressively competitive market, organizations are facing stiff competition, with customers increasingly making unique and unpredictable product demands and expecting much more than satisfactory service, so organizations are adopting competitive strategies that create a symbiotic synergy between mass customization and continuous process improvement. Mass customization is premised on the idea that product and service components can be quickly adapted and rearranged to create a new product or to meet the precise needs of a particular customer, while continuous improvement is based on the idea that processes are capable of continuous change and innovation and both require an architecture that enables flexible and rapid change to support a constantly changing business environment, rather than meeting predictable needs.

To do this, the architecture must be adaptable so that it can meet both predictable changes and needs that cannot be anticipated. Certain things are more likely to change and information components that are stable and unchanging need to be separated from information that is dynamic and changeable.

In most large corporations it is difficult, expensive and time-consuming to change infrastructure. Infrastructure should be relatively stable and long lasting, but it also needs to adapt to new business situations and support a wide variety of distinct information processing needs. In practice, the organizational infrastructure is often rigid and inflexible and, as such, it is a serious obstacle to the effectiveness and success of a business. In **rigid and fixed** architectures, information structures are designed to meet a specific need. New types of product, trends and fashions, customer expectations, market demands, competition, changes in the global economy, politics and regulations and many other factors, cause these information designs to become outdated. The responsiveness of the organization – whether this is to customer demands, market forces, or the opportunities afforded by new technology – is constrained by the degree to which its information architecture is flexible and adaptive.

Think of this analogy: in a house or apartment it is relatively easy to change the look of a room by repositioning furniture or hanging new pictures on the walls. Redecorating achieves a more dramatic effect, but would require more effort and, if you are like me, it is not the sort of thing you want to do too often (or ever)! To relocate a washing machine requires new plumbing. Adding a conservatory probably requires foundation and load-bearing changes (and demolition and reconstruction if you are living in an apartment). The effort, pace and frequency of change vary, depending on whether they affect the structure, services, or contents of the building. We expect the foundations of the building to be stable, while we want the flexibility to rearrange furniture for different social occasions. As Steward Brand puts it in his revealing study of how buildings learn, structure persists and dominates, skin is mutable (Brand, 1997). The spaces and shapes of the building limit the degree to which we can rearrange furniture. In a similar way, the flexibility of information is constrained by its architecture.

One of the characteristics of information is its amazing flexibility. As we talk, we instantly analyse, assess, compare and store information that we receive, at the same time as we send out more information. If we keep receiving the same old news it becomes boring because it ceases to be new. As soon as we organize and store information in a mechanical or digital form it starts to lose its flexibility. The structure and design of a database and the functionality of software immediately limit the flexibility of information and once this foundation is in place it becomes more difficult to change. The dynamics and flexibility of the whole system is limited by its architecture.

Given contemporary need for and dependence on sophisticated uses of information, how can we create a stable infrastructure that retains and supports the dynamic nature of information itself? With a **flexible and adaptable** architecture, information is more responsive to our needs, and therefore more valuable. When requirements change the architecture is designed to meet those needs with minimum effort. A good design is even able to meet needs that could not have been predicted at the time when the infrastructure was created.

There is a very simple rule at work: separate things that are stable and unchanging from the things that are dynamic and changeable. When we understand the difference between items that are stable and those that are dynamic we can build infrastructures that are long lasting and adaptive. This concept is sometimes referred to in business theory as 'dynamic stability' and it is the foundation behind the popular business ideas of mass customization and sense-respond (Haeckel, 1999). Organizations that have flexible infrastructures are based on well-designed information architectures.

Dynamic and changeable components should be grouped into hierarchical 'families', which are designed for rapid change. At the highest level of each family hierarchy are the components, features, facilities and parameters that apply to all items lower down the hierarchy. Moving down the hierarchy, constraints and limitations are introduced that are necessary at each level; constraints restrict the flexibility of this structure at lower levels, so they should only be introduced at the level when they actually apply. This type of analysis helps to create architectural components that are structured into loosely coupled cohesive units, rather than creating elements that are tightly bound together. Each unit should be engineered into plug-and-play building blocks that can be quickly changed and recombined to meet continuously evolving information needs.

Surviving without information architecture

If architecture can provide such a powerful and distinctive capability, how do organizations get away without using it? We have already stated that *information architecture is not optional*, so organizations that appear to manage without architecture are just not managing it.

Organizations survive using weak, *ad hoc* architectures for three main reasons. **Their customers accept low information quality or service**, partly because information management standards are generally low across many industry sectors. Also, although many customers try complaining, organizational change is often slow and therefore appears unresponsive, so people put up with poor quality information. A second reason is that **their employees deliver strong efforts, which hide a suboptimal**

information and knowledge infrastructure. If information structures have been less than perfect for any period of time, then people create workarounds and fixes to get their job done. It is not until you conduct an information audit that you realize the extent of these makeshift arrangements! Finally, **they invest in solutions to address the most pressing problems**, a hit-and-run approach that fills the cracks. Although this only works in the short term, for a time it looks as though everything is under control.

The resulting unplanned architecture therefore appears adequate in many situations, but such architectures emerge as a reaction to various pressures and they are always trying to catch up with the latest emergency. Unplanned information architectures do not work very well because they are based on shifting sands and constantly require fixes and patches. It is like living in a house that needs the constant attention of builders to keep it in shape. It is all too easy to overlook costs that are incurred when there is no information architecture, and where information management is at best *laissez-faire* and at worst totally anarchic. Here are some stories caused through inadequate information architectures.

Utility companies are fighting tooth and claw to gain and retain customers. One utility company estimated that it lost an average of 30 customers per day, or more than 10 000 customers per year, because staff did not have access to the right information to handle customer queries. This was equivalent to $5.5 million in lost revenue.

Inconsistent information and structures between systems often means that the same data have to be entered into more than one system. A study at a UK bank estimated that duplication of effort totalled more than $3.2 million per year.

An insurance company spent $67 million developing a replacement information system. After acquisition of another company, they found that it would cost nearly the same amount to adapt the system to their new requirements. If the system had an adaptive information architecture this effort and cost would have been avoided.

An insurance company wrote off a sum of around $16 000 every year because accounts from two separate systems did not balance, as they should have done. Each system was developed many years previously and was not designed to interface with other systems. Although the problem was recognized, it was regarded as too difficult to correct because each program was complex and poorly documented. It was assumed that the cost to fix the problem would be far greater than the $16 000 per year to balance accounting *figures. Eventually the problem was identified – at a key point in the calculations one system used fixed decimal arithmetic and two decimal places, while the other system used floating-point arithmetic. If the difference had not been corrected it would have cost $16 000 every year for the life of the two systems.*

Change is a perpetual feature of all organizations. Without an architectural framework for change organizations muddle through using some form of *implicit model or template* for seeing the big picture, managing change and using information. Things get done, but not being aware of the architectural context there is a danger that changes fight against each other, that there is a lack of synergy in using resources, that important things get overlooked or ignored, that there is all talk and meetings with no action, or that there is a clear business case, but no commitment to change. These are the organizations that we mentioned in the preface. A rough estimate of the typical costs in not having an explicit information architecture is 10% of the organizations total expenses (i.e. $400 000 on expenses of $4m).

Identify the circumstances when architecture is most useful and find specific examples of problems that these situations cause or opportunities for resolving problems with information architecture. Be aware of factors that hide the need for information architecture. If there is no adequate architecture in place, people will learn to make do with it: they will expect that information is difficult to find, that information quality is low, that customers are dissatisfied and that an inordinate amount of time, energy and cost is spent on fixes and workarounds. If this is acceptable, then all is well; otherwise – you need information architecture.

There are many advantages when change is better organized and more disciplined. **Everyone is working in the same direction**: a company in the music industry achieved planned targets 2 years earlier than expected through coordinated effort. **There is less duplication of effort**: a financial institution saved $5m p.a. by reducing project overlap. **More can be achieved with fewer resources**: an Australian bank reduced their contract force from 4k to 1k. **Obstacles to change are easier to address**, because it helps to understand the principles that are directing or constraining changes.

The word 'architecture'

There is increasing use of the word 'architecture' in the world of information and knowledge management. Some of the most common are information systems architecture, business architecture, enterprise architecture, data architecture, information architecture, application architecture, network architecture, and process architecture! Each one is distinguished largely through differences in the scope or subject matter that it covers. The popularity of this term highlights the need and value of *architecting* as a process. The principles, guidelines, and dimensions described in this book are relevant to all information-based architectures, because the basic *process of architecting* is the same in each case.

This is a good time to explain the difference between 'architecting' and 'architecture'. Charles Savage (Savage, 1996, p. 121) made a similar distinction between 'knowledging' and 'knowledge', arguing that knowledging was much more than just knowing 'because it suggests an active and continual *process* of interrelating patterns' (our italics). Architecting change creates a *capability* rather than a commodity. It is the *process of using* the principles and discipline of *information architectures* to achieve practical organizational benefits, by creating *a management toolkit* for orchestrating change. Architecting is a way of thinking that is disciplined and structured, is based on explicit principles and standards and approaches the subject matter holistically. An organization can only architect change and information when it has people with the necessary skills, expertise and knowledge, and an enabling and supportive environment. In contrast, most architectures describe a set of outputs that they create; they produce a commodity. Architecting embraces the *artifacts and deliverables* produced by all types of information architecture; these commodities are part of the management toolkit created by the architecting process.

Architectural style

Architectural styles emerge from the techniques and principles that are applied, the availability of materials and technologies, the preferences of culture and fashion and the ideas and experience of individuals or groups of architects working together. Despite the many characteristically distinct styles of building architecture, such as Gothic and Byzantine, they all share certain basic architectural principles. The principles that are selected determine the style, with different selections resulting in dissimilar designs – a traditional brick-arch bridge is based on the principle of compression, while a suspension bridge is designed using the principle of tension – yet both serve the same function.

This is true in architecting information just as much as it is in the construction of buildings. Although styles come and go like fashion, the basic principles and techniques of information architecture remain constant. Here is a (slightly tongue in cheek) list of some of the more common information architecture styles:

- **The enterprise information systemists**. This style is designed for and best suited to the development of enterprise information systems. It is one of the earliest styles of architecture, emerging in the late 1970s and early 1980s to help manage the development of large-scale software systems.

- **The datists** put their emphasis on the management of data – in databases, data structures in programs and in data warehousing. Data modelling, in one form or another, is at the heart of this style.
- **Business process re-engineers.** Whereas the datists made data their starting point, this group put process and workflow first, with a corresponding emphasis on process models.
- **The modellers.** Data and process models demonstrated the value in using graphical representations to simplify complexities of business practice and modellers took this a stage further by developing models of other types of information and integrating these into a single corporate information model or map (instead of having a separate data or process models for each project, system or business process).
- **The objectists** started from the basic premise that everything is an object. They built upon the knowledge of data and process modelling, adding techniques to analyse more complex situations and placing a greater emphasis on reusable components.
- **The webbist movement**. In the late 1990s information architecture was given a new boost, with the need to design well-structured websites that were easy to navigate. As well as providing a new focus in the form of web content, the webbist movement was noted for bringing skills and techniques that originated with professional librarians.

Understanding architecture through analogies

Architecture is conceptual and abstract, so analogies and metaphors are commonly used to make it easier to grasp and understand. Comparisons with other disciplines or professions help define or clarify what we mean by information architecture. It is equally important to know the limitations of such analogies. The most common analogy is with architecture in the construction and building industry.

The analogy or analogies used will affect the success of architecture in your organization. People find it easier to work with analogies that are closer to their existing experience and knowledge. The building analogy is popular partly because it is easy for anyone to imagine. *The wrong analogy can mislead or confuse*. Analogies that omit vital characteristics may explain the basic ideas but miss more subtle features. The parallel with building architecture is useful if it really helps to identify principles of information management.

The analogy with building architecture was particularly common with early information architectures. John Zachman famously used the analogies from classical building architecture and military aircraft manufacturing to help define the Information Systems Architecture (Zachman, 1987, p. 282). (Some architects in the building industry argue that the word 'architect' should only be applied to their profession.) It is a comparison that is easy to understand: 'architecture' is most commonly associated with buildings and we are aware of the features and design of buildings through living and working in them. The outputs created by building architecture are blueprints, drawings, plans and parts lists – which also compare well with information architecture. Each building design must be placed in the context of things like planning regulations, the availability of components and materials and conformance with architectural, engineering or design principles. Developing a standalone system is very much like constructing a building, so this analogy is particularly useful when the final outcome is a system and the architecture must describe the components used to build it.

The building analogy has some limitations. Information is an intellectual rather than a physical resource, so it uses materials that are very different from those used to create a building. Information can be reused in ways that are not possible with more tangible resources: if I have a penny and I give it to you, then you have the money and I do not; but if I give you a piece of information then we both have it. Information gains in value with reuse, while each component can only be used once in the construction of a building. Building components by nature are long-lasting, while information structures are more prone to change. And there are aspects to information architecture that are not found in buildings. For example, the spatial dimension is important in building architecture, while the epistemological dimension (whether knowledge is explicit or implicit) is a key factor in information architecture.

Using the analogy of a city plan, rather than a building plan, architecture becomes a mechanism both for designing individual structures and for siting them as part of an integrated and coordinated whole, shedding light on a diverse collection of information structures that form and are used as a cohesive enterprise resource. Richard Nolan and Dennis Mulryan point out that,

> City planners must design in the face of many unknowns, such as future transportation technologies, changing work, living, and commuting patterns, and so on. To deal with the complexities and unknowns, city planners set guidelines on, for instance, building height, set-backs, and zoning. They can ill afford to delve into such detail as prescribing building materials. As a result of this level of planning, our major cities are able to accommodate new technologies for transportation and communication which remain viable for hundreds of years, and which make a major contribution to each city's brand of urban culture (Nolan and Mulryan, 1987).

Joe Podolsky, in an opinion column for *Datamation*, said that what our information systems need is landscape architecture not building architecture, to provide 'bottom-up ecological and evolutionary models of system growth'. He concluded, 'We may wish our systems portfolio with its hodge-podge legacy of applications and processes to be a planned community of buildings and roads, but it ain't so. And the kinds of plans we need will come not from the IT version of Frank Lloyd Wright, but from the inspiration of the parks of Frederick Law Olmsted' (Podolsky, 1994, p. 90).

Using a balance between building, city and landscape planning might suggest that information architecture within the control of the organization relates to city planning, while landscape planning is everything beyond the organization's boundary and each buildings corresponds to the information needs of an individual or group or people (these needs are referred to as 'views' within this book).

Using an analogy with music reveals more clearly the need for several different factors that interact to form the information architecture. There are a number of factors to making music – each of which is necessary and important – including tone, pitch, scale, duration, volume, harmony, orchestration and melody. You do not need to know all about them in order to listen to music, but if you are a composer then you need to know more of this theory and if you are a performer then you need practice and experience. Information architecture is very similar – there are eight factors that need to be taken into account, and you will need a different knowledge of these factors depending on whether you are creating the architecture, using the architecture, or simply using information.

Cooking is a good analogy for reminding us that information architecture is about *information* first and *technology* second. Focusing on technology is like trying to prepare a wonderful meal by equipping the kitchen with cooking utensils then ignoring the quality of the ingredients! The information architect is equivalent to the chef or trained cook: as architects we must understand and apply a thorough knowledge of our raw material – information. Ingredients are the equivalent of information content, and recipes are guidelines for using information, making the knowledge of experienced architects (or chefs) available to a wider audience. Menus provide a more sophisticated combination of recipes, allowing recipes to be reused in many different ways.

There would be no point in kitchen equipment, ingredients and recipes if we did not use them to create nutritious meals and yet there are plenty of organizations that have far more information (ingredients) then they can ever expect to use; or more equipment (information technology) than they need to cook (use the information effectively). This analogy demonstrates how organizations need to rethink their investments to gain a balance between technology and architecture.

It is often necessary to use more than one analogy to explain what is meant by information architecture and help people understand its benefits. Each analogy emphasizes some characteristics of information architecture, while at the same time failing to explain other equally important features, so one must be careful not to take comparisons too far. The best analogies illustrate benefit and value, explain limitations or problems that the organization is facing, or help demonstrate the need for investment and change.

Key points

Architecting information is a disciplined approach for managing the complete information resource.

The most expensive challenge facing modern organizations is the lack of a simple and straightforward architecture that provides the big picture and is used by everyone in the enterprise to coordinate organizational changes.

Every action we take and every decision we make requires and uses information. The diagnostic in Appendix A helps identify the main benefits and value from architecture by asking people to think about information as a distinct organizational resource.

Architecture is inherent and necessary in every information structure. Therefore, we need to learn new skills in using and architecting information. Smart organizations use the discipline of architecture to control their vast information and knowledge resources.

The future is increasingly difficult to predict and a strong information architecture provides the capability for an organization to adapt quickly as necessary.

Unplanned architectures appear adequate in many situations, but constantly require fixes and patches, and can never match organized and disciplined changes.

We use the phrase 'architecting information' to describe the processes and techniques that form the foundation for the many different styles of information-based architecture.

Analogies help expand our knowledge of information architecture and explain the benefits and value in architecting information.

The essential eight factors

Attentiveness to context, not to self-expression, is the skill we have
to foster, to encourage, to share . . . The context, not the boss, has
to become the manager of what is done, and how.
John Chris Jones

Each pattern describes a problem which occurs over and over
again in our environment, and then describes the core of the
solution to that problem, in such a way that you can use this
solution a million times over, without ever doing it the same way
twice.
Christopher Alexander

There are eight factors that are essential for effective information
management that need to be taken into account when forming an
information architecture. These factors are drawn from experience and
practice in information architecture, knowledge management and
organizational change. The eight factors are:

- Categories
- Understanding
- Presentation
- Evolution
- Knowledge
- Responsibility
- Process
- Meta levels

These eight factors are at the heart of all information architectures, forming
a checklist of key points to make sure that important concerns are not

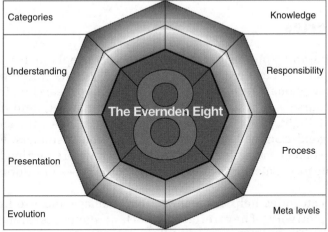

Figure 2.1 The essential eight factors.

forgotten. The eight factors are based on our experience in implementing and using information architectures and they are used on their own or in combination as the starting point when creating the fundamental information architecture tools. Just as we describe space in terms of the dimensions of height, depth and width, so we can describe information architecture in terms of these eight separate factors. When a factor is selected as part of an architecture, it becomes one of the 'dimensions' of that architecture. Dividing the architecture up in this way makes it much easier to discuss and use.

Think of this comparison with the various factors that impact the design of a garden. Its aspect will determine the effect of the weather, while a slope from the back of the house will affect whether to add a terrace or steps. You might want to emphasize a view, or use its shape to optimize the space and, of course, much will depend on use of the garden. Neighbouring gardens are quite distinct, even though they are based on the same set of variables, because each factor is customized to meet different needs and preferences. The eight factors work in a similar way, representing the key areas that need to be addressed in creating or customizing information architecture.

The eight factors allow you to decide which bits you need as you need them. It is generally easier to start architecting with one or two and gradually introduce others when a more sophisticated approach is needed or as organizational capability develops. Unlike a pre-defined architecture, the eight factors are readily customized – by *ignoring* factors that you do not need, *adapting* them if they are not quite right, or *extending* them if you need something extra – before the architecture is established. What follows is a brief overview of the essential eight factors (popularly known as the Evernden Eight).

Categories

Classifying and grouping our thoughts, using concepts such as 'furniture' or 'transport', is a technique we all use daily. We grade children at school, arrange telephone directories alphabetically, group meals into first course, second course and dessert (or starter, main and sweet), and distinguish long-haul flights from short-haul, English from Spanish, family from friends, good from bad and customers from non-customers. Every time we label someone as a 'customer' or 'prospect' we are putting him or her into a category. Categories help us identify the types of information that we need.

Good categories help to organize, find, manage and use information more effectively. They reflect important concepts and ideas, by distinguishing one thing from another and are essential for comparison and analysis. Categories are also helpful as a checklist. For example, if someone gave me a checklist of all the things I would ever need to do to renovate my house, then I could quickly use it to see an overview of what had been done, what needed to be done and to plan the renovation process. A reasonably complete set of information categories provides an excellent high-level scope tool, as well as giving an overall structure to the architecture.

Standard categories are as necessary to information management as a consistent accounting structure is to finance. They allow everyone to use the same language. It is a myth that standardized categories force a single viewpoint on everyone; in fact it is vital to the success of the architecting process that differences of opinion are taken into account (we will discuss later how this is achieved using responsibilities to manage diverse viewpoints).

Poor categories limit full use of information. Using categories is a very powerful organizational tool, and it is important to note here that unless some effort has been taken to define a standard set, use of such classifications will be at best informal and at worst ineffectual.

A simple example is a directory of local companies on a town website that are categorized alphabetically, but cannot handle a company name starting with a number, such as 1st Options or 4th resource. A more sophisticated example, but one that is equally common, is categorizing a person on the basis of purchase information, which can work well if all of the purchases relate to that individual. Then again, a set of credit card transactions of music CDs, clothes and make-up may suggest the purchases of a teenage girl, when in reality the items were bought by a 40-year-old man on behalf of his daughter.

This type of misclassification really does happen, and can result in marketing efforts that are aimed at the wrong person to total alienation of existing customers!

Inconsistent categories cause confusion. Categories work because they belong together as a set, while anything that sticks out like a duff note in a musical scale does not feel right. Comparing totals month-by-month causes misunderstanding if it does not take into account variations in the number of working days or seasonal differences. Using the wrong label for a set of categories will make them appear inconsistent. Coffee, chocolate and tea make sense as types of beverage, while blue, red, coffee and chocolate are all example colours – but they are not all drinks!

Understanding

We gain understanding and find meaning in information in a variety of ways – we become familiar with the language by *defining* and *explaining* the words that are used and we clarify with *descriptions* and *examples. Guidelines* and *procedures* provide assistance, business *rules* formalize links and dependencies, *theories*, assumptions and hypotheses help us interpret information, and we build *models* to simulate situations that are harder for our brains to comprehend. Data become information through our interpretation because of the understanding and meaning that we give them. Understanding provides the means for extracting information from data.

A definition explains what a word means, an explanation and examples show how it is used, but it is not until you interpret its use in a context that it gains real meaning and value. To gain the most value from information requires tools of understanding that help us to gain clarity. Good tools take us beyond our current knowledge by introducing us to unfamiliar mental models, showing us new analytical techniques, or combining and linking information items in original patterns.

In competitive situations, understanding must also provide insights not available to our rivals and innovations that differ from mainstream thinking. The huge investments made in data warehousing or data mining are largely aimed at making sense through finding patterns or discovering new archetypes to form the basis of competitive advances.

Differences of understanding cause disagreement, confusion and frustration. Even something relatively simple can have more than one interpretation – if there is 50 ml of water in a 100 ml glass, is the glass half full or half empty? The highly normalized data structures of the IT professional are very different from the way that a business person sees the same information. Discussion and debate can reveal differences in meaning, resolve uncertainty and create insight, thus preventing the expensive mistakes.

The CIO of a bank wanted a single, enterprise-wide definition of customer. An initial study showed that there were at least 49 distinct uses of 'customer' across the company – from individual to corporate customers, casual versus regular customers and single or multiple product users. After some debate he conceded that there were practical business reasons for differentiating between these alternative meanings and they finally settled on 31 valid definitions of customer. This understanding allowed the bank gain a better sense of direction, and over time it plans to focus on the 'top ten' while phasing out support for the other 21.

This transition would not have been possible without recognizing these differences of meaning.

Each era has its popular beliefs and such habits and preconceptions can inhibit new ways of thinking and influence our understanding. A common 21st century example is the assumption that loyal customers are better customers and that customer loyalty is encouraged through points schemes. This is true in some, but not necessarily all, situations and it is difficult to verify without putting a loyalty scheme in place and testing it over a number of years. Opinions tend to vary more when information is used in new and less familiar situations, or when information requires a greater degree of interpretation, which are the type of situation when understanding is most important.

Presentation

Information is presented in various formats and styles. The same data could be represented in textual or pictorial format, in a mass of detail or summarized to show salient points. Instead of seeing information in a report or on a screen we could listen to someone reading it. The pinball wizard 'felt' information through the suppleness of his wrists. We receive information through a formal meeting, or informally at the coffee machine through word of mouth. Organizations are storing more diagrams, pictures and photographs than in the past; there is more spontaneous, unstructured information than well thought-out formats, while the use of audio and video is likely to increase in the future. The bias today is toward visual information on screens and in printouts, in text and diagrams, but increasingly information architecture will need to encompass a much wider range of presentations.

Presentation determines how well information is understood or used and can suggest new meanings or reveal hidden patterns, for example by showing trends in a chart. Good choice of presentation will expose information and help understanding, while poor choices, accidentally or deliberately, obscure the facts.

By considering the same information in a different way organizations have achieved insights that would otherwise have been less obvious.

A company marketing advertising space in journals and magazines found that regional sales figures showed a dramatic drop in July, August and December when these numbers were summarized graphically, which was not apparent in the detail of unconnected tables of data. As a consequence they adopted new tactics for those months that made better use of the sales force's time. An electronics company used a simulator and joystick that enabled analysts to 'feel' resistance and attraction to different product features, giving them a better 'sense' of customer emotions. An IT company distributed customer reports and news digests on audio files which enabled a sales force to listen to important updates on the drive between calls.

A good example of a radically different way of representing information is the use of cartoon faces to improve the reporting and communication of accounting information (Smith and Taffler, 1996). Each cartoon drawing represents four key financial ratios through different facial expressions. The eyebrows represent liquidity, the size of the eyes shows the companies financial leverage, the shape of the nose indicates working capital position and the mouth shows profitability. A distressed face shows a company that is in poor shape, while a happier face means that all four indicators are healthy.

The faces are not intended to replace numbers, but to complement them, while combining numbers and faces enhances the financial message. The cartoons are a visual aid that helps provide an overview of the performance of a company. Large quantities of data are often overwhelming and to understand how well a company is doing over time requires simultaneous tracking of several important variables. Malcolm Smith and Richard Taffler argue that traditional ways of representing accounting information are either too complex to integrate the key features of the accounts or indicate separate aspects of performance rather than the overall picture.

Presentation is a vital component of any information architecture because better decisions are made when information is presented in a more understandable format.

Evolution

Information changes over time: new information emerges, while some becomes out-of-date and irrelevant and additional knowledge aids understanding. Time qualifies information. We distinguish one budget from another by saying that one is the current version while another was last year's financial statement. We describe the frequency that information is updated when we talk about daily newspapers or monthly reports. We have archived information, future regulations and plans and proposed changes.

Time stands still for no-one, thus acknowledging the element of time helps to focus on what is relevant at a given time, prioritize different needs and keep everything up-to-date. Unless there are periodic reviews of objectives, action points and the use of information, we risk a widening gulf between the information we need and the information that we receive. The length of time that information remains useful varies enormously. It does not have to be the most recent, latest is not necessarily the greatest, and older information is often the mainstay of our decisions and actions. Some information is timeless and long-lasting, while some older information is unreliable and becomes uneconomic in use. It is therefore important for the architecture to take these potential variations into account and make adjustments accordingly. Too often the architecture is regarded as something that is fixed and unchanging, whereas in reality there are frequent shifts in meaning and structures often become outdated, requiring an architecture that evolves over time.

Mailing lists are notorious for being out-of-date; how many of us continue to get mail and calls for previous occupants, long after they have moved on? For a sizeable marketing exercise, a 10% error rate can be a costly mistake, yet studies show that the percentage of outdated records is more commonly 30% or even 40%. The impact of management or consultant diagrams that are used long after the underlying principles cease to be valid is a more insidious problem. Common blunders include applying manufacturing models without modification in service industries, or using models that were developed to explain an earlier era. Many business theories apply to a wide variety of situations over a long period of time and there is a lot to be learned by taking hypotheses from one sector and using them elsewhere, but it is critical to question the underlying assumptions from time to time. Timescales are also frequently unrealistic, resulting in many plans and projects that are too ambitious.

An international technology company famously displayed a chart showing the major organizational changes it had planned over a 4-year period, when even the year one starting point took 5 years to achieve!

Making time a specific factor in architecting changes, in conjunction with feedback and learning, addresses these issues.

Knowledge

Although knowledge can be codified into expert systems and other tangible forms, it is largely seen as personal, ranging from that of an untrained novice to that of an experienced expert. For example, 'the knowledge' is the detailed information on which London taxi drivers are tested before they are licensed. The use of knowledge results in increased *awareness* and better use of information (among other things), while a lack of knowledge implies that corporations must somehow deal with *ignorance* and poor use of information.

Information covers a broad spectrum ranging from attributive data that are quite formal and structured, to more personal knowledge which is often more spontaneous and random:

- Attributive information, e.g. information in transaction files, databases, or a data warehouse.
- Complex information, e.g. information in documents, spreadsheets, presentations, graphics, multimedia, sound, video, faxes, e-mail, web pages.
- Procedural information, e.g. information in business processes, business rules, conditions, parameters.
- Theory and practice, e.g. information in business theories, management practice, organizational culture, mental models, simulations.
- Corporate knowledge, e.g. information about organizational history, products and services, intellectual assets, skills and competence, organizational experience.
- Personal knowledge, e.g. information about explanations, interpretations, ideas, bias, assumptions, opinions, feelings.

Knowledge management tends to focus on the more abstract, fuzzy end of this scale, while information technology is more likely to cover the routine and predictable. Some information in the middle of this continuum does not fit perfectly in either camp. Often there is no single group or function in an organization with responsibility for the full range and no integrated way of managing the full picture. A comprehensive information architecture should cover *all* variations.

Many information architectures have the same scope as information technology and this overlooks the fact that we interpret information through our personal knowledge and world-view. Some people are more optimistic than others, looking at the world through rose-coloured glasses and some people have greater experience or more developed skills than others, which can make a huge difference to the way that information is used. Many companies leave this factor out of their architecture and finish up spending vast sums of money on technology to do something that could be achieved more simply by tapping into employee knowledge.

Revealing and sharing knowledge provides the greatest opportunities for creative and original use of information. Introducing new knowledge has the same potential for significance and impact as introducing new technology. Let us give you a simple example.

Customer relationship management has been in vogue for a number of years and continues to draw a lot of interest. The commercial solutions in this area have similar features, so one of our clients in the banking industry wanted to do something different. Instead of looking at software, we examined the information about customers, looking at what information was available and how it was currently used. We quickly developed a map showing each type of information and how it was used with other pieces of information. The next bit was the creative step, using the map to think laterally about the information that was available by seeking new connections between information items, or unusual ways to analyse and use the information. We came up with a host of new ideas, but here we will just describe one of the innovations.

In our map, customer was initially described as a role taken on by a person or organization when purchasing or using the bank's products. Exploring the customer role and defining it in more detail led to a suggestion of a new label of 'recipient' for this key role. Changing customer relationship management into recipient relationship management and then treating buyer, client, consumer, customer, end-user and power-user as discrete subroles for recipient, provided a totally different way of thinking about customers, their requirements and their relationship with the bank, resulting in better analysis of product use, which led to new product facilities and a measurable improvement in customer relationships.

New concepts and ideas have a profound influence on how we run an organization. Knowledge management itself is a relatively 'new' function, which has changed the way many companies use their intellectual assets. Similarly, the emergence of the business process re-engineering (BPR) movement in the 1990s has resulted in a leaning towards process-driven analysis of contemporary organizations. This is not to say that knowledge management or business process re-engineering are good or bad ideas, but to illustrate the deep impact of theories on organizational life.

It is not always worth the effort of making knowledge tangible, but there is sometimes value in doing so. An international IT company ran a workshop to find ways to break down national boundaries on sales to multinational clients. Discussing and sharing anecdotes and stories (tacit knowledge) produced many positive suggestions for improving the sales process, but after the workshop the knowledge that had been documented – such as process flows, checklists and diagrams – was destroyed. The opportunity to exploit this explicit knowledge during redesign of the processes and subsequent training exercises was wasted. One of the main reasons for including 'knowledge' as one of the eight factors is the need to decide when personal knowledge should be transformed into corporate information and when codifying knowledge is unnecessary.

Responsibility

Information assets, like other corporate resources, can be managed and used well or mismanaged and wasted. Establishing responsibilities is critical for getting a good return from information.

Responsibility for information is much more than simply establishing 'ownership'; in fact, ownership alone does very little to change the way that information is used, as we will discuss later on. Responsibilities include deciding who will be accountable for:

- Planning and funding changes to the information resource.
- Creating or distributing information and knowledge.
- Designing information structures and organizing information.
- Analysing data and developing new models for interpreting them.
- Using information efficiently and productively.

There are, unfortunately, many organizations that never seem to get anything done. We visit them after 2 years and they are still talking about the same pressing problems and, despite their urgency, nothing has changed. Invariably it is difficult to tell who is responsible for changes and frequently there are bun fights over ownership that never move beyond political wrangling. The first step towards resolving this inertia is to be more specific about the types of responsibilities that are needed.

Assigning responsibilities does not have to be complicated and finding the appropriate person combines accountability as a natural part of their work. The oversights revealed by a more comprehensive set of responsibilities are quite staggering, ranging from the major transformation project that did not have anyone to fund the changes, to the most common situation of information that is collected and stored but never used! Linking responsibilities with categories ensures that the information resource is well managed and used, whereas the link with processes makes sure that planned tasks are accomplished.

Responsibilities should not only be assigned to people within your own organization and it frequently helps when they are shared beyond the enterprise boundaries. Some companies give customers the responsibility to keep information about themselves up-to-date, either through the opportunity to update address details on a monthly invoice or to log on to a website to update personal information. Such procedures are usually simple, with incentives for customers to keep their information current that are often information-based, such as receiving details of special promotions. Another common example of joint responsibilities is in supply chain relationships such as a retail company sharing sales data with preferred distributors.

Process

Information has value when it is used in actions or decisions, so analysing the process of using information is therefore of prime value and importance for:

- Improving decision-making.
- Simplifying work and information flows.
- Achieving action plans and change initiatives.
- Developing information value chains.
- Maximizing use of information.

The process aspect of architecting covers the *use* of information and is therefore concerned not so much with what is done but how it is done – it ain't what you do it's the way that you do it.

> *Studying the use of information by a distributor exposed many work-arounds that were not obvious from a purely task standpoint or by studying the workflows. Addressing these needs reduced the time to fill an order by 31% and cut errors by 24%. When introducing on-line banking, an international bank found that customer use of information via the Internet was unlike that of internal staff users, which therefore required very different types of information. For example, staff at the bank understood the process for verifying a loan application, conducting credit checks and approving the loan, whereas many Internet customers became frustrated by delays in the process that they were not expecting. Adding further information to the website, including a diagram that showed an overview of the process flow, reduced the number of complaints and resulted in a greater number of successful loan applications.*

How information flows from one person or department to another is one of the determining factors for increasing the return from information (RFI). Information value chains are similar to a manufacturing production line in the sense that each step in a process has the potential to take information from a previous step and add further value to it. In practice, people working on one stage of a process often do not know what information their colleagues use in a previous step, so the potential to reuse information or increase its value is wasted.

> *At one financial institution each senior department gathered its own information to analyse key performance indicators, quite unaware of whether the same information was being produced simultaneously by another group. Creating a map of the indicators used made it possible to make the information flows explicit,*

revealing huge overlaps in collating data. Eliminating this redundant effort cut the cost of gathering information, while discovering ways to reuse information helped to maximize its value – resulting in a greatly increased return from information.

Making processes an integral part of the architecting approach is one of the quickest means for getting the most from the information resource.

Meta levels

Meta data are *information about information.* They provide the *language and grammar* for describing, structuring, analysing and managing information, as well as *templates or patterns* to guide more detailed design and construction.

Because meta data are information about something else, there is an implication of layers or levels, with each meta level providing information about the next level down. A TV or radio guide provides *information about* programmes, such as when they were produced, a summary of their content, the names of participants, an opinion about or rating of the programme, and when they are scheduled for broadcast. The information in the TV guide is, at one level, providing a directory or guide to the actual programmes, which have their own information content at a lower level. Another way of thinking about this, is that the higher meta level is an index to the lower level. An entity relationship model contains *information about* corporate data and can be used as an index to understand what corporate data are available. The yellow pages on a corporate intranet are an index to some of the personal knowledge and skills within a company.

Lack of meta data for a subject makes many information management tasks difficult or impossible. Try watching a TV programme without knowing which channel it is on or when it will be broadcast! The meta data allow you to decide which programmes to watch without seeing the programme first. Comparing data structures in one software program with those in another requires information about those structures – otherwise the comparison is unworkable.

Meta data can also be used to create templates and patterns that provide knowledge and advice on how to structure and use information. Style guidelines for a website are meta data about the look and feel of the web pages.

Creating a set of templates for the five most common documents (travel options, booking form, insurance form, travel itinerary, special offers) at a travel company resulted in a consistent look-and-feel, making them easier to read and use, and eliminated set-up times for new documents.

Introducing an architectural meta level above data, process and object modelling teams makes it possible to share the information and knowledge contained in their models, even though each methodology has very different diagramming conventions.

In some respects information architecture itself is meta data about the corporate information resource. Depending on the scope of an architecture it will require at least one meta level, while the most complex and sophisticated ones will require three or more meta levels.

How do we know that!! Where did the eight factors come from?

The eight factors were not simply drawn from thin air! They are a synthesis, blending:

- Years of *experience* in architecting.
- The *practice* of key methodologies.
- And *theory* from diverse disciplines.

Experience in architecting

Architecting changes with time and, broadly speaking, there have been three generations of information and technology architectures. Generations one and two each spanned roughly ten years, covering the 1980s and the 1990s respectively and further advances will gradually replace third generation ideas, which emerged around the year 2000. The continual advancement of architecture is one of the reasons why *evolution* is one of the eight factors. Each generation reflects changes in our use of information, supporting infrastructures, information technology and our levels of skill and experience in architecting. As use of architectures has evolved, so the list of factors has expanded.

First generation architectures were those published and described in the 1980s for developing standalone applications. Because of their focus on software development they only used information *categories* directly relevant to technology of the day, were restricted to the *processes* of software development and mainly catalogued *presentations* used for requirements specification and design.

The second generation took these initial ideas and applied them at an enterprise level across more than one application. Their broader scope extended *processes* to a wider range of information uses, increased the number of information *categories* and introduced new forms of *presentation*. In addition, the use of industry reference models established a layered approach to *responsibility* that differentiated between vendor-supplied models and customized enterprise versions, and opened up new uses for *meta data*.

The current or third generation has a focus on information rather than technology, which is evident in the need for better *understanding* and the increasing relevance of personal *knowledge*. There is greater recognition of the need to manage change and *evolution*, the role of *responsibilities* and a consequent need for broader information *categories*, better management of *processes* and more sophisticated forms of *presentation*.

Table 2.1 summarizes the features of each generation (for a more detailed discussion of these three generations see Evernden and Evernden, 2003):

As well as countless private architectures developed by organizations for their internal use, there are a number that are published or widely discussed on the Internet or at conferences. These might be called reference architectures, because they are frequently used as a starting point for developing organization-specific versions. Some of these were developed for a particular industry, while others have a more general outlook. (Examples of such architectures include Information Frame Work (IFW), the Purdue Enterprise Reference Architecture (PERA), Computer-Integrated Manufacturing and the Zachman Framework – also known as Information Systems Architecture or Enterprise Architecture. If you are interested reading more about these architectures, the companion website for this book provides references at http://www.4thresource.com.) Inevitably these various architectures have a great deal in common and their shared features and best practice were the foundation for our eight factors.

Some of the lessons from architecting include the need to divide architecture into a number of distinct factors, the value in defining a consistent set of items or elements for each of these factors and the benefit of grid diagrams or tables to summarize and compare factors.

The practice of key methodologies

There are scores of methodologies for analysing and managing information. As with architectures, there is quite a wide overlap between methodologies, despite the fact that almost every methodology has some unique techniques. No single approach can or does cover everything, so the most practical and common strategy is to use a mixture of the most appropriate techniques, whatever their source. There are a few organizations that stick rigidly to one method, but from our experience these are rare. It is far more likely that an organization has adopted sundry approaches at different times, leaving a unique mixture of legacy procedures and contemporary practice.

The eight factors draw upon the customs of information modelling methodologies, such as information engineering or object-oriented approaches, software development methodologies and practice in knowledge engineering and change management – to name but a few. It would be impossible here to list all of the methodologies that have influenced the eight factors, but some of the more common ones include information engineering, dimensional modelling, software engineering, the Integrated DEFinition family of methods (IDEF) and object-oriented approaches.

Table 2.1 The three generations of information architecture

Generation	Focus	Driven by	Content	Factors used
1st Generation: the 1970s and 1980s	Information systems as standalone applications within a single organization	Increasing functionality and sophistication of standalone applications	Explanation of the need for an architectural approach. Analogies with building architecture. Simple 2-dimensional diagram or framework that provide an overview of the architecture	Categories Presentation Process
2nd Generation: the 1990s	Information systems as an integrated set of components within a single organization	Growth in the complexity and interdependence of information systems. Demand for software reuse	Extension and adaptation of diagrams from 1st generation architectures. Population of frameworks with industry reference models and architectures	Categories Presentation Responsibility Process Meta data
3rd Generation: late 1990s and 2000s	Information as a corporate resource, with supporting tools and techniques in information technology	Emergence of the Internet, e-commerce and an increase in business-to-business applications. Growing interdependence between organizations. Adoption of knowledge management, systems thinking and a more holistic view of information as a resource	Explicit definition of principles and background theory. Development of multi-dimensional architectures. Customization of information frameworks to the needs of each organization. Generic information patterns and maps	Categories Understanding Presentation Evolution Knowledge Responsibility Process Meta data

Lessons from methodologies include:

- the expressive power of formal diagramming notations to depict information structures and designs and facilitate the sharing of ideas,
- the ability of models to capture complex business logic and rules and simplify reality by suppressing irrelevant details
- the advantage of step-by-step guidelines that explain how to perform routine tasks while principles and policies help guide decisions in more involved situations.

Theory from diverse disciplines

Architecting is an umbrella discipline, by which we mean that it draws upon research and theory from a wide range of arts and sciences. Some of these disciplines include:

- Systems, complexity and chaos theories
- Knowledge management, artificial intelligence and knowledge-based systems
- Organizational behaviour, change and learning
- Workflow and business process re-engineering
- Librarianship and information retrieval, schema and domain analysis
- Information and computer science and software engineering
- Communications, linguistics, psychology, cognition, sociology and anthropology
- Visual and graphic design and human-computer interface design
- Management and business practice.

There are therefore many similarities and parallels to the eight factors in these related spheres. Some of the lessons from, and comparisons with, these diverse disciplines include the wide use of categories: e.g. in the Dewey book categories used in libraries, or classification systems in biology for plants and animals; discussions about how we understand and learn from the cognitive sciences and psychology, and from experiences in teaching; guidelines for presentation of information from graphic designers, artists and mathematicians; or various theories for managing organizational change.

The result is a working set of eight factors that are as fundamental and necessary to information management as pitch, scale and harmony in *music;* colour, shape and texture in *art*, or ingredients, recipes and nutrition for *cooking.* They underpin all of the procedures described in this book, providing an integrating *frame-thought* for coordinating effort through the use of, and changes to, information. Through use of the eight factors, information provides a bridge uniting the more attributive, factual aspects of information supported by IT with the more abstract, tacit aspects covered by knowledge management and the high-level strategy planning and designs for process improvement with detailed organizational change and project management.

Every architecture is a subset of the eight

Information-based architectures include business architecture and enterprise architecture, which usually encompasses data architecture, technology architecture and network architecture. (For further examples see http://www.4thresource.com.) A frequently asked question is, what is the difference between each of these labels and much time is wasted when these terms are used without a clear understanding of their meaning. Basically the word in front of 'architecture' describes its scope; we will introduce a simple technique using categories to analyse and compare what each phrase means later in the book.

All information-related architectures are a subset of the eight factors. Knowing this makes it easy to see what each architecture offers and how one relates to the others. It also follows that the eight factors are a synthesis of the dimensions used by the architecture community and therefore represent best practice in information management.

For example, every architecture describes the categories of information that it covers; by implication, this is the one factor that is completely necessary for all information-related architectures. Categories are also referred to as subarchitectures, types of information, or views. Here are the categories of information as they appear in three popular architectures:

- The **enterprise architecture** described by John Zachman (1987) includes data, function, network, people, time and motivation.
- The **information framework** (IFW) (Evernden, 1996) includes strategy, structure, skills, data, function, workflow, solution, interface, network and platform.
- The **computer-integrated manufacturing – open-systems architecture** (CIM–OSA) includes function, information, resources and organization. [http://www.eil.utoronto.ca/entmethod/cimosa/cim.html]

In our experience there is a great deal of overlap – some of it obvious through the use of the same category name, such as function in the examples above and some less obvious in the use of different words, such as motivation and strategy, covering the same concept. Overlap and the lack of standards across architectures was the inspiration behind the eight factors – to identify and list items that are common practice, with the aim of improving the understanding and use of information architecture.

We are often asked why it is necessary to have eight factors – surely having it makes the architecture more complicated? Imagine an orchestra playing a magnificent symphony, creating a rich tapestry of sounds through the combination of different instrument types, melodies, harmonies and rhythms. A sizeable organization, with a large information resource, tackling complex changes, like the orchestra, will need all of the factors to a greater degree. A smaller company, dealing with a small part of its information and undergoing fewer changes, like a solo instrument, will still require the factors but to a lesser degree.

Attempting to remove any of the factors will alter the nature of the architecture. Some omissions are tolerable and the architecture will still succeed. To go back to our musical analogy, a pianist could play the melody and some of the harmonies, but would not be able to simulate the timbre of a full orchestra, whereas removing the timing and rhythm would destroy the piece. In a similar way, removing some information **categories** is possible when they are truly unnecessary, but having no **knowledge** or **understanding** of using a type of information will render it useless.

- **Each factor is necessary to a greater or lesser degree**. The importance of each factor depends on the requirements that you are going to place on the architecture. More sophisticated uses of information architecture require a greater use of each factor.
- **The eight factors are the essential ingredients for architecting**. If you know the ingredients and how to use them you can create an architecture for all occasions. Understanding the factors enables us to select those that are necessary for each occasion.

Using the eight factors – creating the management toolkit

Looking after and managing any type of resource effectively is a difficult task. The eight factors are used individually in the form of checklists or combined to form a comprehensive collection of diagrams, making a management toolkit that provides the means for architecting organizational change. The toolkit is the architectural equivalent of the balanced scorecard for senior management, making it easy to control and use the information resource.

Consider this scenario – an office uses a two-drawer filing cabinet for storing information and every time that an important piece of information is created it is added to one of the sections in the filing cabinet. Documents and files are often retrieved, used and updated, before being replaced in the cabinet. In this scenario, the information architecture includes the categories and labels for the files, the order that they are filed in the drawers and the procedures and responsibilities for using and updating records. Because the system is relatively simple and there are a small number of users, the architecture is implicit in the position of files in the cabinet and the way in which the information is used. The filing cabinet itself is a simple information management tool.

Corporate use of information is much more complex than a two-drawer filing cabinet. More users and greater volumes of information across diverse locations require a more explicit architecture and management toolkit. The complete set of factors act as a checklist to ensure that you choose the ones that are relevant to your needs. They all apply to greater or lesser degree, so some will be more useful to you than others. How do you decide which are relevant? It depends largely on *what* you want to achieve, the *scope* of the consequent changes, senior *commitment* to the process and the availability of *resources*.

Assuming that commitment and resources are available, here is an overview of some of the more common architectural objectives.

- *Categories* are used to decide what information is required in a given situation. It includes eliminating categories that are not really needed and adding categories that might have been overlooked or ones that encourage the creative or innovative use of information. Categories are also an excellent comparative tool that can be used to identify overlaps between projects and across departments or functions and to find opportunities for cutting costs or gaining synergy.
- *Understanding* is used to clarify meaning by formally defining and explaining terms or by developing hypotheses and explanations. It aids interpretation by applying a model or theory, or by comparing alternative readings of the data. Understanding is a tool for getting the full potential out of information and extracting the maximum meaning from data.
- *Presentation* is used to identify patterns and trends by using graphs and charts or by summarizing and reviewing information. It can be used to think differently by changing the format of information or using another sense (e.g. hearing or feeling instead of seeing). When there is a good understanding of information, presentation is the tool that communicates this understanding to someone else.
- *Evolution* is used to allow for changes through periodic reviews of results and assumptions, by including realistic timelines and deadlines and by anticipating future needs. It helps to keep information useful by keeping it up-to-date and accurate and by ensuring relevance and availability. Without evolution the information and its architecture gradually and inevitably become useless.
- *Knowledge* takes advantage of personal experience and skills by inviting people to interact with information and by encouraging collaboration and sharing. It is used to develop personal and corporate knowledge by using knowledge and information and by capturing knowledge in tangible forms. Applying knowledge is a powerful way of creating unique and innovative uses of corporate information and maximizing the return from information.
- *Responsibility* is used to manage information as a resource through organizational principles and policies and through shared acceptance of responsibilities. It ensures that things get done by establishing accountability and by linking requirements for change with responsibilities. Responsibility is a great way of getting everyone involved with the effective use of information.

- *Process* enables information to be used effectively, in both operational and management processes, by examining its use in key processes and by designing processes to take full advantage of it. It improves the processes of managing the information resource by developing suitable skills and capability and by building a supportive infrastructure. Without process, architectures manage information in a more static, structural way.
- *Meta levels* are used to improve the structure and organization of information by describing and comparing information structures and by developing the necessary links between structures. They are used to improve the use of information by capturing information about information through an in-depth understanding of organizational information.

Let us illustrate the eight factors by looking at a study of customer behaviour at a UK charity organization. Their objective was to acquire new donors and raise income from existing donors. One of the first issues was to decide the categories of information that would be used for the study. It was decided not to use external data, partly to keep costs down and partly because of the limited availability of external information that was deemed relevant. There was also a strong feeling that analysis would be more effective with a limited set of data. These two constraints resulted in analysis of a small set of categories, including information about people, households, locations (postal sectors), donations, and issues facing the elderly. Understanding the information was largely through creating data-based behavioural models and using these to help define new marketing campaigns. Little thought was given to presentation, relying on formats that were available in the software that was being used. Evolution was used to analyse past household response rates and current data to project the chance of future support. The knowledge of employees, donors and the aged was only used indirectly. The two main responsibilities were for analysis of data by external specialists and for marketing to act upon the results. Apart from the process of analysing the data, the main business process affected by the project was the mailing of propositions to households. Finally, the project used fairly simple meta data of information in operational databases. This project improved the cost-effectiveness of campaigns and progressively improved response rates.

As well as providing a quick overview of the architectural framework for this project, the eight factors can be used to examine alternative tactics. For example, use of a broader set of categories would certainly discover different patterns in the data and could result in alternative marketing campaigns. Understanding might suggest the use of external models, possibly from a different industry sector, for analysis, rather than rely on potentially limited models that could be derived from internal data. As well as making marketing decisions, the analysed information could also have been presented to potential donors to persuade them to support the charity. Evolution of the data could have been used to project further into the future and describe new scenarios, possibly with the addition of new categories of information, such as predicting life events that might happen to relatives and friends of donors and lead to greater empathy and support of causes. Opinions and viewpoints could have provided insightful knowledge without the need for detailed data analysis! Exploring additional responsibilities often suggests ways to get additional value from the same information; some options here might include the responsibility for reusing information or redesigning operational databases. Feedback from data analysis might suggest changes to the process of data collection, while new processes could be introduced to target donors by different channels, such as e-mail. Use of an additional meta level might suggest alternative ways to organize operational information that also supported easier analysis of trends. Instead of the fairly moderate achievements, this organization could have achieved similar results with less cost or more innovative changes by making more of the available information resource.

So the first step in using the eight factors is to decide which factors are relevant in a given situation. The next step takes each factor to the next level of detail. Each factor consists of one or more sets of items, which are sometimes referred to as examples of a type, instances of a class, or values for a schema. The best way to understand this is through an example. 'Categories' is the first factor and arguably the most important one because it determines which types of information form part of the architecture. If we ask what categories are available, we end up with a list of one or more items, which include *information about* 'places and locations', 'people and roles' and 'products, goods and services'. It is possible that each of these categories contains further subcategories, which could also contain subcategories and so on. The best way to visualize this is to think of a hierarchy or tree structure, branching out into more and more detail. These detailed branches can be defined as you use the architecture, or a standard set can be specified at the outset. Later in this book we provide example hierarchies for each of the eight factors, drawn from the practical experience of architecting information. These lists and hierarchies of items for a factor are frequently used as checklists.

They are also used in combination with items from other factors in diagrams that provide a high-level picture of key parts of the architecture.

The most common use is in a two-dimensional table, providing a simple tool that is used as a basis for planning and developing the architecture. Such tables show and guide – among many other things necessary for successful architecting – what needs to be done, when and how it is to be achieved and who is responsible for achieving it.

For example, the rows might be used to list *responsibilities*, while the columns show the main *categories* of information. The cells, being the intersection of responsibilities and categories, could show who is accountable for, say, *funding* changes to information about *products, goods and services.*

The rest of this book shows you through detailed examples and case studies exactly how the eight factors are used in practice. These techniques develop and build the organizational capability for architecting information, which grows the more that the architecture is used. The book was designed to provide assistance at all levels of capability for the eight factors. The diagnostic – 'to what extent are you using the essential eight factors' – in Appendix K, will suggest which of the eight factors need further development. To find out which level your organization has reached, compare each information category against the levels of capability (introduced in Chapter 3).

Key points

There are eight factors that are essential for successfully architecting information and organizational changes. Each of these factors plays a different role in the information architecture. Depending on your needs, some will be more worthy than others. Table 2.2 is a summary of the key uses for each factor:
The eight factors are derived from experiences in the three generations of information architecture, the practical application of key methodologies and theory from a wide range of diverse disciplines.

Table 2.2 Summary of the eight factors

Factor	Uses and value
Categories	Classifying and grouping items together Distinguishing one thing from another Dividing something large into smaller sections Organizing and structuring information
Understanding	Extracting information from data Interpreting and using information in innovative ways Discovering new meaning, patterns and trends
Presentation	Improving the use and understanding of information Communicating ideas and messages Persuading others by portraying information with impact and passion

(Contd)

Table 2.2 Contd

Factor	Uses and value
Evolution	Keeping everything up-to-date and relevant Prioritizing and controlling changes Recognizing changes and new ideas
Knowledge	Codifying personal knowledge as a corporate information asset Applying personal experience and skills to information Learning through feedback and practice
Responsibility	Assigning accountability for changes and information Reconciling differences of opinion Coordinating efforts throughout an organization
Process	Improving the efficient, effective and productive use of information Increasing the value and reuse of information Maximizing the return from information (RFI)
Meta levels	Providing a language and grammar for managing information Developing templates and patterns for improving use of information Providing an index to the information resource

Every information-related architecture uses a subset of the eight factors. The factors they use or ignore influence the purpose, scope and function of the architecture.

The factors are used on their own or in combinations to create a management toolkit, consisting of checklists and diagrams, which are used to manage the information resource and manage organizational changes.

3

What and why, and when and how

The world stands aside to let anyone pass who knows where he is
going.   David Starr Jordan

Pick battles big enough to matter, small enough to win.
                                                           Jonathan Kozol

To improve is to change. To be perfect is to change often.
                                                         Winston Churchill

Who and what

The main questions at the outset of an architecting project include:

- What changes are required?
- Why does it need to change?
- When are the changes required?
- How should it change?
- Who wants the changes?
- What will be the impact on the information architecture?
- What information is needed?
- How will it be used to manage the changes?

Each question is closely linked, so what is the best starting point? People
are ultimately behind everything: if they did not face challenges, have
ambitions and seize opportunities, there would not be the same urgent

need for changes! It is therefore important to identify and list the stakeholders – the people or groups of people who are involved in change. At this stage we only need to know who they are so that we can find out *what they want to achieve.* While people are directly linked to architecture through their acceptance of information management responsibilities, they are not part of the architecture itself. Later we will need to assign responsibilities for action!

It is also worth noting in passing that it may not be possible to get a consensus of opinion as each stakeholder has his or her own viewpoint. Later we will explain how to resolve these differences, but to start out we will assume that we are dealing with a group of stakeholders who share the same point of view.

Once you know who is driving change, the first question you need to ask is *what* they want and *what* changes are required! 'What' is a good entry point for architecting as it brings strong organization and structure to change by working directly with the information categories. It is also a 'good' starting point in the sense that without knowing what needs to change, architecting efforts are directionless. By implication, it is impossible to move on to 'how' or 'why' questions until there is some understanding of what.

'What' questions ask about *change* issues with questions such as:

- What are the challenges and difficulties?
- What is the ideal?
- What do stakeholders want to achieve?

They also deal with *information* issues through questions that ask:

- What information is needed to understand the change issues?
- What information is needed to manage or implement the changes?
- What information structures need to alter as a result of the changes?

Using information categories

The information categories, the first of the eight factors, are essential for answering 'what' questions as they provide a high level *checklist of the areas of change*, which helps to pinpoint *what* you want or need to change, and *the information that is required to understand and make the change*, which helps by focusing on collecting the right information.

Although the precise names or labels may vary slightly, lists of categories are found in all information architectures. It is important to have a set of categories that work well for your organization, so you must be prepared to adapt and extend them. A consequence of this is that your list or hierarchy of categories is not likely to be the same as those in other companies. Information performs a different role in each organization.

For some it is information about customers that is of paramount importance, so understanding customer needs is key to delivering the products and services they expect. For others information about their core business processes is essential for the efficient and low-cost operation of the business. While in some cases technology is of such crucial importance to their success that information about machinery or computers is a prime concern.

Some architectures use a single word for the high-level categories, such as 'people' or 'product'. In our experience using two or more words for each high-level name makes the categories more generalized, and helps clarify the meaning and content of the category. For example, using 'product' as a category, it is not clear whether it also includes services; whereas the label 'products, goods and services' shows that products *and* services are both part of this general group. 'Business environment and competition' suggests that we are very broadly interested in information about the many factors that affect the overall position or context of the organization.

Knowing which information is important in your organization is a vital role of the architecture and categories provide a catalogue or index of the crucial information, which is comparable to the classification of books and materials in a library. The arrangement of books in the library corresponds to their grouping by subject matter and their identification by a reference number within the overall classification. In a similar way, categories determine how information is organized, grouped, subdivided and classified and have a big impact on how well people find, navigate and use information. The emphasis of certain types of information over others produces a profile that is distinct to your organization and categories are the mechanism for deciding what information is included or excluded in the architecture.

Information about. . .

Whenever you do take action or make a decision you need information, but different types of information are needed for different situations. A quarterly review of product sales might need a list of products, sales figures by salesperson and region and comparative figures for the previous quarter. To decide resource allocation for the next budget you might want to know what changes the organization will go through in the next 18 months, which areas are critical for growth and development, what projects are planned, expected costs for different business units, plus figures comparing planned to actual spending for the previous budget.

The information required in these scenarios is quite specific to the situation and how the information will be used. Because the information is described *in context*, even the presentation of the information is implied in the description: the products are presented as a list; the comparative figures are side-by-side in a table; and the figures for each region could be shown in a bar graph. Categories provide a more neutral way of describing the information that is required, because they tend to separate the information from its context – just as the Dewey classification system for books has no connection with your reasons for reading a particular book.

Going back to our example situations, a simple technique for identifying categories is to think about the types of information that are needed instead of thinking about the detailed information that is required. The difference is quite slight, but the subtlety is important because it helps identify the categories that are important; for example asking the question 'what *type of* information do you need to review product sales?' might elicit the response, '*information about* products and *information about* sales'. Thinking about the types of information that are needed in different situations helps categorize and classify information. So the simple trick that helps to think in terms of types of information rather than detail is to preface a potential category with the phrase 'information about'. *Information about* products suggests 'product' as a candidate category, while *information about* a list of products shows that 'list' is not needed at this stage.

Providing a simple and powerful structure

Categories describe what information is needed by distinguishing one piece of information from another depending on its subject matter or topic. In common situations the types of information we need are fairly obvious, but when contexts become less familiar or more complex and the volume of information increases, so categories become more important for deciding the scope of the architecture. The set of categories determines the focus of the information architecture and the name given to an architecture usually reflects this. Thus business architecture includes *information about* the business, such as its processes, customer data and details of products and services; and enterprise architecture covers *information about* the organization as a whole, but with a strong emphasis on its commercial operations and supporting information systems. A data or process architecture contains *information about* data and processes respectively. Note that there is a degree of overlap, with some categories included in more than one architecture. Each architecture uses a subset of the possible categories and a comprehensive list of categories provides a tool for comparing one architecture against another.

Information categories work in a similar way to a thesaurus. A thesaurus structures words using a sophisticated concept index, which is described as 'a semantic hierarchy of the most common concepts we use' (Roget's 21st Century Thesaurus). All other words fall under one of ten concepts – actions, causes, fields of human activity, life forms, objects, the planet, qualities, senses, states and weights and measures. Words with similar meaning are conceptually alike; for example, looking up the word 'structure' offers construction, configuration, arrangement, composition, organization, form and shape as alternatives.

Separating one piece of information from another is determined by conceptual differences, while several items are grouped into the same category based on their conceptual similarities. Similar types of information have similar characteristics, so techniques for analysing, structuring and using one type of information can be reused for similar types within the same category. For example, action plan, goal, and requirement share similar characteristics and could therefore be grouped together in a category called 'strategy and purpose' because they share a sense of something that must be completed within a set period of time. A room, a vehicle and a document could be categorized as types of 'property and equipment' and, as such, they could all have owners, users and value.

Just as the real life items are similar, so there are similarities in the structure and use of *information about* the items. This is a very powerful problem-solving technique that makes it possible to know a great deal about less familiar information simply by knowing how to structure and use other types from the same category.

What information should we manage?

At many organizations the basic question – what types of information do we want to manage? – is not asked, let alone answered and yet the most important decision to make about the architecture is to decide its scope. Too many organizations choose a scope that is too narrow, or one that does not reflect their true needs, so not surprisingly, the architecture fails to deliver the benefits that were hoped for.

Another common mistake is to try to cover everything at once, which is the consequence of failing to decide what information is directly relevant, necessary or strategic. Because there is no clear statement of what is important, efforts at information management lack focus, resulting in the classic story of the organization that embarks on one information-related project after another with no improvement in the overall use of information.

Deciding which information categories form the architecture makes it easier to identify information that is relevant, necessary or strategic, information that is not as important and information that has been overlooked or ignored. This can be done either for the enterprise as a whole, or for a particular project, product, business unit or marketing campaign.

An insurance organization at the forefront in adopting the latest technologies did not stop to examine its relevance to executives, staff or customers, making the assumption that the latest technology solutions must be relevant and useful. Information-

related projects included database marketing, customer data analysis, mobile data services, customer relationship management, business retention, data mining, and e-business solutions. Using a checklist of information categories with managers from fourteen business areas identified the types of information that were really important. When these were mapped to recent technology projects they showed little significant impact on critical information. The technology projects created some new information that was not useful at all, improved the usefulness of information that was not particularly relevant and even took away information that had previously been useful! Using information categories beforehand would have prevented wasted cost and effort.

As a general rule it is better to choose a broad scope, based on a comprehensive set of categories or a list that is easily extended and implement it gradually using an evolutionary approach, rather than picking a smaller scope and find it is difficult to extend or change later.

Prioritize the information categories that are most important, as it is impossible to manage all types of information at once. Prioritizing ensures that time and effort are invested where it can deliver real value. Focus on information that needs to be managed or structured and work out which information will benefit from a formal architecting process. It is also much easier to manage a single comprehensive architecture and use subsets of the overall information architecture to show different viewpoints. Basing each view on the full set of information categories and explicitly stating which categories are included avoids confusion and ambiguity. Different viewpoints then become simple subsets, eliminating duplication of effort, controlling inconsistencies between different perspectives and providing an integrated overview.

Be aware that pre-defined architectural scopes will not necessarily meet your needs. They make assumptions about your information requirements and, in many cases, will not be an exact fit to your needs. It is better to customize the information architecture so that it is right for your organization. Selecting the wrong information categories results in structures and designs that are not effective.

Three main categories of information

In more than 20 years of developing and working with information architectures we have discovered three main categories of information. From an architectural perspective these are categories because each has a fundamentally different purpose, which is reflected in the way it is documented, the people who use it and how it is used. Ultimately the three categories are interrelated to one another, which is why they all form part of a single information architecture. While some information architectures do not cover all three areas, it would be impossible for them to show fully how information is used throughout the organization.

- **Organizational or management information** is used to understand and make decisions about the organization itself, such as *information about* organization and management structures, strategy and purpose, and business environment and competition. It is information that assists in the administration of the organization, in strategic planning and direction setting and in managing personnel and their skills.
- **Business or operational information** describes the business (or businesses) that an organization manages, including *information about* its products, goods and services, marketing and sales, customers and transactions. This information assists in meeting customer needs and in providing products and services.
- **Information about supporting technologies** is *information about* the technical infrastructure that supports business operations and management decisions, for instance information about software applications and interfaces, communication networks, and system platforms. This helps develop and manage information systems.

It is helpful to separate requirement analysis using the three broad information types – organizational, business and technology requirements. By keeping each information type distinct we get a clearer picture of what is required because our understanding is not constrained by limitations imposed from the other two categories. Business analysts can discuss how they would use information in an ideal world – without restrictions imposed by staff skills or budgets (organization requirements) or the limitations imposed by applications and networks (technical requirements). Taking these other factors into account limits people's thinking. People know the limitations of 'the way things are now' and project these onto their future needs even when these restrictions do not need to apply any more!

When information is used in a particular context, the organization, business and technology requirements are combined to create a design that accommodates and balances each outlook. Information is only as effective as the weakest link. If you have the best and latest technology but you do not have managers and business people with appropriate skills and experience to use it, then you will be limited by your organizational competence. If you have great strategic vision and strong products in the marketplace, but you do not have the technology to support them, then you are constrained by technology.

As you implement changes in the use of information, there is an additional complication – history. Except in very rare situations you will always have to deal with legacy information systems, legacy processes, legacy thinking, legacy skills – in fact, legacy everything. This is the balancing act between implementing the design as planned and coming up with ingenious workarounds to make it work in reality.

An example checklist of information categories is provided in Appendix B, followed by an outline of the scope of various types of architecture.

Using the checklist of categories

The checklist of categories is one of the key information architecture tools, which is used every time that information needs are analysed – for example, in defining the complete scope of the architecture, scoping a particular project, or identifying the information needs of a business department. The checklist is used to understand the information needs of key decisions – for example, whether to develop a new product or not, deciding how to restructure the organization, or whether to invest in a new technology. The most important categories should be a key part to the information architecture, while any category that is left out should be of little or no importance.

If a category is found to be missing it should be added to the list, making sure that it is not already listed with a different name, while examples can be tailored to represent the specific needs of your organization. By asking others to use and extend this checklist it will quickly become the foundation for managing the information resource. Comparing the categories that are selected by different groups of people gives a good understanding of overlaps and differences in requirements. Asking users to explain the importance or use of their selections helps to prioritize needs and is a starting point for knowing the value of each piece of information by capturing alternative perspectives. (Further discussion of the labels used as categories is included in Chapter 8: Improving the architecture and keeping it current.)

The following questions will help to evaluate the importance of each information category:

- How necessary is each category?
- What would happen if this information were not available?
- Assuming that this information is available, how useful is it?
- What information is needed for daily, routine work?
- What information is needed in extraordinary or unusual decision making situations?
- Which types of information are really important?
- If you could only have access to information in three categories, which ones would they be?

Another way of using this checklist is to decide which information needs a formal management process or structure, as opposed to being left to an informal or casual approach. As with most resources in an organizational context, formal approaches will reduce costs and increase value in proportion to the value and importance of the resource itself.

Identifying information needs in different contexts is important for making sure that *all* of the right information is available and that the work space is not cluttered with too much information. The information, the right information and nothing but the right information – so to speak.

Developing a website

Web technology has been adopted at such a pace that there are very few genuinely green-field sites, where an Internet site or corporate intranet is being built totally from scratch. A holding company, with well-established operations throughout the world and more than 100 000 employees, had already built both a DOT.COM Internet presence and numerous intranet sites. A quick analysis of the content of the intranet pages, mapped against the information categories, revealed the ones that were fairly well covered:

- *Organizational or management information: Business environment and competition; People, groups and roles; Skills and competence*
- *Business or operational information: Places and locations*
- *Information about supporting technologies: Communication networks*

The heavy emphasis towards people, skills, locations and communication networks was mainly because early intranet development was based around the notion of corporate yellow pages, serving as a directory to help staff contact one another when solving problems that depended on rare knowledge or skills. What was more interesting were these comments about other categories, suggesting improvements to the intranet:

- *Community and culture – we didn't really take into account different attitudes towards sharing knowledge and ideas across the web. In some countries the yellow pages were seen as a way to increase personal influence and make social contacts; in other countries there was a general reluctance to put any personal information onto a web page.*
- *Intellectual assets and knowledge – we didn't view the information and knowledge on the web pages as intellectual assets. We should have spent a lot more effort in formalizing this knowledge in a way that made it really accessible. Because the focus of the intranet was on the individual, it was difficult to get a corporate-wide overview of skills or knowledge; we don't know what we know as a company.*
- *Measurements and key indicators – there was no mechanism for*

evaluating skills and knowledge. Anyone could say they were an expert, but there was no scale for measuring what they meant by this. There weren't any links to the key indicators we were trying to measure, so we couldn't use the intranet to work out whether we were achieving those targets or not.

- **Organization and management structure** – we quickly found out that the organization structure varied enormously worldwide. Job titles and descriptions weren't standardized and there were very different needs from one place to another. We found that staff wanted to know more about the position of people that they were talking to – they wanted to know where they fitted in and what their responsibilities were.

- **Strategy and purpose** – we saw strategies as sensitive and confidential. More of this information could have been made available – it would have helped people to see where their skills applied and given them a clearer sense of direction. One comment we heard was that staff found out more about company plans from newspapers and radio.

- **Processes and events** – we encouraged people to describe their skills and capabilities, but we didn't ask them to describe the processes where they used these skills, nor did we ask them to link skills to processes. It was very difficult for managers to see whether skills were being used, or even whether they were necessary when they were listed devoid from any process context.

- **Property and equipment** – as an organization we use a lot of equipment, but descriptions on the intranet forgot to mention this; people just assumed that a reader would know which equipment was used to solve a problem. It would probably be useful to have an inventory of equipment.

- **Software applications and interfaces** – this is very much like property and equipment: we don't have the same software all over the world; people develop or buy the software they need for their job, but that same software could be useful elsewhere.

The study showed that there were significant benefits in extending the scope of the intranet. New developments use information categories to allow developers quickly to identify the type of information being added to the website and reveal opportunities for linking it to other information.

Selecting criteria for a twin

A financial institution based in Spain wanted to find 'twin' companies for comparing ideas on best practice. Which criteria should be used for selecting a twin and what information would they share with their new-found twin? The starting point was to *highlight categories that were thought relevant, keeping notes of any comments and observations that were being made. A pattern quickly emerged, with the same points being made by different commentators. Once the main categories were chosen, two workshops decided which information to share and how it would be used.*

Three strong themes emerged. The main driving force, supported by analysis of the business environment and, in particular, opportunities from new technologies, was the idea that the customer experience could be significantly improved by including people who would normally be considered as outside the organization boundary. To do this effectively would require the sharing of knowledge, information and experience, which would require the development of new skills and responsibilities. There would be different types of 'team', involving people from outside the organization in key roles, and a need for better communication between those inside and outside the organization structure.

One of the recurring comments during this exercise was that the executives involved felt that they had considered the full spectrum of possibilities by analysing all of the categories and that their final selections were not just based on what they thought of or remembered, but were the result of a logical and rigorous process.

Synchronicity with a data warehouse project

A common complaint about information technology is it does not always bring the return or benefits that one might expect, given the huge sums invested. Although this is a story about a data warehouse project, it could apply equally well to other technology investments. A leading national retail organization spent large sums of money installing and populating a data warehouse, with the intention of discovering exciting new connections and patterns in its data.

A data warehouse is limited to the data that are available for populating it, which often means that it is inclined towards business or operational information. Organizational or management information is the expected output, rather than a possible input, which means that information in these categories is not included in the data warehouse. In this example the warehouse was populated with customer, product, location and transactional information. Although some interesting patterns emerged from the data, it was difficult to see how these discoveries served a useful business purpose. We asked senior managers to select the five information categories that they considered most lacking, keeping a detailed record of why each category was chosen and how each manager thought that type of information would add value. The five categories most frequently chosen were:

- *Business environment and competition – managers felt it was necessary to put findings into a context, which included an understanding of what their competitors were doing and the factors that caused changes to patterns in the data. For example, customer purchases vary widely by season, especially in holiday periods; some of the connections were obvious, like sales of Christmas pudding in December, but the triggers for other seasonal variations were not so clear.*
- *Measurements and key indicators – managers felt that traditional measurements were not appropriate to the large volumes of data that were now being handled (with an average 8 million customers per week and more than 25 000 products on the shelves). Using new types of indicator could give the company an edge over its competitors.*
- *Skills and competence – managers felt that they were not trained in how to use data, either through accessing them directly, or interpreting and using them. They felt that there should be different ways to access and view the information, depending on the skill of the user.*
- *Strategy and purpose – managers felt that, at the time of the study, the direction of the company was not clearly defined and that goals and objectives kept changing. This hindered their use of information from the data warehouse – if their objective was to increase sales of particular product lines then they would require different information than a goal to focus sales around weekly special offers.*
- *Agreements and contracts – managers felt that they needed more information about contracts with suppliers because some of the ideas that emerged from data analysis were limited by clauses in agreements, making it difficult to modify buying schedules.*

Even at a high-level the categories provided an excellent structure for analysing information, by providing a neutral checklist for assessing whether it was suitable for business and management needs or not. Categories also made it easy to solicit the views of different users, whether they were senior managers or operational staff, by providing a framework for asking questions about what information is required, how it is used and how it might be used.

Why

Using a checklist can lead to the danger of wanting everything and it is very easy, especially with a comprehensive inventory, to get carried away and 'tick all the boxes'. The importance of each item on the list is often a matter of degree and, to a certain extent, everything *is* necessary when dealing with larger, complex changes that touch numerous areas, or when using a systems thinking approach that encourages us to find associations and dependencies between items.

What we need and *why* we need it are very closely related. Asking 'why' something is needed helps to narrow the scope to what really matters by explaining why it is important, by justifying why a change is required and by giving evidence to prioritize one view over another. It reveals underlying challenges and difficulties that are causing problems with the current situation, as well as exposing the possibilities and options for improving things, for the ideal or at least for something better.

When faced with a demand for everything or for more than can reasonably be achieved, the best procedure the information architect can adopt is to repeatedly ask, why? There is a technique called a 'why-why diagram', which is useful for capturing the response. Say you are told that information about the business environment is a requirement, by asking *why* it is needed you are informed that it will help to understand what competitors are doing and make it easier to respond to changes in the market. Asking *why* to these two explanations reveals that understanding competitors will provide new product ideas and help avoid their mistakes, while the ability to respond is necessary to catch opportunities that provide a high-return but only during a very short period. Each response provides a clearer explanation of *why* the information is required. (There is another technique called the how-how diagram that is used to find out what information is needed and *how* it will be used; for example starting with the requirement to net high-return opportunities, asking 'how' may propose 'by making it easier to respond to changes in the market', and asking 'how' a second time might recommend 'analysing information about the business environment'.)

So when someone selects a category, ask for an explanation of why it is important and how it will be used. This can be recorded as a text comment, supported by ratings that document the importance, the cost of gathering, the risk in not having and the value from using the information. It is usually easiest to start with personal opinions that can be collected through individual interviews, which are later consolidated into a group viewpoint. An alternative is to gather the key stakeholders for a joint discussion and capture group comments. This works well both when there is a consensus of opinion and when there is an open debate of differences, although the latter requires more effort to record all comments. The checklist of categories should be used to make sure nothing important has been left out and, in some key situations, an explanation of why something is *not required* shows that this has been considered and rejected and not simply forgotten.

> *A furniture retailer wanted ideas for new product developments. Carol and Pete had different views on what information was required for this task. Pete selected information about people, groups and roles because it would identify their main customer types and could be used to create a standard set of customer archetypes for testing new product ideas, but Carol didn't think this type of information was important and so didn't select this category at all. Carol and Pete both selected information about business environment. Carol wanted to know which operations and products made sense, while Pete asked if they knew enough about future requirements and whether they could cover all of the possible options. From this simple example it is clear that opinions can vary widely from person to person, and even more so from one department to another. Table 3.1 shows the two opinions classified according to importance, value, cost, and risk.*

Table 3.1   Individual selections and ratings

Category	Person	Importance relative to other categories	Value from using	Cost in using	Risk if not available or not used
People, groups and roles	Pete	High	High	Medium	Medium
	Carol	–	–	–	–
Business environment	Pete	Medium	High	Low	High
	Carol	High	High	Medium	Low

> *Capturing the comments for each category of information makes it possible to share ideas on use and to agree how the information will best serve the purposes of the organization, resulting in more powerful arguments for positive organizational change.*

Even though only two people were involved in this example, there is already quite a wide divergence of opinion. Making these views explicit produces a wide range of ideas and options, including many that would otherwise remain unvoiced and suggests uses of information that often bring significant and swift benefits. Furthermore, it exposes any differences that could hamper changes and provides the justification or business case for decisions and action. If these differences of opinion remain buried they often come to light at a later stage when plans have been made and resources allocated, making it difficult to accommodate new ideas and sometimes jeopardizing work that has been completed. Publishing the results of this analysis and telling people what you have learned builds a deeper understanding of how information is used and how it provides benefits.

At the other extreme, spending too much time capturing purpose and rationale leads to analysis paralysis. It is only worth recording as information things that really benefit and help. Some ideas and opinions are better kept as personal knowledge, used dynamically as events progress.

When and how

So far information architecture has been used to reveal:

- *What* needs to change.
- *Why* changes should be made and the benefits they will bring.

This has been achieved primarily by using the information categories to find out what information is needed to plan and implement the change. It also highlights information itself that will need updating, restructuring, or new uses.

The key decision at this point is whether something is going to be done or not. If the answer is yes, then there has to be an action plan of some type to explain *how* it will be achieved and a realistic schedule and deadlines to make clear *when* it will happen. *When* and *how* serve as a double check against *what* and *why*, by showing that the necessary resources and commitment are given for the changes to succeed. If nothing is going to be done, then there must be something wrong with the what and why! Either nothing is ever going to change, which is unlikely, but in this situation the whole exercise has been pointless and you do not need to continue reading this book, or something is going to change, but not to the categories originally selected, or for the given reasons. If an action plan is not forthcoming, then you may need to start this chapter again to select more compelling categories and reasons for change!

An action plan is the most important management tool and is used to show how information changes over time, to identify planned changes to the information resource over time and to provide management with a tool to control these changes.

The main types of architectural evolution

Architecting information needs to look at organizational change from a number of perspectives:

- **A timeframe** is used to track change over time, for project management and for allocation of resources. Timeframes can be divided into stages or steps to distinguish between short- and longer-term changes. The four timeframes that are most commonly used for architectural changes are: 3–12 months, 1–3 years, 3–10 years and 10–30 years, which are subdivided into weeks, months, quarters, half years and years.

- **Degrees of change** determine the type of modification that is necessary, ranging from making existing structures more efficient (*optimization*), through adding new value or quality (*augmentation*), to their complete redesign (*transformation*). A fourth type covers information structures that need to be created for the first time (*creation*).
- **Capability** is used to determine how much *competence* an organization has to support a type of information. Competence is based on a combination of experience, knowledge, infrastructure, tools and skills. The approach used here is based on different levels of capability, ranging from the introductory or entry level through to the expert level. For example, at the introductory level there is little or no knowledge of information architecture, while at the proficient level the organization has used its knowledge of information architecture in several situations or projects.

Each of these three types of change can be used in an action plan, typically matrixed with information categories. (Information categories are shown along one axis of the diagram, with the type of change shown as the other.)

Developing a high-level action plan

The high-level action plan combines all of the elements discussed so far:

- **What?** In terms of which information categories are required for or affected by the changes.
- **Why?** In terms of explaining the challenges and difficulties that are faced and visualizing an ideal or better situation.
- **When?** In terms of deadlines or targets and a timeline for achieving them.
- **How?** In terms of what needs to be done to make the changes.

It is a combination of information and knowledge, some of which is highly structured while some is not so formal. Table 3.2 provides an overview of the look of a completed action plan. The 'what' column is drawn directly from the selected information categories, while the two 'why' columns are derived from the reasons for selecting these categories, with the information summarized and split into a description of the challenges and difficulties within each category and a description of the opportunities or ideals if there were no constraints affecting that category. This provides an excellent summary of the required changes. Between these are a number of columns, representing the steps between the current situation and the anticipated future situation.

Information in the action plan is given its structure through using the

Table 3.2 The high-level action plan

What? Selected categories, e.g.	Why? Description of the challenges and difficulties	When? When? When? When? *The action plan for moving* *from the problems to* *their resolution*				Why? Description of the opportunities and ideals
Products, goods and services		How?	How?	How?	How?	
Key indicators and measurements		How?	How?	How?	How?	

eight factors (we are *architecting* the information). Within this structure it is easy to consider less information to see a broad overview of the action plan, or to look at more detail for a particular section of the plan, because each of the eight factors progresses from a high-level through to greater detail. Items within a factor are arranged hierarchically, for example at the top of a hierarchy are high-level categories, which subdivide into more specific categories that could split at lower levels into more and more detailed types of information. For a financial institution the high-level category products, goods and services might break down in lower levels as follows:

- Products, goods and services
  - Loan products
    - Loan products requiring collateral
      - Mortgage loan
      - Executive car loan
    - Loan products without collateral
      - Car loan
      - Personal loan
      - Home improvement loan
  - Credit card services
    - Credit service
    - Cash advance

The appendices provide more detailed examples of hierarchical structures for the eight factors. Moving towards the top of a hierarchy makes it easy to scale up, for *seeing the big picture*, while drilling down becomes more specific, *to see more detail*.

Using timeframes

Time periods form part of the 'evolution' factor and are particularly easy to scale up or down. Four 3-month periods can scale up to a single period covering a year, while a 5-year period can be broken down into five 12-month periods, or ten 6-month periods and so on. In the action plan, a short period of time will contain more detail of the actions that have been planned, while a longer period of time will contain a summary of the expected changes.

Different time spans are used for different purposes. For architecting changes we have found that a 2-year range of four 6-month periods is best for high-level planning, while 6-months is long enough to achieve measurable goals and provide timely review points. Periods of 5, 10, or even 20 and 50 years are good for comparing alternative scenarios or exploring a vision for the future.

Putting this into practice, here is the basic approach for making an action plan using a table with seven columns:

- List the selected high-level categories in the first column
- List challenges and difficulties next to their appropriate category in the second column
- List the situation you want to achieve for each category in the final column
- Each remaining column represents a 6-month period – the full table therefore covers a 2-year period
- List, in the appropriate time column, the steps that must be taken to move from column 2 to the final column.

Table 3.3 is an example action plan based on Pete and Carol's discussions in the last section, showing some of the steps that they decided to take. The actions planned for each 6-month period are quite realistic and it is easy to see progress towards their mutually agreed objectives. The chart makes it easy to see if there is a conflict between one task and another and is particularly useful when checking dependencies between one step and another. For example, in the following chart the competitor information gathered in the first 6 months could be used to check the archetypes in the following period.

If Carol and Pete wanted to see more detail for their action plan then they could expand *People, groups and roles* to cover more specific types of people and role, such as individuals, organizations, teams, workgroups, customers, prospects, or suppliers. Similarly the *time periods* could be merged to cover broader intervals, such as 12 months or 2 years, to give a clearer picture of long-term change, or expanded to show actions every 3-months or every week. Moving up a hierarchy, items are broader, covering a wider and more general scope, while down a hierarchy items are more specific, with a narrow scope and more detail.

This type of action plan makes it easier to spot and allow for dependencies between changes. If dependent tasks appear in the same column, the situation can be corrected by sliding these tasks along to a later column. The chart can also be used to think about priorities and

Table 3.3 Example action plan

Category (Information about . . .)	Now	6 months	12 months	18 months	24 months	Objective
People, groups and roles	No standard customer archetypes	Analyse existing customer data. Identify criteria for separate archetypes	Define draft customer archetypes. Check archetypes against external data	Use draft archetypes to suggest and verify product proposals	Update archetypes if necessary	Standard set of customer roles or archetypes
Business environment	Insufficient knowledge of trends or what competitors are doing	Gather competitor information	Identify the main criteria influencing trends	Compare what actually happened against predictions	Update criteria used to track trends and competitors	Good anticipation of market directions
Etc.						

decide which things should be done first, or which actions make it easier to meet the desired objectives.

If a task requires more than the time period represented by a column, then it can be shown across several columns. It is vital that enough time is allocated for each step to be completed by deciding whether each action point is a 3-month, 6-month or 2-year job. For example, if each column represents 3 months, but an action point requires 9 months to complete, then it should be shown across three columns with an indication to show when the task started and where it continues.

Most organizations try to carry out more changes to their architecture than they can handle and at the same time they also allow too little time to carry out the changes! This simple management tool gives a clear indication of what is possible and what is not possible, avoiding taking on too much at once. When completing an action plan it is better to overestimate how long it will take. Making changes to the information architecture takes time; so do not underestimate the time needed for each task.

The next step is to define the changes in more detail. Because each information category contains a number of subcategories, it is easy to control the level of detail by deciding which types of information within each category need to be changed. A similar table can be used to capture this analysis, the only difference being the use of more detailed categories or more detailed timelines. A detailed example appears in the case study in Chapter 9.

At this more detailed level, improvements will always appear relatively small, but they provide the measurable short-term benefits that gradually build into a better information architecture and that would be much harder to achieve without an architected action plan. Because each detailed category is part of a higher-level one, it is easy to ensure consistency with the overall action plan, by ensuring that each detailed step is part of the high-level step. Exactly the same information-based approach is used to coordinate all architectural changes across the organization. Without this planning, many organizations make changes that are inconsistent and even counter-productive.

Assessing the degree of change

Broadly speaking, there are four types of change. *Optimization* works with the existing architecture, making it more efficient or effective, by improving the quality of what is already in place. *Augmentation* goes beyond simple optimization of existing structures by extending them to provide additional value or allowing them to be used in different ways. *Transformation* is a more radical form of change that throws out the existing structures to replace them with a totally new design and resulting in much greater benefits than either optimization or augmentation. Finally, *creation* introduces new information structures that did not previously exist and this type of change occurs in the rare situations when there are no precedents to deal with. Transformation always involves creation but, in addition, it has to deal with removing entrenched structures and handling resistances to change, whereas pure creation, which is quite rare, has no established structures to deal with. The four types of change – optimization, augmentation, transformation and creation – are described in more detail in Appendix F.

Optimization requires less effort than augmentation, while transformation requires a much longer timeframe and creation depends on how much is being created and the degree to which it has to impact with other existing structures. Looking at the *types of change* required for each information category in a 3- or 6-month period makes it easier to decide whether the changes are practical or not. If resources remain constant, then so should the degree of change across each column! This exercise serves as a check against commitment, resources, skills and timing, and if there are any discrepancies then the action plan should be adjusted accordingly. An example of this analysis is included in the case study.

Building capability

As an organization uses information architecture so its capability, which is a combination of skill, experience, knowledge and understanding, will grow. To achieve the goals of the action plan successfully requires the appropriate capability. If this is not available within the organization, which is quite likely at the early stages of development, then it will need to get the help of more experienced information architects. There are a number of levels or steps that an organization will pass through as it develops capability, starting at an *introductory or entry level*, where there is little knowledge about information architecture and progressing through the *basic or competent level* to the *intermediate or proficient level* and possibly to the *advanced or specialist level*. These are described in more detail in Appendix G.

The levels of capability are not the same for each type of information. An organization may be *proficient or advanced* at handling customer information, while remaining at the *introductory level* for information about key indicators and measurements. As an organization becomes more proficient at using information architecture, the quality of the information resource increases and the productivity of information users increases. Risks from misunderstanding and misuse of information also decrease. A table comparing the information categories against the levels of capability will help determine the level of architectural capability for each type of information and this will quickly show organizational strengths or weaknesses. The descriptions for each level of capability in Appendix G can be used to determine your organization's capability in each information category. Comparing capability against detailed information categories provides a good indication of whether the organization has the necessary capability to carry out changes defined in the action plan. A higher level of capability is required when the changes are more complex and the changes are expected to *transform* the situation, while a lower level of capability will suffice for a simple *optimization*. Capability can only be developed gradually; it is not possible to jump from the entry level to the proficient level without first becoming competent.

Long-term transformation

The same approach also works for more complex changes, involving a longer period of time and a greater degree of transformation, but with this slight variation, which is based on a 4-column chart:

- List the selected high-level categories in the first column
- List challenges and difficulties in the second column
- List the ideal situation in the third column. The ideal in this case is a vision that is difficult to attain or that will take a long time to achieve
- In the remaining column put a realistic estimate of how long the ideal will take to achieve. This may be 2, 20, 50 or 200 years – the important thing is that it must be as realistic as possible!

An organization had grown rapidly as the result of an aggressive mergers and acquisitions strategy and, as a result, customer information was stored in many different places, systems and formats. As an ideal they wanted to hold customer information in a single, standardized format, stored in one, centralized location, or in multiple places with real-time synchronization. Because of other priorities, technical issues and language differences they decided that a realistic deadline for this ideal was 15 years.

Note that such long range plans covering 8 or more years will not work in some organizations that use shorter-term planning horizons and only deal with changes that can be accomplished in a small time frame. A deadline of 8 or 15 years still includes significant deliverables in the short term, but these achievements build to a momentous transformation. Long-term transformation is necessary when there are major hurdles that prevent achieving the objectives in a shorter time. Typical stumbling blocks that impede faster progress include dealing with cultural variety, political pressures, limited resources, conflicting demands, or uncertain sense of direction.

An organization recognized that players in their market were strongly competitive, resulting in 'follow the leader' strategies, rather than ones based on a sound analysis of the true situation. They wanted to improve information about their business environment to enable a thorough analysis of their markets, resulting in unique strategies that differentiated their offerings in the marketplace. Although this was regarded as a vital transformation, they recognized that they would need to change attitudes and infrastructure within the organization to take advantage of such knowledge, making this an 8-year programme.

The next step is to turn ideals into actions. For each row in the chart divide the realistic deadline in half – so 50 years becomes 25, or 4 years becomes 2 – and describe what could be achieved at this halfway point, which should be some combination between the ideal and the current situation. Take this halfway point and again divide the timeline by 2 and write another description, until you reach time periods of less than 2 years, when you can start creating a detailed action plan, as described earlier. Starting with a far-sighted vision of the distant future, more and more information is gathered until there are realistic and practical short-term steps that move towards it. Architecting the information makes it easier to manage changes.

Evolving the action plan

Because actions in the plan are based on a standard period of time it is easy to keep the plan up-to-date. Our examples use a 6-month time period and at the end of each period the high-level action plan is reviewed and updated. Anything that was previously overlooked or unrecognized is added, irrelevant and unnecessary things are removed and unrealistic plans (what, why, when or how) are adjusted. The review may require updates to the list of categories as new types of information or new subcategories are added to the architecture. Anything that was scheduled to take place but did not should be given a more realistic position in the chart. One of the most common changes is that timelines have to be extended, which means that actions in the chart simply slide further across to the right.

Pete and Carol's new chart (Table 3.4) now has a history because it shows what has been achieved so far, while a new column has been added to keep the 2-year horizon visible and some of the tasks have shifted because progress has not been as swift as they originally hoped.

In a more complex environment the chart is invaluable for monitoring changes and seeing the big picture. Later we will explain how each step in the chart is linked to the other eight factors, providing a simple information-based tool that ranges from the top-level sketch to the highly detailed blueprint for change. Reviewing the chart provides valuable

Table 3.4 Developing the action plan

Category (Information about...)	Start	6 months	12 months	18 months	24 months	30 months	Objective
People, groups and roles	No standard customer archetypes	Analyse existing customer data	Identify criteria for separate archetypes. Define draft customer archetypes	Check archetypes against external data	Use draft archetypes to suggest and verify product proposals	Update archetypes if necessary	Standard set of customer roles or archetypes

learning and feedback. The achievements demonstrate organizational capabilities and strengths, while slippages show weaknesses and over-optimism.

Changes within the organization always require changes to the information architecture, due to the changing uses of information or the need for new information. Similarly, changes to information structures necessitate change within the organization if the new configuration is to be productive and useful. For example, intranets allow users to take responsibility for creating and maintaining their own information, but to be effective this requires major changes in skills, in responsibilities for organizational data, in the design of information architectures and in culture to allow for sharing and collaboration.

Key points

The starting point for an architecture project is to find out what changes are required, what information is needed to understand and manage these changes and what information structures need to alter as a result.

The checklist of information categories is the primary architectural tool for defining the areas of change and identifying the information required to make the change. A simple technique for keeping focus on the architecture is to preface potential categories with the phrase 'information about'.

Categories provide a simple and powerful structure for managing information about an organization, its business and supporting technologies. It is easier first to decide the overall scope of the information architecture and then subdivide it into sections to facilitate an evolutionary and iterative development.

Capturing comments about why information is required and how it is used quickly builds a detailed map of information requirements. This understanding of the unique use of information by an organization makes an architecture distinct from that of competitors.

Information categories provide structure to the action plan and help to assess the degree of change and whether an organization has the capability to complete a proposed change. The tools described in this chapter do not require sophisticated software and can be used on whiteboards and flipcharts during architecture planning sessions.

What and why (the information categories and why they are required) and when and how (the action plan for changing the information architecture), are the two most important architectural tools.

The eight factors

In this chapter the essential factors used were:

- **Categories**: used as a checklist to identify areas of change, to identify information that is required to understand and make the changes, and to identify information required in a specific context or situation. They are also the foundation of the action plan.

- **Categories – understanding**: used to capture explanations about why information is required or how it will be used.
- **Categories – evolution**: used to show when changes are expected to take place, to define the type of change that is required and to help assess whether the organization has the appropriate capability to handle the change. A chart based around these two factors can also include *understanding* about the current and desired situations, together with the *processes* for achieving the changes.

Who's responsible for what: assigning responsibility for changes

4

It's not because things are difficult that we do not dare; it is because we do not dare that they are difficult.   Seneca

Each man is architect of his own fate.   Appius Caecus

Responsibilities for information must be carefully defined if they are to make any difference. Ivan Shutte, speaking of the architecture experiences of Standard Bank of South Africa, asked his audience to remember that 'models don't solve problems, methodologies don't solve problems, tools don't solve problems – people solve problems, and I can't emphasize how much the organization is essential to the success of this' (Ivan Shutte, Information FrameWork Conference, 1994). The eight factors and the management tool kit derived from them are the foundation of any information architecture, but at the end of the day it is people who make architecture a success by accepting and carrying out their *responsibilities*. A practical approach for assigning responsibilities to information is therefore critical for sharing accountability for the information resource, securing the effective use of corporate information and ensuring that planned changes are carried out. In the previous chapter we discussed what, why, when and how, but now we must find out *who* will put up their hand and take on the responsibility for change.

Ownership does not go far enough

The common practice of assigning 'ownership' does not adequately describe the *obligations* of the owner. In other spheres of life ownership means legal accountability, so owning a car means that you are legally *responsible* for road tax licence and keeping the vehicle roadworthy, whereas in the corporate world the legal owner of information is the organization, in terms of duties such as Data Protection, rather than an individual or department that is assigned 'ownership'.

The legal and political connotations of ownership often cause unproductive turf battles. Ownership is not very good at handling overlaps between roles or departments. It does not explicitly describe a *commitment* by saying what the owner is going to do or describing the consequences of ownership. It also gives everyone else (the non-owners) a wonderful opportunity to say, 'it's nothing to do with me' and, consequently, it does not work unless responsibility is also assigned.

Shared ownership is even harder to make operable. In contrast, shared *responsibility* is easier to accept as it is more common in everyday life and suggests a more cooperative and collaborative arrangement. Talking about types of responsibility clarifies and makes explicit what people are going to do. By asking, 'what responsibilities do you have?', rather than 'what information do you own?', you are more likely to find out what is actually being done for each category of information.

In a case of forgotten ownership, an international bank spent 18 months allocating owners for every data item defined in its repository. Most owners could not remember what items they owned and the exercise did not make any difference or result in any changes.

Responsibilities for views on information

It is widespread practice to assign ownership for a particular piece of information, for example to appoint the accounting department as owners of information about sales transactions. A better approach is to allocate responsibilities for a *view* on information, meaning that accountability is not directly for the information itself, but rather for a viewpoint or perspective, which allows for many different views on the same information. This is better than defining a single owner because it permits differences of opinion and multiple uses for the same information.

To illustrate this let us assume a very simple information architecture that only contains four categories of information, covering customer, product, sales transaction and invoice. The product manager is only responsible for maintaining accurate information about products, so from her view there is only one category of information. The accounting department record and track sales transactions and invoices, so their view covers two categories. The marketing department analyses customer, product and sales transaction information. The product manager and marketing department both have an interest in product information, but the product manager needs information to show that a product can be manufactured at a cost below its sale price, while the marketing department are not concerned with manufacturing costs but rather that the price appeals to the customer. The information categories are exactly the same in each case and the information covers the complete needs of each stakeholder, but their separate 'views' are quite different.

A view identifies a set of *information items* that have been selected for a stated *purpose* by a person or group of people. This is an important concept for architecting information. Responsibilities can be defined for individual data items, but they are more useful when they are applied to a group of information items that belong together, either because they are used for a common purpose or conceptually they feel right together. The number of information items within a given view ranges from a few to several hundred, depending on the context in which the information is being used; thus a critical, but isolated, decision may depend on three key pieces of information, while the process to establish a multimillion dollar loan for transnational corporation could depend on the interaction of more than 150 information items. So a view lists the information that is required in a given context, but equally importantly it explicitly records that purpose and it states who is responsible for the view.

Information is used as the basis for defining responsibilities because it is:

- *Explicit* – it is easily described, making it tangible and measurable.
- *Universal* – it is required by everyone in the organization and is necessary for all decisions and actions.
- *Comprehensive* – it can be used to reveal and record the viewpoints and perspectives of all stakeholders.

Defining responsibilities in this way is about managing people *through use of information*. Architecting organizational change falls apart if you do not have people to do it, they do not know what is required or when and they are unaware of the consequences of not doing it. Assigning responsibilities *involves* people by explicitly describing their commitments and *motivates* them by describing the purpose and use of the information, thus demonstrating benefit and value.

An international bank ran three workshops to list, define and assign responsibilities for key performance indicators in corporate banking. Over the following 6 months more than 100 data sources were simplified to eight responsibilities for creating and sourcing information, use of information from an internal economist group tripled, while external information sources were cut by 38%. A map of key performance indicators increased sharing of that information from 4% to 68%.

Ultimate responsibility for information should lie with its users, not with information technology departments. If any of that responsibility is delegated to technical staff, then they should be directly accountable to the users. Some information architecture methodologies have a strong technical bias, and either ignore or pay lip service to an independent understanding of business requirements or the alignment of information systems with organizational needs. In our experience, around 40% of information systems departments develop or apply information architecture with little or no involvement from users and by excluding business professionals, often alienate them. Melissa Cook has said that 'the business community has been convinced that it can't possibly understand information processing anymore' (Cook, 1996, p. xviii), resulting in the delegation of information responsibilities to technologists. Architecture requires a deep understanding of business and managerial information needs that requires the active participation of the business and management community.

This technical bias forces an undue reliance on information technology for all of our information processing needs. A well-defined information architecture provides a comprehensive framework for managing and using information that works both with and without technology. 'We need to stop waiting for technology to magically solve the human side of our commercial information processing problems. Without an information processing framework or architecture within which to apply them, faster processors are probably going to make things worse in the enterprise, not better' (Cook, 1996, p. 6).

An information architecture based largely on technology is an incorrect analysis of the problem and results in inability to solve it. It is important that the architecture is recognized as a benefit to both technical and business professionals, with both business and technical responsibilities and commitment. Although a specialist group may be put in charge of architecture, everyone must be involved in explaining and defining their information needs. Information is a crucial business and management resource, so there should be a detailed inventory of that resource in the form of an information map and established measurements for studying both its costs and its value.

Views describe the information required from a particular viewpoint or perspective and always show a subset, or a filtered selection, of the information map (described in Chapter 5). To understand the information needs of an organization requires building the set of views that cover the needs of each information user. While each view is distinct, there are inevitably overlaps from one view to another. Views are also used to capture snapshots of the information architecture at different points in time and are, therefore, the mechanism used to map and manage changes.

Deciding the types of responsibility

Information architecture should take into account four types of responsibility:

- **Governance responsibilities** – responsibility for the overall *direction and control* of information. It is usually governance that organizations are thinking about when they talk about information 'ownership'. Ownership does not convey what the owner will do, whereas more precise words such as fund, plan or control are more specific; saying that the accounts department *funds* information about budgets and financial transactions is more exact than saying that they *own* this information. Governance responsibilities include funding information systems, planning information development and supporting the information architecture.
- **Stewardship responsibilities** – responsibility for the *quality* of the information resource. It includes activities for looking after information, such as creating it in the first place, archiving information that is not used very often and deleting it when it is no longer required. The same information is often created more than once in an organization, simply because the responsibility for creating or sourcing it is not defined. Other stewardship responsibilities are repeated unnecessarily, or not carried out at all. Verbs used to describe stewardship responsibilities include create, update, distribute, archive, delete, enhance, source, generalize, transform, optimize, specialize, normalize and gather, used as in create information, update information, distribute information and gather information.
- **Infrastructure responsibilities** – responsibility for creating the right *environment* for using information. It is responsible for defining and setting up appropriate information structures, including information technology responsibilities, such as defining database structures and links between information systems. Typical verbs include define, design and structure, for example in define information items or design information structures.
- **Usage responsibilities** – covers the *efficient, effective, productive and innovative use* of information. Usage responsibilities are often forgotten because of the focus on responsibilities at the 'ownership' end of the spectrum. We may 'own' our house, but everyone who lives in it shares other responsibilities because we all use it in different ways – eating, sleeping, working, painting, or entertaining. Usage responsibilities include using, analysing, deciding, evaluating, validating, verifying and assessing information.

Thinking about specific actions or activities makes it easier to understand and allocate responsibilities. Most types of responsibility are present and they should be made explicit for all categories that require change. Responsibilities for funding and providing resources are likely to lie with senior executives and linking each information category to the four high-level responsibilities is a quick way of seeing which categories lack the necessary executive commitment. It is also important that information is used.

> *A form requesting a loan asked applicants whether they were male or female, but once entered onto the system this information was never used again.*

This responsibility is more than simply using information – where appropriate it should ensure that the information is used efficiently, effectively, productively and creatively. The time and date for transactions could be used *simply* as a record of an event, or it could be used *effectively* to analyse purchase patterns according to different times of day or seasons. Common problems are keeping information when it is no longer useful or necessary, having more than one department create the same information and having information that is not used to anywhere near its full potential.

> *A company specializing in developing software had multiple intranet sites running to many thousands of pages. When it looked at the responsibilities for the content of these pages it realized that no-one had responsibility for removing pages when they became outdated. They decided that anyone posting material had to give it a 'sell by' date to show when the information was no longer useful. In addition, the web architecture group took responsibility to archive all pages that had passed their 'sell by' date and introduce new meta data to capture information about which pages were accessed and used.*

Deciding the levels of responsibility

It is impossible to define all responsibilities for information at the same level within an organization because some responsibilities only make sense in part of a company, information may be unique to certain departments and opinions will vary from person to person or from one team to another. Consequently, the architecture must have several levels of responsibility to handle these variations and differences. Most organizations have three or four distinct levels, while some organizations need seven or eight layers adequately to cover their needs.

The most common level is one to cover information that is consistent enterprise-wide, which is mirrored in the frequent use of the phrase 'Enterprise architecture'. While it is often desirable to have homogeneous information structures for economy and simplicity, standardization can result in suppressing individuality and difference where it is most needed. The development of new products or new markets often requires original and creative use of information, which might be impossible if enterprise standards are too constraining. A practical solution is to have what Paul Strassmann has called a 'federated governance model', with responsibilities for information being defined at the most appropriate level (Strassmann, 1995). He states that 'Well over 80 per cent of the labor costs associated with application development and maintenance are caused by the need to define elements that would already exist if you had global, enterprise, function and business layers in place'.

Above the enterprise layer are levels defined elsewhere, such as standards specified by international bodies, or generic information models and architectures that are available for various industries. These higher levels, which can save a considerable amount of time and effort, are often overlooked by organizations which insist on 'reinventing the wheel' when developing their own information architecture. For example the American National Standards Institute (ANSI) is a membership organization founded in 1918 that coordinates the development of US voluntary national standards in both the private and public sectors. The International Standards Organization (ISO) sets international standards. Founded in 1946 and headquartered in Geneva, it carries out its work through more than 160 technical committees and 2300 subcommittees and working groups and is made up of standards organizations from more than 75 countries. Among its many standards are ISO 3166:1974 which sets out a two-letter and a three-letter alphabetic code for representing the names of 'countries, dependencies and other areas of special geopolitical interest' for purposes of international interchange, ISO 4217 defining standard values for currencies and ISO 8601 which defines an international date format, showing dates in the format yyyyy-mm-dd. In this format, the 25th June 1953 is written as 1953-06-25.

Below the enterprise level are tiers that recognize the information needs of different business units, products, projects, or regions, as well as the opinions of individuals (as we saw with the views of Carol and Pete in the previous chapter).

An enterprise-wide level is almost certainly required, unless the information architecture is only to be used in one or two departments. The geography level is only required if your organization operates in more than one country and the architecture needs to be adapted to meet regional differences. It is very important not to underestimate cultural differences; forcing a 'standard' architecture across a multinational organization does not work. The local level is usually subdivided into a number of sections, with responsibilities allocated to separate projects, business units, locations or products when their needs are not identical to those at the enterprise level. The personal level is most often used as an interim step in gathering requirements for a local level.

Table 4.1 gives an example of the levels of responsibility used by a typical multinational corporation.

There are many geographical levels, but these only cover variations of components in the architecture that are defined and managed at the enterprise level. Local levels are responsible for using components at the enterprise or industry level whenever possible and for defining new components or for variations from the enterprise standard.

> *A multinational organization was made up of a number of different companies, some of which operated with a high degree of autonomy, while others had very close controls with the parent company. Information needs were different in each country, so it was important to clarify responsibilities for information that was shared between the parent company and its subsidiaries, particularly accounting information that had to be passed up to the parent company for inclusion in the consolidated accounts and annual reports.*

Appendix C provides definitions of suggested levels of responsibility, which should be adapted to suit the specific needs within your organization. Decide what levels are required based on differences in the use of information and potential differences of opinion, knowledge or experience; then arrange these into a hierarchy of levels. At the lower levels, add details that are specific to your organization, for example adding the names of business units or current projects, or listing countries and regions that require differences. Although we have discussed the levels

Table 4.1 Example levels of responsibility

Main levels of responsibility	Sublevels of responsibility	Further subdivisions
Industry level	Insurance industry, retail industry, petroleum industry, etc.	
Enterprise level	Regional level, such as Europe, Asia, United States and Canada, and South America	Country levels, such as France, Great Britain, Germany, Japan, Thailand and Brazil
Local level	Project level Business unit level	Project one, Project two, etc. Accounts department, Loan products department, etc.
Personal level	Sue, Dan, Christopher, Rosie, Lindsay, etc.	

of responsibility in terms of using the information resource, they can actually be applied to *any* resource that is owned at multiple levels within an organization.

Levels of responsibility help share the cost and effort of the information architecture. Without this formal approach in place it is difficult to share resources and infrastructure. Internal accounting procedures are one mechanism for allocating and sharing costs and levels of responsibility are a similar mechanism for defining obligations to look after and use information.

Assigning responsibilities

The checklists given here for levels and types of responsibility can be used in many different ways – but their prime use is to make sure that the important information types are adequately accounted for. A simple matrix between information categories and the four types of responsibility provides a quick, high-level overview – as shown in Table 4.2.

Table 4.2 Assigning responsibilities

Information category	Governance	Stewardship	Infrastructure	Usage
Customer information	All customer relationship and marketing departments. Facilitated by the enterprise architecture team	Customer. IT department	Enterprise architecture team. Human resources. IT department. Process support team	Process support team. Business units. Customer relationship roles. Marketing roles. Enterprise architecture team
Transaction information	Sales and marketing. Accounting. Warehousing and distribution	Accounting. IT department. Branch managers and staff	Accounting. IT department. Location managers	Sales and marketing. Accounting. Warehousing and distribution
Etc.				

For customer information, funding and planning change is the responsibility of the *business* through the relationship and marketing departments, while customers are given direct responsibility for keeping their own information up-to-date. The business units are also explicitly given responsibility for using the information and would therefore be accountable to show that they used information efficiently and productively. The enterprise *architecture team* plays a key role in facilitating study of requirements and changes, designing information structures and gathering feedback on the use of information.

With transaction information the story is quite different. Here the *governance* is split between three groups, reflecting their different *uses* of transactional information: for tracking of sales and the impact of marketing; as a key operational input to the accounting teams; and as part of the feedback necessary to maintain product supplies in warehousing and distribution. Whereas in customer information the architecture team played the key role, here it is *accounting* that is involved throughout.

Healthy interaction between the four types of responsibility – in particular governance, stewardship and infrastructure – helps to manage the impact of changes, which are mainly felt by people who *use* the information. Note also that there are often overlapping responsibilities, with two or more groups sharing responsibility for the same information category. Drilling down to more detailed categories or more detailed types of responsibility would show whether the overlap is exactly the same or not. When two groups, such as two projects, have exactly the same responsibilities it suggests that the projects could easily merge into one. The overlap between projects aimed at improving information architecture in some way is often quite large. Where there is more than one type or level of responsibility, it is vital that all parties acknowledge who is ultimately responsible!

> *A petroleum company used its information architecture to scope all information-related projects, with an estimated 48% reduction in project overlap.*

By increasing cooperation and team-work across projects and business functions we can combine the efforts of separate project teams by working together on common elements, and only working separately on components that are unique to a single project, thus taking advantage of analysis that has been carried out in other parts of the organization. Many of the problems and issues facing individual organizations are very similar, so instead of working on these problems individually it makes a lot of sense to work with other organizations to solve the issues. Forming alliances, even with organizations that might previously have been considered competitors, can be a very effective way to get benefits. This type of cooperation is increasingly common among organizations in a particular industry sector.

Responsibility for changes

Just as some responsibilities are assigned for information, so someone must be responsible for each change in the action plan – otherwise the changes will simply not occur. A problem with ownership is that it rarely seems to reside with those responsible for funding or carrying out changes. Making the responsibilities explicit removes the possible stalemate that occurs because a key duty is omitted. In many cases the responsibility for changes is the same as that for information, making it easy to add this detail to the action plan.

More collaborative plans require a higher degree of shared responsibilities, so it is important to make sure that someone is ultimately responsible for success! Remember that responsibilities should be allocated to *views* on information. In effect these defined viewpoints combine a set of information requirements with associated responsibilities and actions for change.

> *In a project to improve the management of customer relationship information, funding was shared proportionally across the budgets of all relationship and marketing departments, sourcing and analysing information was the responsibility of relationship and marketing departments and defining and designing information structures fell to the enterprise architecture team and IT department.*

There are some situations when external people may be needed, for responsibilities that require special knowledge and skills, such as architecting and modelling information, to transfer or develop new skills, or to facilitate agreement on disputed issues. External support can be shown in responsibilities for information or changes in exactly the same way as internal staff.

Key points

Ownership does not adequately describe the obligations of the owner and instead it is better to describe explicitly what is meant by ownership – such as *responsibility for* legal compliance or funding change. Assigning responsibility for information is critical for architecting organizational changes because it describes explicitly how people must collaborate to ensure success.

Responsibilities are defined for *views* on information, which makes it easy to represent accurately differences of opinion and overlapping accountability. The types and levels of responsibility show who is accountable and where responsibility must be shared.

Many architecture programmes stumble because responsibilities are not well defined, the single most important issue being who should fund changes. The types of responsibility are designed to span all accountabilities for the key information categories. Levels of responsibility help share the cost and effort of the information architecture.

Responsibilities provide an accurate way of adding information about accountability to planned changes and linking individual changes more directly to an overall blueprint for change.

The eight factors

In this chapter the essential factors used were:

- **Responsibilities**: used as a checklist to identify the types and levels of accountability for the information resource.
- **Categories – types of responsibilities**: used to show who takes each type of responsibility for each type of information.
- **Categories – level of responsibilities**: used to show the level at which responsibility is assigned for each type of information.
- **Responsibilities – evolution**: used to show who is responsible for each step in the action plan.

Developing an information map: how to navigate the information resource

You only learn something relative to something you understand.
Richard Saul Wurman

Once the organization knows how to determine what information is valuable, its investments in information gathering become more focused and productive. Stephan H. Haeckel

What is an information map?

An *information map* can be any *diagram*, from a simple graphic to a complex software model, *depicting corporate information*. As with a geographic map, the information map may provide complete coverage of the information resource, or it may just cover the most important features in the info-scape. It can also provide a historical record of how things were in the past, or a chart showing how it will be in the future.

An information map is used to catalogue, understand, organize and navigate the information resource. It describes what information is available and, to some extent, what is not. Just as roads on a route finder are colour-coded to distinguish highways from byways, so symbols and colour can be used to show what information is needed and what is not required. (An earlier chapter showed how the information categories are used to identify what is in and what is out of the architectural scope and this forms the basis of what is included on the information map.) The information map may include annotations explaining why information is needed or not needed, what value it adds, who uses it and how it is used. This can be recorded on paper, but it is usually much easier to document using a software package designed for this purpose.

There are four components to an information map:

- **Big picture** overviews.
- More detailed **neighbourhood diagrams**.
- **Views**, which show the information required from a particular viewpoint or perspective.
- **Information value chains**, showing how the information is used.

A *big picture* shows a *broad overview* of the information map and the most important *links between items on the map.* It is *large scale*, equivalent to a map of the world, showing the most important or key aspects but without much detail.

Detailed *neighbourhood diagrams* are based on a *focal concept*, such as information about a 'sales transaction' and only show *links from and to* this focal concept. There is a separate neighbourhood diagram for each focal concept, which is placed at the centre of the diagram with links radiating out to show related information. A neighbourhood diagram is *small scale*, showing plenty of detail and is the information equivalent to a map of New York City, London or Sydney.

Big picture and *neighbourhood diagrams* both represent the same information architecture, but at different levels of detail. If the big picture were a *map of the world* showing oceans, land masses and key cities, then our neighbourhood would be *a detailed map of each country*; if the big picture were a *map of the USA*, related neighbourhood diagrams would be *maps of Boston or Chicago* – the detail in each case is a matter of degree, relative to the what is covered in the big picture. *An enterprise-wide information map* (big picture) would be related to neighbourhood diagrams of conceptually distinct information categories, such as information about *products and services*, or information about *places and locations*, while a big picture *map of key performance indicators* could have neighbourhood diagrams providing *a detailed map of each indicator.*

Views and *information value chains* can be applied to any part of the information map and are therefore used with both big picture and neighbourhood diagrams.

Views group together information items that have *something in common*, such as grouping together countries where Spanish is spoken, grouping information items that are recorded in a stockroom inventory, or listing all items that are dates. A view operates in the same way as a relief map in a museum with a push button that lights up all of the historical buildings. The items included in a view are typically spread across different parts of the map and it may not be obvious that they are connected until they are highlighted as such. The same items can appear in many different views, just as another switch in the museum lights up all buildings that are factories – some also being historical.

Views can also represent information that is selected as *part of a responsibility*, such as information items used by the accounting department, or information items subject to changes funded by marketing and sales. (Ideally software handles different views based on a single information map, just as coloured light bulbs highlight the 'views' of buildings in the museum.)

Going a stage further, an *information value chain* is a special type of view. Not only does it show a subset of information required from a particular viewpoint or perspective, it also indicates how the flow from one piece of information to another creates value. This is very important for maximizing the use of information, because an information value chain highlights the accumulative value from using certain pieces of information in a particular sequence and this value is in addition to any value that each piece of information has in its own right!

A sales department at a car supermarket conducted a survey of the customer experience to find ways to improve customer satisfaction and increase sales. The survey produced a wealth of information that had significant value in its own right and helped the sales team achieve their objectives. The information map was used to identify how the results of this study could be combined with other information to gain further value, suggesting a value chain that reused customer experience information with market research and information about availability of second-hand cars to help purchasing decide which stock to buy. Without looking for the information value chain, information from the sales study would only have been used once.

Scope and scale

Scope and scale are deeply related characteristics of an information map. Scope determines what the map covers, while scale governs the amount of detail on the map.

Just as a geographic map could cover the whole country, a city, or a single suburb, the information map can cover the entire enterprise or one area, such as a department, product or project. The coverage of an information map is referred to as its *scope*. Whether large or small, the entire scope *or* a partial scope of an information map can be shown using a big picture diagram. A map that only covers the information needs of a small project will have a narrow scope. On the other hand, a 'complete' enterprise map evolves into something much more complex to cover every information need.

Cartographers publish a range of maps of the same location at different scales: one-inch-to-a-mile is a good general-purpose map, while three-inches-to-a-mile is excellent for walking and a quarter-inch-to-a-mile is better for long distance driving. Whether an information map is high-level or very detailed is referred to as its *scale*. A big picture diagram provides a high-level overview with a relatively small amount of detail shows all or part of the information map at a *small-scale*, while a neighbourhood diagram provides a low-level detailed view of part of the information map at a *large-scale*.

The highly detailed entity relationship model of an insurance company was so big that printouts covered the entire length and height of a 30-foot wall in the IT development 'war room'. Standing at a distance did not help to see the big picture, because the model was both large-scale and detailed. At the same time trying to see the context for a particular information item was also impossible due to the difficulty in tracking links to and from it because of the enormity of the map. Although the modelling team made the distinction between conceptual, logical and physical models, in practice they were all painstakingly comprehensive and the map lacked any ability to increase or decrease the scale, or to zoom in and out of detail.

In contrast, a logistics company used a high-level diagram of the twelve core information categories in their business. This big picture was used to control more detailed analysis, with each of the twelve categories expanding into more detailed diagrams. Whenever a detailed diagram became 'unmanageable', because its detail made it large-scale, it was divided into a high-level overview and a set of more detailed diagrams. This simple approach made it easy for users to change scale by zooming into detail or zooming out to get the big picture.

The content of an information map depends on its purpose and use and will be reflected in the scope and scale of the diagrams used to depict it.

Getting started

The hardest part of almost any task is getting started and starting an information map is no exception, partly because of the variety of choices that affect the type of map that is created. We have listed the most noteworthy questions under three headings:

- **Deciding objectives**: what challenges are you facing and what changes are required? What is the purpose of the information map? Who will use the map and how will they use it?

- **Starting large or small**: can you jump straight in and do everything at once, or is it best to start with a simple project? Should the information map cover the whole enterprise or have a smaller scope? Do you have to develop your own map or can you buy one ready-made?
- **Using software**: is it necessary to use software or not and, if so, which software?

Before you start it is worth remembering that there is *no ideal or perfect way* of creating and using an information map and you will therefore need to balance the various options to develop a map that meets your requirements. Because your approach is inevitably based on a variety of factors it is essential to follow a mapping discipline, which is provided by the architecture. Just as geographic maps are based on the grid structure provided by longitude and latitude and use standard symbols and colours to represent features such as elevation, roads, rivers, railways and vegetation, each component in the information map must be designed to fit with the rest. Let us examine some of the issues and tradeoffs that will influence the information map, before we go on to describe the steps for creating big picture and neighbourhood diagrams.

Deciding objectives

Some information architectures have a technical focus, while others are aimed at getting the best out of operational information, or supporting the innovative use of information. What you want to accomplish has a strong bearing on the content and design of the information map. It has been said that if you do not know where you are going, then it does not matter which direction you take and if the architectural objectives are vague then there is no way of proving their achievement. Despite this, it is amazing how many organizations embark on architectural programmes without a clear understanding of what they expect to achieve.

It helps to think about the audience or customers for your architectural services. Who is going to benefit by the creation of an information map? The people who benefit directly are information users, and an information map will help them understand and navigate the information resource, resolve information-related problems and identify better ways to use information. Then there are people who benefit indirectly from your efforts, such as information technology departments that can reduce their storage and processing costs through better information structures, or business analysts who can understand requirements in a shorter time by reusing the information map.

It is worth making a list of everyone that will benefit in some way from the information architecture and map. These people need to *know* what they gain from the map, by explaining how it helps them and describing benefits from their perspective, which also helps ensure that their interests are represented in the architectural objectives.

> *Before developing their information map, a bank drew up a list of benefits described from the perspective of various stakeholders, in order to get their support. Loan officers were told that the map would reduce the amount of information required to complete a credit check and reduce the time taken to check credit status of loan applicants. The sales force were advised that it would improve information about products, making it easier to explain them to customers, increasing sales and resulting in better sales commissions.*

Peter Weill and Marianne Broadbent conducted detailed research in the 1990s (Weill and Broadbent, 1998) into the creation of business value through information technology. Although they examined investment in technology rather than investments in information architecture, we have adapted the portfolio approach that they adopted to help you decide your architectural objectives. By sorting objectives into the four investment categories you will get a better impression of what the information map will include.

Investing for *leadership* is aimed at creating an advantage over competitors, for example through leadership in an industry, in a market or segment, or showing leadership in a product or process. Leadership objectives are important for proactive organizations that want to lead the way, requiring a map capable of analysing complex interactions between information about the business environment, competitors, products, strategies and skills. Typical objectives might include:

- Developing a competitive advantage.
- Addressing competitive forces.
- Positioning the organization within a market.
- Developing innovative services.

Management investments are designed to support the information needs of management and decision-making. When key decisions have a significant impact, management investment is critical, calling for information about key indicators, measurements, resources, action plans and objectives. It includes:

- Providing new types of information.
- Improving information quality.
- Improving decision-making.
- Improving the effective use of information.

Operational investments support the information needs of the business and the need to take action. A well-established organization with old-fashioned processes and legacy systems will need to invest more in operational changes which demand an information map covering operational data, processes and technology. Objectives are typically aimed at:

- Increasing process productivity.
- Improving operational efficiency.
- Cutting costs.
- Increasing sales.

Infrastructural investments build a sound architectural foundation for the future. Infrastructural investment allows an organization to respond quickly to new demands, needing a comprehensive information map of products, processes, organization structure and skills, and technologies, with objectives such as:

- Integrating the information resource.
- Developing flexible and agile information structures.
- Increasing the capacity to share responsibility for information management.
- Standardizing definitions and structures.
- Reducing overlapping and unnecessary redundant effort.

If the problems are purely technical in nature and require a software solution that can be developed with absolutely no input from business or management, then it is safe to have a very specialized information map, such as a detailed class diagram that uses object oriented programming terminology.

However, in most situations the map must support operational or management situations and therefore be accessible to a wide range of users from both business and technical backgrounds. Business people use diagrams that are similar to those of more formal information modelling disciplines and the most practical information maps often use a simplified version of the notation prescribed by these methodologies. If the information map adheres to the same basic principles and techniques, then it is relatively easy to turn the map into a detailed technical specification or to extract the map from a more detailed diagram.

Starting large or small

The best information map is the one that fits your needs and meets your objectives. As there is no generic solution that meets everyone's needs, an information map is created using a balance between buying reference components from a vendor, customizing purchases to meet the exact needs of the organization and developing components in-house. The precise balance varies from one organization to another, but here are our recommendations for keeping budgets as low as possible, demonstrating a quick pay-off from investments and achieving a high-quality architecture!

As we move further into the information age, generic information maps are starting to become more common, although many still have a strong leaning towards their technology origins rather than focusing purely on information. Information maps are also known as information models, references models, industry models and information meta models. Industry models are available from the major technology vendors and consulting firms, while more generic information maps are likely to come from companies specializing in information architecture. A search on the Internet should reveal the main sources. The cost of a generic information map varies between $100K and $700K, although more expensive does not always mean better quality or more suited to your needs!

These pre-defined components are generally of high quality, save considerable time and effort and are less expensive than re-inventing the wheel by trying to build everything from scratch. If you want carpentry tools to work wood you do not need to invent them first because you can easily buy them from specialists that design and manufacture saws, planes and power tools. Similarly, there are now specialists who develop and supply components for information architecture and buying a solution delivers results in a shorter timeframe. As few organizations have the necessary specialist skills or resources to build a complete enterprise map from scratch, purchasing a generic information map is generally considered the best starting point.

While it is impossible to buy a map that exactly describes the info-scape of an organization, a lot of information is actually similar from one company to another. Work using information maps and industry reference models shows that as much as 60–80% of enterprise level requirements are covered at the industry level, cross-industry and global levels. Effectively the *responsibility* for creating an information map has shifted from the enterprise to the industry level or the more generic cross-industry and global levels, leaving the responsibility for customizing the map at the enterprise levels or lower levels within the enterprise. The remaining percentage is met either through customizing reference materials or developing new components. As customizing takes time, it is best to adapt the reference model as you need it, rather than attempt to tailor it as a one-off exercise at the start.

In most cases, unless the scope of the information map is small, going-it-alone and developing it in-house is a final resort and should only be used when the components you need are not commercially available. Developing from scratch takes longer, costs more and is higher risk than purchasing something that is readily available. A detailed enterprise information map or model will take between 2 and 5 years to develop, will require the time of the most knowledgeable business experts within the organization and will need the facilitation skills of highly qualified and experienced modellers. Westpac's CS90 (Core Systems for the 1990s) project has been estimated at nearly $200 million (Boynton, Victor and Pine, 1993). Even with extensive resources (both in terms of money and time), there is no guarantee of success and very often costly developments are stopped, incomplete, after several years of investment. Typical difficulties encountered in these projects are finding suitably knowledgeable business experts, getting agreement on the structure and definitions of the model, dealing with inconsistency and incompleteness, lack of clarity, insufficient resources or time and a result that is too broad and arcane for non-technical people to comprehend.

Assuming a full-time-equivalent figure of $1000 per day, a team of 15 people working solidly for 3 months would cost $900K, which is a good deal more than the cost of most generic information maps; moreover, it would be impossible to create a complete enterprise map in that time and would involve many managers and business people in addition to 15 architects. So in comparison, a generic information map at $250K is a bargain!

The best approach strongly parallels the work of a building architect, who, in the majority of situations, will design an edifice using standard components selected from manufactured parts that are readily available. The architect uses his or her skills to combine and configure these standard materials to meet the unique needs of the client. It is only in rare circumstances that an architect designs something so extraordinary that it necessitates totally original components and when this happens development is more experimental, inevitably increasing both cost and risk.

A credit card company bought a data model developed as an industry reference for the financial services industry. Before using it they initiated a 3-month project to customize it. The model they purchased contained 2573 pre-defined information items, to which they added a further 381 items during customization.
Approximately 75% of the resulting corporate information model was derived directly from the purchased industry model.

So, if 80% of information architecture is very similar from one company to another, it is the remaining 20% that differentiates. Instead of re-creating something that has already been done, your time and effort should go into the 20% that is unique to your organization. Following Pareto's 80/20 principle, many of the benefits of an architectural approach accrue by starting with a generic information map or model, which is quickly adapted to a particular situation.

There are several things to consider when seeking vendors for architecture components. Remember, there are different meanings for the term 'information architecture'. In a narrow sense it might mean the design, structure and navigation of a website, or refer to the development of information technology. Using the phrase in a broader context will find a wider range of skills, techniques and components, which can be refined if necessary to find more specialized areas. When you are searching on the Internet, use a variety of words and phrases, such as those used in this book, to find suppliers, for example, try 'reference model', 'industry model' or 'concept map' as well as 'information model'.

Compare commercial materials against the information categories to see which types of information they cover. A traditional information systems approach will only cover data supported by applications and technology, whereas you might need to analyse information about products, key indicators and roles.

The information map should be well defined from the perspective of the information user. Many models start life in the design of a software application and this is readily apparent in definitions that are obviously written for a technical audience. Technical models are necessary for the detailed design of software, but they are unfit for a thorough understanding of information use. Find a model that is comprehensive and is based on an explicit information architecture. Make sure that there is a methodology for using it that includes the basic architectural tasks. Look for software that is quick and easy to use. Functions that allow you to filter out unnecessary details or to drill down from an overview into more detailed layers are particular useful. The ability to define subsets or views of the model is essential for recording the information needs of various users.

It is a poor worker who blames his or her tools, but it is vital that the right tools are available for the job and if an information map does not really match your needs, then it is going to be of little help. A diagram downloaded from the web is not a quick-fix information architecture if it results in wasted or failed effort.

Finally, consider working in cooperative ventures with other organizations, as there is a growing trend for organizations to work together to define architectural elements that are standard for an industry. This can even include collaborative projects with partners who might previously have been considered competitors. Providing the focus is on the percentage that is common to all, then there is no threat to the components that distinguish one organization from another.

Using software

The next step is to consider what the map will look like, deciding its shape and form and thinking about how it will be presented. Development options range from a simple hand-drawn sketch to an entity relationship model developed in software for computer assisted software engineering (CASE tool), while presentation options range from a casual discussion around a whiteboard to a flash presentation on a web page. Software support will almost certainly be necessary in most situations, due to the probable size of the map, the need to filter out discrete viewpoints and to allow for its evolution. While it is impractical to discuss particular software packages here, we will describe the main features to look out for.

There are approaches that are good at mapping information on a small scale, but which are not so successful for the quantities of information that are required when architecting changes. Mind mapping, popularized by Tony Buzan (Buzan, 1993), is one example of a tool that is used to structure and organize information, but like many similar techniques it works best when the result fits on a single page (although there are some notable exceptions to this rule: *The Mind Map Book* mentions a 25-foot long mind map created at Boeing Aircraft with information condensed from an engineering manual). The techniques discussed here use similar principles to those found in mind mapping or concept mapping, but with additional rigor that ensures consistency across even the largest of information maps.

There are other methodologies, such as the information engineering and object-oriented modelling approaches, that are excellent for the level of detail necessary to design and implement software solutions, but not so good at stepping back to see the big picture.

Architecting information needs to preserve a balance between the big picture and a mass of detail, with an approach that mixes the rigour and discipline of formal modelling, with the naturalness and insight that comes from conceptual mapping approaches.

At the time of writing, there is little serious software support specifically designed for architecting information. Most of the tools in common use were intended to support software development rather than understand and improve the use of corporate information. On the other hand, there is a point with anything where you need to have the best available tools for the job and software is often the easiest and quickest way to document information architecture and manage change initiatives.

There is no single piece of software providing a complete architecture solution, but at the same time, new software appears all the time, so what follows is a summary of the key features to look for rather than a definitive recommendation. (Further discussion can be found at http://4thresource.com.)

In our opinion the most important software need for architecting information is functionality supporting node-and-link diagrams. In our discussions so far we have mentioned three forms of node-and-link diagrams:

- The use of *hierarchies* to document details of the eight factors, for example, showing high-level information categories that expand into lower and lower levels of detail.
- The use of *extended node-and-link diagrams*, where each node can have links to any other node in the diagram. The big picture diagram is an extended node-and-link diagram.

- And *radiating node-and-link diagrams*, which start with a central node and extend with a branch-like structure, as in the neighbourhood diagram or mind maps. In fact, this form of node-and-link diagram is similar to the hierarchy diagram, with the nodes and links arranged in a different manner.

There are many diagramming tools that support node-and-link diagrams, including PowerPoint, TreePad, eMindMaps and CMap.

The next step up is to use software supporting entity relationship diagrams or object relationship diagrams that has quite sophisticated support for capturing node-and-link information, but it is aimed at an audience with a more technical background. The big advantage of such software is that it uses a database for storing information, which provides greater flexibility, analysis and reuse than software that is aimed mainly at *presenting* information. We use an entity relationship modelling tool that has the option selectively to switch off certain diagramming features, giving us the best of both worlds – the underlying database means that we only have to capture information once before it can be used in many different contexts, while the selective use of features means that we can produce documentation and present our findings in a format that is suitable for both information users and system developers.

Using a database allows the capture of definitions and comments for both nodes and links, information that is particularly important for understanding how information is used and building a solid information architecture. It is also essential for implementing the notion of *views,* which is indispensable for handling the complexity and scope of a typical enterprise architecture. A database search allows a user to zoom-in on exactly the information that is included in a view, making it easy to isolate the items that are relevant, to the person or for the defined purpose, for that view. Even more sophisticated functionality allows comparisons between one view and another.

Unfortunately, there is a down side in using computer assisted software engineering (CASE) tools for information architecture tasks, as many are slow and unwieldy to use because they are based around complex software development methodologies. Many software engineering tools attempt to cover *everything* in great detail, making it more difficult to use as an information map because it is trying to encompass both full scope and small scale. Before the knowledge in such tools can be used for architecting changes, the information must be converted into big picture and neighbourhood diagrams, or filtered to show the information from a small number of relevant views. Consequently, it is difficult to find everything you need for architecting organizational changes in a single package, although we can expect this to change gradually as software catches up with current best practice.

Creating a big picture diagram

If a generic information map is not available as a starting point, the two main options for developing an information map are to create a big picture and work towards more detailed neighbourhood diagrams, or develop the detailed neighbourhood diagrams and merge these to form the big picture. Whichever approach is adopted, a consistent mapping discipline is essential.

A big picture diagram shows the key pieces of information in a particular context. Just as there could be many separate maps illustrating a piece of the landscape, there can be many big picture diagrams, each showing a different part of the complete info-scape.

The first step in creating a big picture diagram is to identify what information is needed to gain an overall understanding of the context under analysis. If there is an existing information map, then this is simply a question of reviewing the complete map and highlighting the relevant information for the situation at hand. Alternatively, you can use the information categories as a checklist of items that could be included. Effectively these selections form a 'view' of the information categories and it is good practice to record the reason why a category is required, as described in the previous chapter.

Our example diagram (Figure 5.1) is based on a project to gain a better understanding of how products meet customer needs. Within the category 'people, groups and roles' we have selected information about customers, person and organization, recognizing the role of both individuals and institutions as customers.

As a rule of thumb a big picture diagram should not contain more than 20 information items. There are exceptions to this rule, but a larger number makes the diagram more complicated, thus losing its clarity and intelligibility. If you find yourself including more than 20 information items, then the situation you are trying to describe may be too complicated for a single diagram and you should consider breaking it down into a number of sections or themes. Another way of simplifying the picture is to use the hierarchy of categories to provide more general categories, basing the big picture diagram on higher-level categories. Likewise, the hierarchy can be used to suggest more specialized categories if the big picture is not sufficiently detailed.

An international software company, facing significant threats from new competitors, created a big picture diagram to show the changes needed to survive. The diagram grew more and more complex, until they were forced to break it down into several smaller diagrams and create a new higher-level overview. Breaking a complex change into discrete chunks made the changes more manageable; not only this,

the exercise required further scrutiny of the categories, creating a
better understanding of the issues and the information these
required to make the transformation. The information categories
were used to identify overlaps, making it easy to group changes into
meaningful 3-month steps, each covering a smaller information
scope. The high-level big picture overview showed the overall effect
of the changes, while supplementary big picture diagrams
illustrated each 3-month change within the complete plan.

The next step is to position these categories in the diagram, together with
the network of links between them. The emphasis is on finding links and
relationships that are logical, because they make sense and are useful. It
does not make sense to link every information item to all of the others,
as some connections are useless or nonsensical.

In our example, there are obvious links between 'customers' who
have 'requirements' to purchase 'products'; 'products' may have
'conditions' that apply to their purchase, but not all products
require 'collateral', although this may be a requirement for a 'loan'
product.

Requiring an explanation or justification for each relationship imposes
rigour on the design of information structures, as it did with the selection
of categories and the quality of these explanations plays an important
part in determining whether the architecture is useful or not. Information
structures that are difficult to use and do not make sense to users are
generally those that do not have a satisfactory rationale behind them.
The following questions help discover the rationale behind links between
categories:

- Why is there a link between these two categories? How is this information
  used? How important is this link?
- What other reasons might there be for linking these categories? Are
  there any other explanations that you either do not use or have rejected?
- What other links between categories are possible? Would it be useful
  to include these on the information map? How could these additional
  links be used? What additional benefits would these links bring?
- What reports, documents, web pages, or other outputs do you want to
  create and publish from this information? Is it possible to produce
  these outputs with the links that are included on the information
  map?

Our example uses twelve information categories. The big picture
diagram shows that 'customers' can be an individual 'person', or an
'organization'. A 'customer' has 'requirements' to resolve a
'problem', which is an 'opportunity' to sell a 'product' that meets

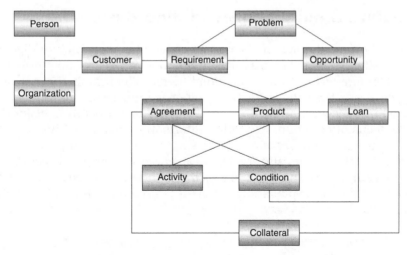

Figure 5.1 Example big picture diagram

these 'requirements'. There are certain 'conditions' which apply to the product, that affect whether a customer will buy it or not and the key product is a 'loan', which requires 'collateral'. There are 'activities' to sell and support each 'product' and when the 'customer' purchases a 'product' they enter into an 'agreement' listing the 'conditions'.

Creating this big picture diagram involved recording each required information category, on paper or on screen and drawing lines to show the links between categories. The rationale for selecting categories and the links was also documented. When the first draft was completed, the diagram was redrawn to clarify patterns and shapes and highlight the main links between items. In some cases it is necessary to do this several times until a clear picture emerges.

Information architecture should be a practical tool that really helps people to use information and architecture that ignores explanations is overlooking vital background knowledge that gives users tips and clues for using the information effectively. The role of the information architect is not only to organize and structure information, but also to demonstrate what can be done with the right techniques, tools and ingredients, in the same way that TV programmes on gardening or cooking inspire their audiences. More than this, we also need to show users what can happen to their information when they use techniques and theories that are out-of-date or inappropriate. The big picture diagram helps users identify and explore new ways of grouping and analysing information.

Creating a neighbourhood diagram

A neighbourhood diagram is easier to create than a big picture diagram because it is a detailed map exploring a particular category of information and therefore has a strong conceptual theme. The information category that serves as the subject for the diagram, in our example 'product', is placed in the centre of the diagram to signify that it is this concept that is the focus of attention. Any other information that has a link in some way to product information is added to the diagram, with a line from 'product' to the other category. Only categories that have a direct link to product are shown, and again, for each link there should be a reason why it is necessary, an explanation of how it is used, or a description of the value that the link adds.

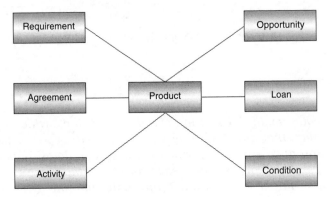

Figure 5.2   Example neighbourhood diagram

Our example uses the same situation that we used for the big picture diagram, in order to emphasize the differences between each diagram type. Unlike the big picture diagram, the neighbourhood diagram only shows other information that is in the immediate neighbourhood for 'product', showing the information that directly interrelates with *information about* products. In our example, all of the links on the neighbourhood diagram are also shown on the big picture diagram, but in practice this will not necessarily be true, as the big picture diagram summarizes only *the most important links* between categories.

Neighbourhood diagrams are like a mind map or a concept map, exploring a single category in detail. This type of diagram, which is more commonly found in knowledge management than information management practice, provides an excellent bridge between the architectural outlook of the information map and the detailed modelling techniques from software engineering. The neighbourhood diagram makes the complex information links with a single information category, like product, much easier to understand by centring on that concept and exploring the value that is brought into being by each link with other information types.

Linking neighbourhood diagrams with the big picture

Neighbourhood and big picture diagrams are closely related to each other. If there are questions about scope or coverage, then a big picture diagram helps clear this uncertainty and should always be created before drilling down into the detailed analysis of neighbourhood diagrams. Alternatively, when circumstances need a detailed study as a prelude to understanding the topic, it may be necessary to create several neighbourhood diagrams, which can then be merged together to form the big picture.

Neighbourhood and big picture diagrams always form part of a *single* info-scape – they are simply different types of information map. Since they are based on the same information categories and have the same links between them, it is easy to convert one into the other.

Merging several neighbourhood diagrams to create a big picture is a question of identifying the main links between information categories and using these to draw the big picture. The links are already implied in the connections from the focal category to its neighbouring categories, but they should only be included in the big picture if they help to understand key relationships between different types of information.

Neighbourhood diagrams can be created from a big picture by systematically taking each information category in turn and using it as the focal point of a neighbourhood diagram. Some of the links to other categories will already be defined in the big picture diagram, but there are likely to be more that were not significant in the big picture, but are relevant for the more detailed understanding of how a particular category of information is being used.

Mapping change

So far we have described the two diagrams as tools for analysing the links between information categories. As such, the two diagrams are useful for understanding the ways in which information is *currently being used* and for showing possible connections between information items *in the future*. Understanding the existing situation and planning future designs are both vital for architecting changes. Potential changes can be shown by using two sets of diagrams – one for the present and one for the future, or by marking what needs to change on a single diagram.

Making multiple versions of each diagram is time consuming and like playing 'spot the difference', with complex changes it can be difficult to see the changes from one diagram to another. Unfortunately, even two diagrams, showing the 'as is' and the 'to be', are often insufficient to document the changes that are taking place because there is a need to show information structures at several stages in the transformation. So a

2-year change might require nine snapshots showing the situation every 3 months.

> *A succession of takeovers and mergers left a travel company with customer information in several different formats, information systems and databases. To understand the situation fully they created an information map showing these information structures and the information value chains that rationalized these sources into a single view of customer information. They then developed a separate information map showing how they wanted to structure this information in the future and, using this as a guide, proceeded to make changes to their information infrastructure. Unfortunately, the complexity of the changes meant that comparing the start-point with the end-point did not identify all of the intermediate steps or give much guidance on how to make the changes, causing the situation to get a lot worse before it got better. This situation was further complicated because of an unrealistic deadline of 2 years to reach the end-point.*

Software gives the advantage of mapping changes onto a single diagram, by documenting the original information structures as a foundation and gradually showing changes by adding, removing and modifying the original diagram. Software may also allow filters, so that we can limit what we see to just the components that apply at each stage. Using this approach, each stage in the transition is a 'view' of the complete information map.

> *A manufacturer of electronic goods wanted to improve their component tracking information. They started by creating a map of all the information used to order, track and use components. This was followed by adding to the same map all changes to the information and their structures that were required in the future. Colour-coding was used to highlight the start-view and the end-view, making it easy to pick out the differences using a single diagram. The team responsible for making the changes then identified intermediate configurations of the information that made incremental improvements, gradually leading to the final view. Each configuration, defined as a view using the single diagram, had to improve on the original structure and make sense as a discrete step towards their goal. In defining these intermediate views the team realized that some of the steps required the temporary addition of information or structures in order to make the changes work effectively. They were also able to calculate how long the complete process would take. The transformation was successfully achieved in 18 months, with no disruption to the everyday operations.*

This concept of a *view* of the information architecture is very powerful, as the information map can contain every option for linking and grouping information items that is ever likely to be required, while a series of views layered over the top of this map show only the components and structures that are required for a particular context in the past, present or future. This functionality can be found in many diagramming and presentation software packages and in some of the more recent knowledge and information management tools; for example, Microsoft's PowerPoint allows diagramming elements to gradually appear and disappear on a page. Simulation software can show the gradual construction of a building condensing several months of development into a few minutes; in a similar way, we can expect software designed for architecting information that will be able to simulate and plan changes to an information map.

Exploring concepts in a domain of knowledge

The Athenian philosopher Socrates said, 'the beginning of wisdom is the definition of terms'. Definitions are used in information architecture to understand a domain of knowledge. While a common dictionary definition describes *a thing* according to its properties, a good architecture definition goes beyond this, to describe the type of *information* that is kept *about a thing*, including an explanation of how the information is used, its value and purpose.

Whenever we analyse the language that people use, we are exploring the concepts in a particular domain of knowledge. In a typical business situation the main concepts include customer, product, address and transaction. As the context for using information becomes more specialized, so the language changes. For example, dividends payable, profit forecast and return on sales come from the domain of *accounts and finances* and market attractiveness, competitive forces and segmentation come from the domain of *marketing and sales*. While a popular dictionary is sufficient for looking up many words, a domain-specific dictionary is needed for more specialized vocabulary, such as a dictionary of finance and investment terms to cover the language of stocks, bonds and corporate finance. Specialized domains have a more limited applicability; thus detailed definitions of proprietary medicines would only be relevant in the pharmaceutical industry.

Note that the labels that we used to refer to the domains above – accounts and finances, marketing and sales – come directly from the information categories. Each definition of a specialized type of information provides further detail to the categories and labels that are used to identify, structure and organize the information resource. Here are some questions to find out more about the key concepts in a particular domain of knowledge:

- **In an ideal situation, what information do you need?** This question is prefaced with 'in an ideal situation' because we do not want answers to be unduly limited by any existing constraints. We want to learn about the language that people use to process information – understanding the constraints comes later.

- **What does each key word or phrase mean?** If 'customer' is one of the important concepts, the question would be 'what do you mean by customer' or 'how would you define customer'.
- **Are there any other meanings for each word or phrase?** Continuing our example, are there any alternative meanings for 'customer'? Differences in meaning can cause a lot of confusion. 'Monthly figures' might mean the amounts for a calendar month or figures that are produced for a 4-week working period.
- **Ask for some typical examples of this type of information.** For customer this might include a printout of a customer record, or contractual information that defines the terms of a customer relationship.
- **How is this information used?** What is the purpose of this type of information? What value does it add? What would happen if the user did not have this information?
- **What information is critical or essential?** What information *must* a user have in order to carry out their work, perform activities or make decisions? Without this information, the user would not be able to survive.
- **How important is each piece of information?** Here we are trying to understand why it is important to the user. Why is 'customer' important to you as a concept?
- **What are the main difficulties in using or interpreting this information?** This question helps to identify problems that the user faces when processing the information. There might be no way of knowing whether the information is accurate or whether a report contains all of the relevant figures.

Productive analysis of information requires a detailed knowledge of the associated domain, for instance, to develop an architecture for an insurance company requires detailed knowledge of insurance. Domain analysis is 'the process of identifying and organizing knowledge about some class of problems – the problem domain – to support the description and solution of those problems', (Prieto-Díaz and Arango, 1991) and domain knowledge is a body of reference material that includes data definitions, business rules, processes, functions, strategies, skill profiles and designs for business solutions that are common within a particular problem domain. Lack of the appropriate domain knowledge is one of the most significant factors in the success or failure of architecture. (Research reported in Curtis, Krasner and Iscoe, 1989, indicates that domain knowledge is a principal factor in the wide performance differences among individual developers.)

Without a clear definition of the main domain concepts it is difficult to develop a strong information architecture and poor information structures result in communication and analysis that is prone to confusion and misunderstanding. For example, unless we know that there are different definitions for the same thing, then disparities and discrepancies will go unnoticed – try comparing sales figures month by month without taking into account the fact that a month can have 28, 29, 30 or 31 days in it! The task of architecture is not to force standard definitions upon everyone, but to identify and eliminate areas of potential confusion and to provide new concepts and ideas to work with by identifying variations in and distinctions between definitions. Architecture provides the language for dealing with information.

Many organizations start their architecture by developing their own information map and definitions, instead of tapping into the knowledge and expertise of other organizations within that domain. For instance, there are many data items that are needed by every bank – such as account numbers, balance on accounts, interest rates and sort code numbers, which are well defined as domain knowledge in generic financial service models at an industry-level, thus saving individual banks the trouble of redefining this information for themselves (Evernden, 1994). As noted earlier, it is quicker and more effective to base the architecture on existing domain knowledge by purchasing an information map, instead of trying to build one from scratch. There are a growing number of reference models that cover particular industries, some created as cooperative efforts and some available commercially. Research has shown that domain models can represent at least 80% of the knowledge required to develop and maintain systems and this percentage is generally true for all uses of the architecture. (See papers in Freeman, 1986 and Tracz, 1990.)

Creating a definition

Each definition provides a description of a *type* or *class* of information, so the definition of 'role' includes things that are true for *all* types of role, describing characteristics of roles in general and providing examples to illustrate features that are common to all roles.

A good information architecture definition includes a descriptive explanation of what a particular label means, typical structures for storing this type of information, details of what information it includes, uses for this information and any background theory or best practice that explains how to use it. Here is an example definition for 'product':

Information about anything that is offered to customers in return for payment. For the financial service industry this includes financial instruments such as notes or bonds, as well as services such as cheque accounts, savings accounts, loans and any fees associated with the services provided.

Information about conditions that relate to product and service offerings may be included here or separated as information about 'conditions'.

This information is used:

- *To determine the cost of developing and providing a product.*
- *To decide the price charged to customers.*
- *To influence other factors relevant to products, such as features or terms and conditions.*

Solving differences of opinion

Information is tricky to deal with because its value depends very much on interpretation and experience. Confusion and misunderstandings arise by the use of words with similar but different meanings, as in expecting a *quotation*, but receiving an *estimate*. Different definitions of the same word may be harder to spot until it is too late – when I ask for a *customer record* I expect to get name and address information, but I get details of the last 30 payment transactions because that is another understanding of a *customer record*. When architecting organizational changes, definitions are critical for handling these differences of opinion, whether that means resolving the difference in the interests of standardization or maintaining diversity because it is a necessary part of the organizational makeup.

When information comes from disparate sources there is a high chance that definitions will not be the same and this can be resolved by asking providers to supply definitions for information they source and encouraging them to resolve any differences between their definition and one that is preferred. Manufacturers expect a parts supplier to make components to their specifications and the same standards should be true when receiving information components. This responsibility should also apply to any information that is transferred from another group within the organization.

When faced with inconsistent definitions and information from two or more sources, it can be difficult to decide which is right or wrong. There is rarely a situation where one definition is absolutely better than another, because information is always used in a particular situation, so this context is necessary to figure out which definition applies. Apparent contradictions can be explained through examples that highlight differences in use and draw attention to the contextual factors that cause a difference of meaning.

Some apparent contradictions are variations on a basic concept, which can be resolved by adding a qualifier to a name, such as the distinction between a *retail customer* and a *corporate customer* as separate variations on the basic concept of *customer*. In other cases, differences can be overcome by using different labels that reflect subtle variations in meaning, for instance using *client* to denote a long-term, high-value relationship, while *customer* refers to more casual, one-off sales.

It is often worthwhile recording who was responsible for coining each definition, particularly in situations where there could be disputes over definitions or where there are highly subjective interpretations of meaning. Disputes are more likely to occur with more complex terms than with attributive items. For example, it is normally pretty easy to get an agreed definition for 'marital status' or 'date of birth', whereas defining the break-even point for a new product will vary depending on the variables that are included and the method of calculation. Recording details of the definer makes it easy to contact them if differences of opinion arise in the future. Furthermore, all definitions, theories and interpretations evolve and change over time. The pace of change varies widely and for newer concepts, such as the recent emergence of so-called e-business, definitions are constantly evolving. Just as major language dictionaries are updated regularly, it is worth revisiting architecture definitions to keep them up-to-date.

All relevant variations should be part of the architecture and the criteria for including or excluding definitions should always be based on the value or importance of the information. For example, regional variations account for quite a number of differences in the use of information, so it may be important to know the regulations that apply to customer transactions in different countries, or to understand how address formats vary from one country to another. Meanings and understanding vary because information is used in different circumstances or contexts.

In a dictionary, an accident would be defined as a chance occurrence, an unforeseen event, a mishap or a disaster, but from an information processing perspective we need a more precise understanding of what information about an accident is required, and how it is used. The first step is to decide whether this is a high-level information category dealing within the subject matter in general or a more specific subtype, by asking what type of accident we are dealing with – we would need different information if this were an accident in the home or a car crash. Next we would identify which viewpoints are required. For a road accident the police would want to know who was driving the car, what the road conditions were like, how fast was it travelling, what other cars were involved and who the other occupants were; the hospital would want to know how many people were injured, what type of injury they had received and how serious the injuries were; and the insurance company would want to know how much damage had been caused, whether it was repairable or not, how much it would cost to repair and who was liable for the damage. Other viewpoints might include those of the passengers, the road maintenance authority and the repair garage.

Knowing what information is required, we could then find out why it is important and how it will be used. Will this information be used to support an insurance claim, to establish the reason for the crash, to compare this accident with others at the same location, or to order spare parts to repair the vehicles involved? When dealing with information, context is critical, so common dictionary definitions are totally inadequate for the architecture. The dictionary definition of accident must be refined by asking what information is required about different types of accident, from different viewpoints and for different purposes. In many information processing situations, existing definitions lead to problems in comparing and sharing information. If the police, hospital and insurance company have different definitions of 'accident' it will be difficult for them to swap notes without reformatting, and possibly re-interpreting, the data.

It is impossible to rationalize fully information needs from multiple points of view, but information architecture must be able to *document and manage* these alternative viewpoints. As we explained earlier, the technique for achieving this is to have a *comprehensive* architecture, documented using a list or hierarchy of categories and an information map, onto which all views can be mapped.

In some situations it is possible to combine multiple definitions to create a single, more comprehensive one, thus eliminating the confusion that could be caused by having different definitions. In many cases deconstructing each definition to make a list of all of the separate information elements, rationalizing some items and then creating a single definition by combining the elements achieves this. If there are elements that do not fit the new definition, it usually means that there is a variation or subtype of the main item.

Barcodes contain information that is a key part of the product distribution chain. Barcodes are used at checkouts to print the product description and price on a bill and they are also at the heart of sophisticated inventory tracking and reordering systems. Unfortunately, the barcode does not contain a definition of the product that it refers to, so its meaning varies from one organization to another depending on the description that they have given to it. Having different definitions causes confusion and requires additional information processing throughout the supply chain. The full impact and additional costs are not obvious because they are spread across so many different departments and organizations and, in the case of international products, different countries. Combining all definitions for a barcode could create a single, comprehensive definition that included all of the relevant information and was standard across all companies in the supply chain. (For a good example, see different descriptions given to barcode 5000174701678 by 11 UK retailers in IRI Infoscan, in Financial Times, Inside Track page 15, Tuesday, 1 September, 1998.)

Linking words to their relevant categories and concepts

Some information items have precise definitions that are not open to interpretation and ambiguity, but these items are pretty rare. Because we are dealing with language and semantics, almost everything is open to interpretation and meaning varies depending on context and use. However, linking each type of information with relevant categories and concepts makes it easier to separate one meaning from another and find the right information. Here are some simple examples of ambiguous words, related to possible categories:

- **Drinks:** coffee, tea, chocolate, cocoa.
- **Colours:** coffee, brown, chocolate, red.
- **Confectionery:** chewing gum, liquorice, chocolate, fudge.

An Internet search on the word 'chocolate' could return information about *drinks*, *colours* or *confectionery*, while a similar search on 'coffee' might produce information about a *drink* or a *colour*. Providing contextual links, by linking words to their appropriate categories or concepts, helps users to find and navigate the right information and this is particularly important for words with more complex meanings. For example, a strategy imposed on an organization by senior management is totally distinct from a strategy that emerges out of the collective action of all employees, so knowing the language used to describe different types of strategy origination – in this case *consensus* versus *planned* strategy – helps enormously to find relevant information on this subject. A user searching for information on 'strategy', which is a high-level category, would be guided and directed by the lower-level, more specific categories for strategy information.

Categories are particularly important for less structured and more complex information. The earliest computers handled data that were relatively simple and dealt largely with information that was reasonably well-structured, but increasingly we expect computers to handle multimedia, pictures, sounds and graphics. By identifying user needs for complex and unstructured information and finding out more about the ideas and concepts that are important for this information, we can provide contextual support by the use of relevant categories and concepts.

Definitions should always add value, provide meaning and be appropriate for their audience. User definitions should therefore be in business rather than technical language. Some definitions are useless; for example, defining 'purchase date' as 'the date of a purchase' provides no additional value or meaning to the label, furthermore, it gives the impression that it does not require further explanation and that the term is fully understood and accepted. Definitions that simply repeat the words in the label should be avoided, as meaning is not always as obvious as it seems. Good definitions include synonyms, antonyms, generalized categories to which the information item belongs, more specific labels that refer to specialized examples of the item, related terms, preferred labels and examples of use in different contexts. Single word searches are less likely to find the information you are seeking than a search that uses key words that provide contextual links; in our example of ambiguous words, keywords such as drink or colour help to focus a search on the right information.

Guidelines for writing definitions

Here are some suggested standards that make it easier to write or review definitions:

Labels or names

Each item should have a unique name or label. If the information is part of a larger unit, such as component part of a product or an attribute of an entity, then the label should be unique within the larger part. PRODUCT. Identifier or Identifier (for Product) would show that *identifier* was part of the larger unit, product. *Each name should be as concise as possible.* One reason for this is the limitation imposed by some databases, CASE tools and other software on the number of characters, but it is also much easier to use terms when they are straightforward and to the point.

Only use abbreviations and acronyms if you really have to. We often use acronyms for long-winded word phrases – BPR for business process re-engineering, or CRM for customer relationship management, which can cause trouble when the same three letters are used to mean something else – and a good TLA (three-letter acronym) often gets reused! Use the full name to identify the concept and hold the definition and link the acronym or abbreviation as a synonym. *If you use abbreviations and acronyms use a standard set.* Check out international standards for things like airport codes, monetary currencies and country codes.

Give equivalent items the same name. As far as the information architecture is concerned, a credit card and its representation in the database are equivalent items and should therefore be referred to by the same label. If the database uses an abbreviated or technical label, say CREDCRD, this would be documented in the architecture as a synonym for credit card.

Definitions

Write the definition in terms that are clear to all users. Business people, as well as technical users, use definitions and the more people who use the information architecture, the more useful it becomes. Writing a quick list of the people who might benefit from a set of clear, integrated definitions makes it easy to check that definitions are useful to all of these people. *State briefly what the item is in the first sentence or two.* The basic concept should be clearly explained in one or two sentences, after that you can go into more detail by explaining the value and importance of the information, how it is used and providing examples. Avoid waffle.

Remember that these are not just general definitions, but definitions of information items. To remind yourself, try starting the definition with the words, 'information about . . .' to avoid simply repeating a dictionary definition. We all know roughly how a dictionary defines customer, but the architecture definition should explain what we mean by customer *information. Clarify specialist key words, phrases or jargon.* Most people using information architecture will not be subject specialists, for example not everyone working in a bank is familiar with the language of finance. *Do not use abbreviations unless they are directly relevant to the item.* Definitions are easier to read and use when they avoid abbreviations. *Try to avoid using the name of the item in the definition.* It may make writing the definition a bit harder, but it will force you to explain it more thoroughly!

Examples

Give plenty of examples. These should illustrate the basic concept, or explain points that you make in your definition. Examples are also an excellent way to demonstrate more subtle differences in meaning. *Give examples of different contexts.* If the item is used in different contexts, provide examples that cover each situation. *Give 'instances' of the item.* The definition should explain the item in general terms, but specific instances of a term make it more concrete. Instances of street name might be Charing Cross Road or Hollywood Crescent.

Key points

An information map is the main architectural tool for documenting, understanding and navigating the corporate information resource. It records what information is available, the connections between information items, the main information flows and the information value chains. It shows how *information* is being used.

Information on the map is portrayed at different levels of detail and scope to provide both high-level big picture overviews and more localized neighbourhood diagrams.

The format of an information map depends on the architectural objectives, whether the map covers a small project or the entire enterprise, whether it is developed in-house or purchased from a vendor and the features of any software that is used. As it is difficult and time consuming to develop a 'complete' information map, a quicker and more practical approach is to start with a generic map.

Most software used for information architecture was originally developed for other purposes, such as software development, mind mapping or making business presentations. However, this software is adequate for the architecting capability of most organizations today and software designed for information architecture is starting to emerge.

A big picture diagram provides an overview of the most important information categories and the key links between them. A neighbourhood diagram is a detailed investigation of a single information category. Views of each diagram are used to map change, by highlighting the current and desired situations.

Understanding the language that is being used is the first step in making sense of information. An architectural definition should explain why the information is useful and how it is used. Because information is always used in a specific context, it is perfectly valid to have more than one meaning. Differences of opinion can be recorded as separate views.

The eight factors

In this chapter the essential factors used were:

- **Categories**: used as the basis for developing the information map. Associations between categories determine the links between items on big picture and neighbourhood diagrams. They are also used to classify words that have meaning in more than one conceptual category.
- **Categories – evolution**: used to map changes to the architecture by defining views of categories on the information map.
- **Categories – understanding**: used to explain the meaning of words and phrases, to explain how information is used and how it is interpreted.
- **Understanding**: used to decide how definitions, examples, synonyms, antonyms, interpretative theories, business or management models, or other tools of understanding are documented.

Making it available: adding exponential value

> The question no longer is 'What do I do with this?' but 'Who else should see this so I can understand and use this better?' The issue isn't just *processing* information – it's *creating* information with others.
>
> Michael Schrage

> A discovery is said to be an accident meeting a prepared mind.
>
> Albert Szent-Gyorgi

So far we have used information to understand changes that we want to achieve and know what information is required in order to achieve those changes. We have also looked at the current information architecture and future needs and recorded these in the form of an information map. Knowing what needs to happen, we created an information-based action plan and described how these changes are recorded on the information map.

To architect organizational change using information, the information map and other charts or diagrams from the architecture must be made available to the people who are responsible for carrying out the changes, otherwise there could be a breakdown in communications and the whole exercise will simply have been an information gathering exercise.

Viewing the map from different perspectives

The example information map we created in the last chapter was from a single viewpoint, but each person has their own view on things and wants to be able to see their own perspective, so it must be possible to view the map in different ways. The ability to have alternative views of the same information is generally ignored in most information management methodologies, making it difficult to map the architecture to reality. *Making each viewpoint explicit is a key contribution from knowledge management*, which makes it possible to compare alternative opinions and perspectives, rationalize or resolve differences of opinion and capture enterprise-specific knowledge in the architecture.

Managing differing viewpoints is probably the topic that causes more problems in information architecture than anything else. If everyone used exactly the same information in the same ways, then it would be easy to create an architecture that covered all situations, but everyone's needs are different. Sometimes needs overlap and sometimes they are contradictory. Fortunately, there is a simple technique for managing viewpoints. Imagine a comprehensive map that covers every information need, including any contradictions. Applying a filter to this complete picture allows you to see only items that are part of a single viewpoint. At its most basic, this is how an architectural view works – it is simply a filter that hides the components that someone is not concerned with while highlighting those parts that are relevant.

Filtering out separate viewpoints from the complete information map can be achieved by redrawing lots of separate submaps, colour-coding a single map, or using software to apply a filter. The software option is the most effective approach, while redrawing submaps is really a last resort! It is important that each view is just that – a 'view' of the complete information map – otherwise it is difficult or impossible to compare and contrast views, or to merge views.

Each viewpoint should be given a name and a definition that records the responsible person, business department or project team and explains the purpose of the view. For example, at the start of a project for restructuring address information we might define a view called 'address restructuring', with a definition that explains it highlights information that might be changed by the project and that the view is the responsibility of the project team.

Viewpoints are more powerful when they record the reasons why someone needs each piece of information. These explanations are not usually captured and yet they are crucial for deciding which information has most value or importance. It is also one of the quickest ways to discover innovative ways to use information.

Here is an example of why information about 'people, groups and roles' was selected for a project analysing the core business processes. Information about the people who interact with a process is important in a number of ways. First, different levels of experience and skill can have a profound effect on the type of support that a person needs in order to perform an activity effectively. For example, if we intend to make a service available on the Internet, then information about a product that was previously tacit knowledge for an experienced salesperson has to become explicit information that guides a customer through a website. Second, the personality and attitude of those involved with a process can have a strong bearing on its outcome. Another important aspect is the way in which roles have been defined and interaction between different roles.

Architectures often underestimate the number of viewpoints that exist within an organization and this is particularly common when there are attempts to standardize definitions or information structures. It is actually much easier to have a comprehensive structure that covers *all* needs and filter out the parts that are not required for a particular point of view, than to develop a standard structure that must then be forced onto each situation. What is the optimum number of viewpoints? The short answer is as many as you need! In practice, the number depends on the degree to which information is architected and at a large multinational is likely to run into many thousands of views.

Some of these views can be standardized across an enterprise and one of the key roles of the information architect is to identify which parts of the architecture can be uniform and which parts must remain varied and lacking consistency. Understanding 'how' information is used requires analysis, then consolidation, of all of the alternative viewpoints.

A bank wanted to rationalize the performance indicators used by senior executives to run the company. Because it was impossible to schedule enough time with all of the key managers at once, each was interviewed separately and the results added to a composite information map of all of the indicators and how they were being used. Each interview was recorded as a view of the complete map, including comments about problems and challenges affecting the use of indicators, descriptions of any ratios or spreadsheets using the information and details of decisions that were based on the resulting information. Everyone had their own viewpoint, but before the study there was no corporate knowledge of which indicators were being used, let alone any differences of opinion or overlapping analysis effort. The individual views were consolidated into a single project view, showing which indicators had common definitions and were used in a consistent manner, while separate views were retained to highlight differences – some resulting in information that was inconsistent and impossible to reconcile. A later project, analysing end of financial year reporting, was able to reuse more than 60% of the information map included in the earlier project view and resolved 40% of the differences chronicled in the separate views. This example shows how the information map and views are used to understand and make improvements to actual use of information, while both are also valuable artifacts when they are made available to subsequent analysis or projects.

Three or four thousand views may sound daunting, but views should always correspond to the hierarchy of responsibilities, so that there are enterprise-level views, project-level views, business unit views and so on. Each view at a higher-level in the responsibility hierarchy indicates acceptance of responsibility by a larger group or community of people. For example, a view at the enterprise-level containing the information item 'invoice due date' indicates the agreement of a standard definition and consistent use of this piece of information across the whole of an enterprise, while each lower-level view signifies a divergence of opinion or a difference in needs of a more specialized group.

Views often start life at the lowest level, representing the opinion of an individual or a small group of people, for instance a project team. As more viewpoints are captured, patterns start to emerge and when views are compared with other views at the same level, areas of agreement and disagreement are easy to spot. When there is enough information to be able to spot common needs it is time to rationalize views – for example, when there is total agreement, this area of agreement becomes a higher-level view.

An intranet development project started with thirty individual views, which were merged to become three project level views, with four individual views remaining to record viewpoints that were impossible to reconcile. The three project level views were used to manage a three-stage implementation of the intranet, while the four individual views were not included. After the first project, a second project to extend the intranet created a further eight views, which were compared with the three project views from the first project, and merged again to form a new consensus of opinion. Two new views, based on this agreement, were added at the enterprise level.

This may sound like a laborious process, but patterns quickly emerge and within a short time a strong image of the enterprise level appears and views quickly become the most powerful building blocks in an architecture. Information is most valuable when it is used and reused and views capture detailed descriptions of the specific ways in which information is being used in unique situations within the organization. Some parts of an architecture, such as the information categories, are quite generic and apply to almost any organization, but the specific use of those categories is highly distinctive and difficult for competitors to emulate. Furthermore, it is easy to resolve differences of opinion that curse traditional architectural development because alternative viewpoints are made explicit.

In some industries the process of identifying higher-level viewpoints is much easier because there are externally defined standards. In these cases it is very useful to extend the levels of responsibility beyond the boundaries of the organization and include external levels, covering cross-enterprise, industry specific, or global standard issues. For example, the Financial Services Data Model (FSDM) developed by IBM and forming part of the Information FrameWork (IFW) architecture has been used as an industry-specific view by more than 200 financial institutions. This is a top-down approach for creating an information architecture and a hierarchy of views; on purchase of the FSDM, the entire model is at the industry level and, gradually, through use and customization, sections of the model are adapted to meet enterprise or project level needs. In the health industry, Health Level 7 (HL7) is one of several ANSI-accredited Standards Developing Organizations operating in the healthcare arena producing industry-level specifications or protocols, in this case for clinical and administrative data.

Resolving differences of opinion

Differences of opinion are:

- **Differences of fact or true differences**. These are real differences that need to be maintained as part of the necessary diversity within an organization. When such differences are identified they usually result in extensions or clarifications to the information map itself. For example, it might lead to a distinction between a customer as a consumer or a client, one covering casual purchases, while the other denotes an ongoing customer relationship.
- **The same thing with different labels**. In this case, one of the labels becomes the preferred term by which something is known and the alternative names are listed as synonyms. In this case, consumer and client might be synonyms for customer, indicating that there is no difference in meaning between the three labels.
- **The same thing with a different description**. On the surface this appears to be a real difference, but on closer examination both descriptions refer to the same concept, allowing the two descriptions to be merged, which provides additional richness and depth.
- **Different interpretation of the same concept**. Because this is essentially the same concept, the difference can often be resolved by preceding the label with a qualifier. For example, there may be slight differences in the treatment received by a high net worth customer over a normal customer, resulting in the addition of this variation prefaced by the words 'high net worth'.

All differences of opinion can be managed by introducing changes like this to the architecture. In some cases there are direct changes to the information map itself, while creating a view of the map and including a comment describing the alternative outlook can resolve other differences. The following scenario shows how differences of opinion are architected.

BankMart (a fictitious name) provides financial advice on a wide range of products and services provided by other financial institutions. It receives updates about available products from each of its suppliers on a regular basis, which is put into a database providing information about product features, fees, terms and conditions. The product database is used when discussing and matching customer requirements.

As the information comes from many different sources and information structures differ widely from one source to another, it arrives at BankMart in a variety of formats. Definitions of what appear to be the same item can be radically different; for example, interest rate is one of the basic characteristics of many financial products, but there are different ways to calculate the amount of interest that is charged, some of the options including whether the interest rate is simple or compound; whether interest is calculated on a daily, weekly, monthly, quarterly or annual basis; or the number of decimal points used for variables in the calculation. Differences in even a small number of variables make it difficult or impossible to compare two or more apparently similar products.

This situation is the cause of several information processing problems and BankMart incurs internal costs every time that it imports data, for things like converting inputs into a standard format. There are also hidden problems caused when a source changes an information structure without letting BankMart know. However, the biggest issue is that customers get confused when the information they receive is in different formats and BankMart's customers keep saying that they want to compare different product options, but they cannot do this without understanding all of the product features, costs, rules and conditions. The chief executive at BankMart is determined to solve these problems so that customers know they can trust the information they receive. A project is initiated to:

- *Identify what information needs to be changed.*
- *Decide who has responsibility for the changes.*
- *Determine where the problems lie.*
- *Identify options for resolving the problem.*
- *Create an action plan for solving the problem.*

The first step is to list the information that BankMart needs to work on, using the information categories to select the types of information that are relevant. In this example there is a very clear focus on product information as they focus on information about products, product components, product features, fees and conditions. Other types of information may turn out to be important later – for example, BankMart may select some key indicators to measure how well this initiative improves the customer experience, but they are not going to get distracted by looking at information about accounting or skills.

Next BankMart decides which levels of responsibility are needed to address their problem and, in this case, conclude that a full range of responsibilities is necessary, which includes accountability at their cross-enterprise, enterprise, business unit, project and individual levels. Cross-enterprise is necessary because BankMart wants to coordinate effort across several organizations, each of which has its own definitions and use of information (enterprise level). Business units within an organization also supply information. BankMart is initiating a project to resolve this problem, which may need some temporary or intermediate definitions of its own to cope with the transition to a better structure. And there may be some individuals who have personal opinions to take into account! Ideally definitions and structures will be standardized at the cross-enterprise level – with all lower levels conforming to these standards.

The outputs from the previous steps are put it into a matrix to analyse the problem and record differences of opinion or understanding. Table 6.1 shows differences in how each item is defined at different levels. The cross-enterprise level is where BankMart wants a consensus, so that everyone involved in supplying products or services has the same understanding, whereas other levels explain potential problems caused by differences of opinion:

Table 6.1 forms the basis of detailed discussions with each stakeholder, leading to actions that will resolve the main issues. There are two options for BankMart:

- *They can start an internal project to address issues that depend on information that is fully within their control. For example, they would define a standard list of product features and test this against customer needs, define a standard format for conditions, or train their own staff to think about products in terms of their features.*

Table 6.1   Using responsibilities for change

			Information categories		
Levels of responsibility	Products	Product components	Product features	Fees	Conditions
Cross-enterprise level	Product needs to be understood as a 'package' of components that is sold to a customer	Need to be viewed as the building blocks used to create products. A component provides one or more features	Aspects of a product, including services, that have value for a customer	A sum of money that a customer is willing to pay for a feature	A pre-determined rule that provides the criteria for carrying out a particular action
Enterprise level	Only two suppliers use the concept of a package; it is therefore difficult to implement 'package' across suppliers	Components are not consistent in their coverage or the interfaces between them	One supplier has a good structure for listing features. Others are not well structured	Fees vary widely across suppliers – it will be necessary to create a standard list	Some conditions are obscure and difficult to understand
Business unit level – e.g. product based units such as Loans, Deposits, Pensions	Very difficult to package features from different business unit levels, for example to create a 'package' that includes a loan, current	One supplier, in the loans areas, has very advanced notion of components. How can this be demonstrated to others without upsetting	Huge inconsistencies at this level. Will require joint effort involving several suppliers and internal business units	No standard mechanisms for calculating or deciding fees. This is very confusing to customers. Need to produce a comparative	Need to clarify all conditions in a standard format so that operators can explain to customers. Will need clarification from all business units

(Contd)

Table 6.1 (Contd)

Levels of responsibility	Products	Product components	Product features	Fees	Conditions
	account and savings	competitive positions?		chart of fees	
Project level	Needs some mechanism that provides virtual packaging and this may not be possible to implement	Will need to define components list, with mapping to source. Check with suppliers that each 'component' will work as such	Need to define standard list of features and test this against customer stated needs	Develop internal fee structure using supplier fees as an input cost	Define standard condition format, probably in If/ Then rule format
Individual level	Three senior managers are likely to strongly resist this idea. Need to convince them to come 'on board'		A number of staff will have difficulty thinking in terms of 'features'. Needs training and explanation		

Information categories

- *They can initiate a joint effort that involves their supplier organizations. This could provide better quality information that BankMart could pass on to their customers, resulting in more sales of those products or product components for the supplier organization and the customer would benefit through a better understanding of the products that they were buying. For example, they could work with suppliers to explain conditions that are obscure and difficult to understand, or work with suppliers to put these conditions into a more standardized format.*

Finally BankMart must decide when it can realistically expect to make changes against a time-line (Table 6.2). Anything that it does will be part of an overall plan to improve product information, so steps taken now will improve the situation and make it easier to attack some of the more complicated problems.

In making elements of the architecture available, differences of opinion must be taken into account. The steamroller approach of forcing an enterprise-wide standard without taking the time to explain what differences exist and why they should be resolved will be burdened with resistance, whereas making responsibilities explicit makes the situation clearer, ensuring that everyone is committed to the changes.

Using meta levels as indices

Each information architecture has a number of meta levels. In some architectures there are only two meta levels, but it is more common to find three or four and occasionally more. Each meta level provides an index, guide and plan to the level below and is therefore used:

- To help people find and use information.
- To help check certain characteristics of information, such as its validity or accuracy.
- To help people develop and evolve architectures.

Earlier we compared the relationship between a meta level and the information that it describes with the connection between a radio or television guide and the actual programmes. Just as the TV guide is indispensable for planning your television viewing, so the meta levels are published as an aid to using the information map.

All commercial organizations are in the business of providing products, goods or services to their customers and they therefore have a range of products in the marketplace. There is probably a list of these products, so an electronic consumer range might include the PX77Z personal stereo

Table 6.2 The BankMart timeline

Now	6 months	12 months	18 months	24 months
Define standard condition format, probably in If/ Then rule format	Clarify all conditions in a standard format at business unit level – starting with loans	Clarify all conditions in a standard format at business unit level – continuing with deposits	Clarify all conditions in a standard format at business unit level – continuing with pensions	Explain remaining conditions that are obscure and difficult to understand
Define our own standard list of features. Test against customer stated needs	Train our own staff who have difficulty thinking in terms of 'features'			

with cassette, the PX89Q clock radio and the PX99R MP3 jukebox. These reference numbers and descriptions are information about the actual products – so this might be called the *corporate information level*. The meta level above, which might be called the *information model level*, acts like a template for the corporate information, showing that all information about products include a reference number and a description. It might also describe the format for each of these pieces of information, perhaps explaining that each reference number was unique, that the first two characters referred to a particular range of products and that the last character was a code for the type of product. The information at the *information model level* would help a user to understand the information at the *corporate information level*, by describing what types of information are available and explaining the format and structure of this information. Without the explanation at the higher meta level, the product reference number, for example, would be meaningless.

The *information categories* are at a different meta level than the corporate information that they classify, providing an overview of the information available at the lower level. The information map, based on these categories, helps users to understand how each piece of information fits with other pieces, just as a street map contains 'meta data' about the actual streets – such as their length, orientation, type of road and name. Publishing the information map gives users an overview of the information resource, which would be difficult to see at the level of the information itself. Sometimes it is easier to understand the value of the meta levels by imagining what would happen if they were not available – imagine that you are a stranger in a town that is unfamiliar, but instead of having a street map you must create one as you walk about – eventually the map emerges and there is a good idea of where everything is, but it requires much avoidable time and effort!

A key role of the architect is helping users find the information they need, including discovering information they did not know they needed. The change agent must help and guide people through changes, using information to help understand what is happening and why. Knowledge management makes it easier to learn from the skills and experiences of others, with techniques such as corporate yellow pages providing a directory at a meta level above personal knowledge. In each case, meta levels provide additional help and guidance in the form of indices to the levels below. When information becomes complex, we naturally invent a higher meta level to help understand and manage the complexity. Making these meta levels available makes it easier to appreciate how the pieces of the jigsaw puzzle fit together.

A company that provided automotive parts for the car industry found that problems with orders could frequently be traced to misunderstanding of the part numbers, or difficulty matching part numbers with descriptions. Part numbers were nearly all codes and while staff learned about these codes through experience, there was no easy way for junior staff to acquire this knowledge. It took two weeks to develop and publish a parts number meta model, which served both as a training tool for new staff and helped to cut errors on orders by 38%.

Presenting information

We have discussed the need for the architecture to handle different viewpoints showing *responsibilities* for information and the value in providing information from higher *meta levels* to act as an index or guide. Another major factor in making information useful and usable is its *presentation*, which is another one of the eight factors so important for architecting information.

The same information can be presented in many ways and deciding the most appropriate format or medium can make all the difference between information being understood as it was intended, data causing confusion, or deliberate misleading through misinformation. From an architectural position, an additional consideration is that each piece of information could be related to others, so it should be possible to make links and combine information easily and naturally – which is not always possible if the presentation used hinders the transfer of information.

In everyday encounters we use all of our senses, interpreting the information we receive through sight, taste, touch, smell and sound. But organizations have a strong leaning towards visual information; with a large percentage of the information we receive and use being viewed on paper, or via a screen, such as a phone, computer or television.

A bus timetable was included on a tourist website. Tables are frequently used to provide layout to web page content and provide visual structure to information and, in this case, tables were used to show departure times, days when the service operated and seasonable variations. In addition, colour-coding was used to indicate other variations in the schedule, with the key for understanding these codes at the foot of the tables. A group of blind visitors tried to plan a trip using a web browser designed for blind people that 'reads' the information, but the assumptions made for presenting the information visually were very different than those for its audio presentation, making the timetable almost impossible to understand.

Meeting someone for the first time we form impressions so quickly that it is difficult to tell which sense informed us, yet much formal analysis of information within organizations is done mechanically – devoid of the intuition, feelings and emotion that are important in a personal encounter. The dominance of static, visual information is likely to change as organizations struggle for new ways of using information that are not available to competitors and as computing power is able to support more demanding forms. There is growing use of video and voice recognition is increasingly common on automated phone systems. Although these changes will probably be quite gradual, virtual-reality-like 3-D information spaces, audio and even the sense of pressure and contact, will eventually become a central part of the architectural info-scape.

> *Staff in an IT department had an excellent understanding of spreadsheet technology and managers had first-class knowledge of the business. Together they developed spreadsheets for analysing corporate information. An audit revealed that the purpose of a spreadsheet was not always obvious from the way that the information was presented. Further investigation discovered that neither the technical nor business staff understood the situations when each type of chart should be used, so while the analysis of information was good, presentation was often poor. A half-day training course explained the differences between, and typical uses for, charts such as area, column, bar or pie charts, leading to more effective presentation of the information.*

In the short term it is important to choose the best available presentation for a particular piece of information. In the longer term, and as an ideal, it would be wonderful to separate the information content from its presentation, so that the user could decide how they wanted to view it, or be able to flip from one format to another (this is akin to the use of alternative 'skins' to alter the appearance of the interface to software – the functionality of the software does not change, only how it is seen by the user). Appendix H provides a summary of some of the alternatives for presenting information and some of the criteria to take into account when deciding how to present information. Design considerations for developing web pages has raised awareness of this factor, but there is still much to be learned about making sure that everyone gets the best presentation of the information they need.

Publishing the architecture

Although some components of an architecture are only of interest to an information architect, there are checklists, diagrams and tools that can be used by a much wider audience. For example, the checklist of information categories is an excellent tool for finding out what information is required in *any* context and we have used it in discussions with systems developers, database designers, the board of directors, business analysts and process re-engineering teams. Similarly, the different types of responsibilities apply to any shared resource, while the information-based action plan can be used for any project or change initiative. The use of the outputs from information architecture is only limited by a lack of ingenuity and enthusiasm. Here are some examples of how the materials have been published.

A Mexican bank believed that it was important for everyone working at the bank to understand the language and terminology of banking and wanted to make it easier for staff to improve their knowledge of financial information and its use. The bank bought a finance industry information model and over 6 months the architecture team worked with the vendor to customize this model to reflect their use of information. A core team of seven information architects worked with 84 business experts, resulting in 2382 definitions of key information items, grouped around nine information categories. In this example, an additional complication was the need to translate the industry model from English into Spanish, but apart from this, the content and structure of the original model was largely unchanged. Sixty per cent of the reference model required no changes, 28 per cent received minor changes due to language differences, terminology and examples and only 12 per cent needed significant change. The final deliverable was transferred to Windows Help files for general access by anyone in the bank. Help files were chosen because most of the staff were familiar with the format and because it was readily available throughout the bank.

Using help files is not the most common way to publish and distribute outputs from the architecture, but in this case it proved a simple and effective solution. Intranets and Lotus Notes are frequently used to post deliverables and make them available to a large number of users, although this often results in a passive architecture that can evolve in a random and disorganized manner. Other architectural deliverables are created and stored in software engineering tools (CASE tools) and more recently the use of repositories, which can mean that the materials are only ever used by information technology departments. The most popular publishing medium is often to use non-specialist software, such as spreadsheets, word processors and presentation packages. Like the use of help files, their big advantages are wide availability and user familiarity. Our second example demonstrates the value in using presentation software to achieve a specific architectural objective.

A bank had a dedicated information architecture team working closely with senior executives, business managers and technology departments for 3 years to identify gradually the key information categories. The team sought to promote the architecture within the organization, wanting it to be easily recognized and established as a tool that would be relevant whenever there was a need to discuss information requirements or usage. Descriptions of information categories may be exciting to architects, but they do not make compelling reading for the majority of people! In a situation like this it is better to hide the details by creating an appealing diagram that is the public face of the architecture.

Senior executives were emphasizing a new strategy, so it made sense that strategy was the focal point of the new diagram, surrounded by six further categories, representing the strategic information areas. 'Customer' appeared above strategy signifying their importance to the organization's existence; to the left were 'channel' and 'products', covering the things that customers were interested in and the various ways in which these products and services were delivered to them. On the right, 'structure' and 'functions' covered information about the organization itself. At the base of the chart 'information systems' provided the foundation for delivering information and products to customers, supporting the development of services and providing assistance for managers and staff.

Each of these six categories contained further subdivisions; for example, information systems were divided into information about hardware, networks and applications; functions had subcategories for roles, skills and processes. The organization that developed this diagram has moved on to other public representations of the architecture, while the detailed architecture is hidden in the background. There are two important lessons here – first, there should be a comprehensive and rigorous definition of the categories of information that your company needs for its information architecture, but once these are defined, it is not just useful but highly desirable to create glossy, simplified pictures of that architecture to make it accessible and useful to the widest audience possible. The diagram was published and distributed as a PowerPoint presentation.

Some of the information captured as part of an architecture will already have an obvious outlet for its publication, but it is often knowledge that is tacit and unpublished that holds great potential when it is made public and has the chance to reach a wider readership. For example, an organization may have six million personal customers and store information about these individuals such as name, address, date of birth, and telephone number. This information is typical of that stored in a database, but there may not be an obvious place to store information that the organization learns about personal customers *as a group* – such as their average age, or the ratio of males to females – even though it is this 'group' information that guides product development or marketing decisions. Identifying this information and making it available will release this dormant value, and increase the return from information.

Key points

The effort in architecting organizational changes by developing an information architecture is only valuable and useful if the results are available for people to use.

It must be possible to view the information map and other architectural outputs from the perspectives of all information users. Although information usage is similar from one organization to another, views are unique to a single organization. While having an enterprise-wide information map is valuable and useful in its own right, views make it truly enterprise-specific and add value exponentially to the map.

Multiple viewpoints inevitably expose differences of opinion. Some of these differences can be resolved, while others are part of the necessary diversity within an organization. Both resolving and revealing differences add precious content to the architecture.

Higher meta levels act as an index or guide to lower levels within the architecture. The number of meta levels increases as the complexity of information rises.

The way in which information is presented makes a significant difference to how information is understood and used. Ideally presentation would be separate from content, allowing users to decide the format used to receive information. Training information users in alternative presentations improves the productivity and use of information.

The information map, charts, diagrams, tables, action plans and other artifacts developed while architecting organizational changes are valuable tools that should be available for use by a wide audience. Publishing these artifacts makes it easier to explain and implement changes.

The eight factors

In this chapter the essential factors used were:

- **Categories – knowledge**: used to document the information required in specific contexts capture and the reasons why it is needed. This knowledge is one of the quickest ways to discover innovative ways to use information.
- **Categories – responsibilities**: used to manage differences in opinion, either by resolving them or using them to extend the richness and diversity of the architecture.
- **Meta levels**: used to develop indices that help people find information, monitor the validity and accuracy of information and evolve the architecture.
- **Presentation**: used to determine the most appropriate format or medium for presenting information.
- **Presentation – categories**: used to identify alternative ways to present each type of information.

Using it: making the best use of corporate information

Before sunlight can shine through a window the blinds must be
raised.   American proverb

Nothing is more practical than a good theory.   Kurt Lewin

Information becomes more valuable the more it is used and a management
toolkit based on the information architecture provides the ideal tools for
maximizing the use of corporate information. Information is the most
under-utilized resource; it is only used for a fraction of the things that it
could be used for. As more people become aware of the techniques of
architecting information, the more they will be accepted and used, and
the better the return from information. The information *categories* are
used to identify the information that is most valuable and pinpoint parts
of the architecture that need to be improved. *Responsibilities* and views
recognize the people or groups that use information and assign
accountability for the efficient, effective, productive and innovative use
of information. *Presentation* offers alternative ways to publish information
in order to improve communication and comprehension. *Meta levels*
provide information about information that serve to confirm its validity
and explain its composition. *Evolution* shows how the design of information
structures changes over time. In this chapter we explore how *understanding,
knowledge and process* help make better use of the corporate information
resource.

What is information?

We deal with huge volumes of data every day. There is every expectation that organizational information will continue to increase and we will be forced to cope with more and more information, so it is vital to be able to separate the useful from the useless. Unfortunately, we all spend time processing 'information' that has no value and we often have to clear away the junk before we can deal with important matters. Corporate processes impose routines that were probably important once, but are no longer needed. Monthly reports are still printed and distributed even though they have been superseded by on-line, real-time information systems. Data are still manually entered into spreadsheets when they could be automatically downloaded from a database. Junk and joke e-mails make it difficult to spot genuine and important communications.

The task of information architecture is to remove confusion and frustration, while simultaneously creating information and innovation. This is done in two ways: the first is to ensure that the information architecture itself is designed to make the distinction between information and non-information, while the second is to make sure that everyone knows when they are dealing with information or not. These two responsibilities are at different meta levels. At one level there is a need to train and educate users on the effective use of information by helping them understand limitations in the way information is *currently being used* and teaching them about *how it could be used*. The level above this is concerned with the way in which that information is arranged and organized and at this level the architect works to improve and transform the structural design of information. While information design *can* be done behind the scenes, architects need to become more actively involved in educating users. In some situations this can be done through seminars or workshops, but very often it is done through demonstration and example by working with people to resolve their information-related problems.

> *A company that provides Internet-based directories of company information was having difficulty in accurately converting data on the notes and forms collected by sales staff into the format of the web pages. An information architect spent a week working with the sales staff and the colleagues supporting them from a central office to understand what information was being used and the process of using it. Information categories were used to pigeonhole the information into logical units and this quickly showed that the existing data groupings did not appear to be coherent or consistent. Furthermore, while the process to collect and enter the data matched the sequence in which sales and office staff carried out their work, the information flows were not so clear, requiring the data to be reordered and regrouped several times during the process! Finally, some information did not make sense to those*

working with it. Redesigning the data entry forms and providing a help file that explained and justified each piece of information reduced errors by making the process simpler and faster. An unexpected side effect was that sales staff found it easier to explain the process to prospects, leading to greater number of sales and improving sales revenues by 16%.

Information is not the same for everyone: information that we would regard as useful might have no value at all for you. Architecting information helps people to find and use the information that they regard as useful and relevant. Critical for doing this is an understanding of:

- The difference between data, information, communication and knowledge.
- The features and characteristics of information.
- The distinction between information and non-information.

Data, information, communication and knowledge

The terms data, information and knowledge are frequently used as if they were interchangeable. Throughout this book we make the distinction, using the following meanings. *Data* are unprocessed or raw facts and figures, often, but not necessarily, stored in computers, from which information can be inferred. Data are still open to interpretation. '25th June' is datum and on its own it is meaningless and has no value. *Information* is a meaning or interpretation that has been drawn from data. It is the intelligence, insight or understanding that is derived by analysing and processing data in a context. 'Tomorrow is 25th June' is information, because it is a communication or message that informs me of the next day's date. *Communication* is data that we send with an expectation that they will be interpreted in a particular way. When we send a communication we are sending data to which we have ascribed meaning, in the assumption that the person receiving it will find the same meaning. *Knowledge* is personal understanding and learning that has been accumulated, among other experiences, through the personal interpretation and use of data and information. 'Tomorrow is 25th June, which is my birthday' is knowledge, because the information has a meaningful link to something that is personally important and consequential: the date on which I was born.

Based on these distinctions, information is meaning extracted from data, which provides an answer to a question by filling a gap and providing something that was not already known. It does not matter whether the question is purposely asked or not and some of the most enlightening information is received when we are not even aware that there *is* a question. Information is a matter of degree – the more important the question and the more data provide an answer, the more valuable information becomes. A message has maximum information content when it is maximally 'surprising' (Shannon, 1948) or as Mike McMaster puts it, information is 'that part of communication that resolves uncertainty' (McMaster, 1996).

Thus data are only information to the degree that they inform, but this also implies that the person receiving them is able to interpret or understand them. There is no guarantee that their perceptions will be the same as the person who sent the data. In effect, data have no meaning without interpretation.

Data, frustration, confusion, information and inspiration

All too often, organizations handle vast quantities of data that are not useful in any way. We refer to data as a *source*, because they are raw ingredients that only have the potential to inform, in comparison with information, which is a *resource* that is actually providing quantitative or qualitative value. If data create information and inspiration then they are generating value, but if they are causing confusion or frustration then they are causing unnecessary expense – in terms of poor decision-making, or wasted effort trying to make sense of them.

Figure 7.1 is a simple chart that we use as part of an information audit, to evaluate a situation to see whether it is dealing with information or not. Any piece of 'information' is assessed on two criteria:

- The degree to which the data provide or provoke ideas and answers.
- The degree to which relevant data are available.

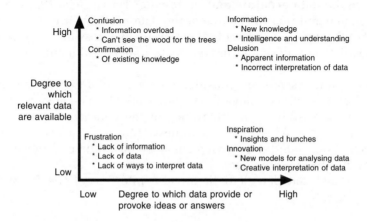

Figure 7.1   Data, frustration, confusion, information and inspiration

The chart can be used to assess whether any datum – such as an article in a newspaper, a piece of gossip from your neighbour, a document describing a new product, or a spreadsheet summarizing costs by location – is useful or not.

The first set of questions examine the degree to which the data provide or provoke ideas or answers:

- **Do the data answer any questions?** Do they resolve a problem? Do they provide a solution? Do they provide something that you were searching for?
- **Do the data provide any new knowledge that is useful?** Did you learn something that was valuable? Does it provide an answer to a question that you had not thought of asking?
- **Do the data provoke you?** Do they raise questions or issues that are important? Do they prompt you to take action or make decisions?
- **Do the data suggest anything new?** Do they give you some new ideas? Do they make you want to find out more?

If the answer to any of these questions is a resounding *yes*, then the degree to which data provide or provoke ideas or answers is *high*. If the answers are all negative then the degree is low. Answers usually fall somewhere between the two extremes. Apart from answering a need, the assessment varies depending on how easy it was to interpret and use the data and the user's existing knowledge of the subject matter, so the assessment is always subjective.

The second axis of the chart examines the datum itself, to evaluate the degree to which relevant data are available; practical questions include:

- **Are there sufficient data available?** Do you feel that there are enough data, or are you aware of relevant data that are unavailable or missing?
- **Are the data accurate and up-to-date?** Do you feel that the data are reliable and that the source of the data is trustworthy?
- **Are the data in a format that makes them accessible?** Do you feel that the data are presented in an easy-to-understand manner?

Once again, answers are considered on a scale of high to low, based on the degree to which relevant data are available. The answers reflect the quality, accessibility and relevance of the data as they appear to the person using it. As with the usefulness of the data, answers are based on personal opinion; interviewing someone else puts different values and relevance to the same data.

The analysed data will fit broadly into one of the following four categories:

- **Information or delusion**. If it is highly relevant and provides needed answers, then it is valuable information, which provides new knowledge, intelligence and understanding. However, there is a possibility that, although it seems relevant and useful, the interpretation placed on it is incorrect and it is actually producing delusion. People often think that they are receiving information, when in fact they are being duped – for example the manager who receives a daily report on the 'latest' sales figures, but the sales results are published a month in arrears!

- **Confusion or confirmation**. If the data are highly relevant, but they do not give the expected insights, then the data are either confusing, or are confirming things that are already known. A large quantity of apparently relevant data that does not provide the necessary answers is typical of information overload, where it is impossible to hear the rhythm for the drums (or see the wood for the trees).
- **Frustration**. If the data received are not the right data and as a consequence there is a lack of information, then users are probably getting frustrated. At least if there were more data it might be possible to discover meaning and find patterns, but without enough input this is impractical.
- **Inspiration or innovation**. Finally, if the data are apparently irrelevant, yet somehow they are producing answers, then users are probably getting information through inspiration or innovation; they have found new ways to get a lot of information out of a small quantity of data. Many organizations make the mistaken assumption that a lot of data are required before information can be extracted. In fact, getting better information out of smaller quantities of data is one of the biggest benefits of a good information architecture.

Figure 7.1 provides a very quick way to assess how well data are being converted to information, to evaluate the value of any piece of data or information and to analyse the real information needs within an organization or business. Information architecture techniques can be used in all four quadrants of the diagram to improve the use of information by making it more useful and understandable, and identifying opportunities to increase the relevance and usefulness of data.

Getting a better understanding of information use

Richard Wurman, who claims to have coined the term information architect in 1976, has said that there are only three businesses involved in communication:

> The first is the transmission business, all companies that start with tele: television, telephone, telex, etc. . . . The second is the storage business. There, the technology is exploding because of the compression of storage: laser, compact disk, ROM, CD-ROM, GDI

and all kinds of floppy and hard disks. The third business is the understanding business and nobody is in it. You might not want to hear this but the best writers serve two gods. They serve the god of style and the god of accuracy but not the god of understanding. Graphic designers, graphic design magazines . . . and all the universities serve one god and that is the god of looking good. They don't serve the god of understanding. They don't have courses in meaning (Richard Wurman – quoted in Smart Yellow Pages, *Communication Arts*, Jan./Feb. 1988).

Information architecture *is the business of understanding* and it serves the god of meaning by providing tools:

- To help find the information that is required or the right information.
- To help information users gain understanding and find meaning.
- To develop new models that accurately reflect how people use information.
- To generate new information and knowledge through using information in innovative ways.

In each case, the process of understanding is the same: starting by understanding the language that is being used, then exploring how people think about the information they use and finally checking our intellectual or theoretical grasp of information against its use in practice.

Finding the right information

Information architecture provides tools to make sense of the available data, by helping us find the right information in the first place and then providing techniques to use it effectively.

Detecting relevant data depends on good retrieval, navigation and filtering mechanisms. One practical way in which architecture helps users find the information they want is by making sure that information has appropriate labels and is well classified using relevant categories and key words. If the same information is known by alternative names, it must be accessible using these words as synonyms, which should be added to the list of categories as substitutes. From a user perspective it should not matter whether they use the 'official' label or the synonym, because any word that refers to the same concept should return the information they are searching for. When someone cannot find the information they need it is an opportunity to improve the architecture by adding new information categories, synonyms, keywords and other guidelines.

Learning more about the keywords that people search on and ensuring that these words are linked to appropriate information sources can improve the search process. Not all information is stored in computer searchable formats and even the most sophisticated search engine only provides a limited implementation of the information architecture. Unless there is some connection between the words and phrases that are in the mind of the person doing the retrieving and the information they are searching for, then it may never come to light. The most important information items are indexed and classified by building an information map of key words, key information items and the links between them. Although there is a heavy bias towards text-based information, which may show a direct link to the information categories in its choice of words, a growing volume of information is in graphical, picture, audio, video and other non-text formats. Searching through these types of presentation is even more dependent on good indexing, descriptions of content and use of keywords to help users to find what they need.

Users often navigate from one piece of information to another, so the overall structure must be logical – which means logical to the user and not just logical to the information designer. This is where an information map is critical, because a good map shows all information items and their connections. It serves as a reference point when making navigational links between information items and should therefore be available to users as a meta level above the information that they are actually using, providing direction and advice. The information map must be updated and navigational structures refined, based on feedback from, and observation of, users.

To separate useful data from unwanted noise requires an awareness of the reason for retrieving the information and the use that it will be put to. Explicit knowledge of analysis techniques should therefore be part of the architecture. For example, Michael Porter's Competitive Forces Model describes the interaction of five forces, which include 'new entrants', 'existing players' and 'new products', which affect competition in a market (Porter, 1980). So if someone is searching for information about 'new entrants' to a market, based on their understanding of this model, then they are also likely to want information about 'existing players' and 'new products'. Including these items from the Competitive Forces Model as part of the information map would mean that potentially useful information was explicitly shown through associations in the map, even if a user was unaware of background theory. If any user searched on one of the five competitive forces, then the architecture would 'know' that the other four might also be relevant; the information map guides the user to find information, including information they may not know they need.

As we mentioned earlier, information is not the same for everyone, because we do not all have the same needs. Patterns of use help predict the type of information that someone will need in a specific situation, so instead of being presented with a vast quantity of information, users can *view* information through a filter based on usage of that type of information within the organization. This reduces the time taken to find relevant information and makes accessed information more useful and, by including feedback loops, the architecture is extended to document the most important viewpoints.

Rigid information flows are more likely to force upon us information that we do not want or do not need, as opposed to flexible information flows that allow users to seek additional information. Rigid information flows may provide the *wrong* information, or prevent us from assimilating and acting on the *right* information. Regular complaints occur when there is no easy way to introduce relevant information or knowledge from non-routine sources, or when someone needs to refer a decision but does not know who is responsible. Bringing in new information is a necessary function of learning, while being able to channel information to someone who can act upon it is a key part of coping with information overload. Asking information users to rank key business processes in terms of whether the information flows are too rigid or not quickly pinpoints problem areas by tapping into knowledge of how the business really operates.

Sometimes ill-defined or confusing information categories make it difficult to find the right information and instead generate unnecessary information processing effort. A good case in point is the concept of 'customer'. While companies spend millions of pounds to integrate customer information from various sources into a single database, relationship management or contact system, surprisingly few identify the different *meanings* of 'customer' throughout their organization. It is difficult to have a single view of customer if data are scattered across multiple storage locations, but it is impossible if there are different *understandings* of what customer means. For example, customer can be an individual, an organization, a department within a larger company, an account, an anonymous entity that uses your services, or someone that buys products for use by someone else. Trying to rationalize these variations into a single definition does not work if the meanings are hidden and are legitimate alternatives. Without them the organization would not be able to continue in business and clarifying meaning often makes it easier to identify which type of information is required.

Helping information users to find meaning

Most architectures focus on structuring and navigating information, but do not include the mental models and theories that explain how information is used or create an environment that adequately supports the interpretation of information, and yet this is the area where information architecture frequently offers most value and benefit.

Information architecture facilitates learning by helping users find meaning in three different ways. The user must be *familiar with the language that is being used,* so the architect's role here is to provide tools to check the meaning of terms and labels, including the ability to look up words (dictionary, explanation of word roots and origins), to find alternative words that make more sense to the user (thesaurus, synonyms), or to provide a deeper knowledge of alternative meanings (contextual examples, comparative definitions, explanations of common misconceptions). People like things to be easy, so where possible the language that they work with and use should be clear from the start. If users are mainly working on-line, then these tools can be integrated with their work environment. Another option is to provide a help desk that users can call for clarification.

We all analyse and interpret information through a personal frame of reference, based on mental models or theories with which we are familiar. An accountant analysing financial information uses a framework of accounting principles and policies, and would be familiar with a set of interrelated concepts that include the balance sheet, the profit-and-loss account, accounting ratios such as return on capital employed and statements of recommended practice. Each user has their own personal model of the real world that provides theories to help them use information effectively. The role of the information architect is to *make relevant models and theories available to users* in a way that enhances their use of information. Some theories can be incorporated into the design of information structures – for example, the notion of debit and credit accounts is deeply embedded in structures that hold accounting information. Contextual help files can be added to computer programs, providing look-up help or step-by-step guidance. Users can be trained in new or different theories. The information map can be extended to include a much greater wealth of background theory, rationale and explanation than such models normally contain. Theories provide structure to information, thus reducing the volume of information that needs to be handled and increasing our capacity to make sense of it.

A company wanted a better understanding of how customers experienced their services. Initially the information that they gathered – through customer interviews and questionnaires and by asking staff for customer related stories – was largely anecdotal. To provide structure to the information we took eight dimensions of quality (performance, features, reliability, conformance, durability, serviceability, aesthetics and perceived quality) that had been described by David Garvin in the Harvard Business Review (Garvin, 1987) and expanded this to cover other relevant facets of the customer experience. The result was a set of sixteen focus areas that were used to structure the information. For each focus area we listed specific features or characteristics, which could then be measured – increasing the capacity to process and make sense of the information.

There are huge opportunities to break new ground with outstandingly original and creative use of information. At the same time, we have to deal with the weighty burden of the legacy thinking that comes with established models and theories. When familiar concepts and ideas do not fully explain information, users introduce slight variations and adjustments to make them work, making a gradual but steady refinement to existing theories. Information architecture can *help users to explore these alternative interpretations and anomalies*, which can be recorded as variations to existing theories or models. These accumulative changes lead to radically different ways of using information and new interpretations of information lead to breakthrough products and services.

> *For years, banks charged interest on mortgages and paid interest on savings accounts, creating the predicament of encouraging a customer both to take out a loan and make savings. A different mental model suggested that savings could be offset against a loan, so that instead of paying interest on savings the savings amounts were used to reduce temporarily the interest paid on the loan. This produces a very different information flow, causing a tremendous shift in the nature of a mortgage loan.*

Information architecture should *provide the tools and environment for users to be able to experiment*. A musician needs freedom, confidence, theory and expertise before he or she can improvise, instead of just reading and interpreting music from a song sheet. Improvisation with information requires an environment that allows reflection, experimentation, communication, discussion and play, which permits the generation of possibilities. Users are often willing to talk about alternative ways of using information and will frequently offer shortcuts, new uses for information, different ways of presenting information, or alternative viewpoints. When architecture is open to change there is no shortage of suggestions for improvement. Exploration of business and management theories or the development of new theories often results in more efficient models of understanding, which require *less* information.

> *A common example of this occurs whenever we use an abstract or more generalized concept as our basis for gathering information. If there are 6000 individuals working for a company, but only 25 different job titles, then gathering information by 25 job titles is easier than collecting information on 6000 people. This works on the assumption that the 25 job titles have sufficient detail and subtlety to cover the work characteristics of 6000 separate people. Without using this generality, the task of analysing work patterns would be prohibitively complex. Grouping information by categories of work – or job titles – makes it much easier by reducing the need for information.*

Patterns are another common tool for making sense of information, which can be discovered by mining corporate data or by defining a pattern at the meta level above corporate data. The first approach is highly dependent on technology searching through vast quantities of data to reveal a prototype pattern that is then tested against further data, which will result in confirming, modifying or rejecting this model until meaningful or useful patterns emerge. The alternative approach, which is commonly found in object oriented texts, creates the pattern by studying a meta model of the corporate information and extrapolating patterns based on business and modelling theory. In both cases, the pattern is at a higher meta level than the data – the mining approach starting with detail and revealing patterns bottom-up, while the more theoretical method starts with a more generalized map to create a hypothesis top-down. Technology and personal ingenuity both have a place in spotting patterns and associations, and the learning process is accelerated when the two approaches are combined – patterns always start as a hypothesis until they are proved useful in practice.

> *Every night the data warehouse, at a bank in the Asia Pacific region, is used to generate sales leads for existing customers. A program searches for unusual events, which become the basis for new patterns and hypotheses. For example, a large deposit amount going into an account might suggest the need for investment advice. These events are passed on to the sales team, who follow-up with a call to the customer to ask whether the bank can provide additional services. Each customer call is effectively a test for the hypothesis. Each interaction with the customer results in a record of their needs, creating new information, which in turn might initiate further marketing activity. Data mining technology, together with smart use of the information map, are used to find the new patterns and hypotheses, which add to knowledge of the information architecture.*

Every day someone struggles to find the information they need. Most people have not been taught how to use information and we are all too busy doing our jobs to stop and learn. Documenting business and management models and educating users in productivity techniques provides an environment and tools to make it easier to interpret and use information more effectively.

Finding out how information is actually used

Information architecture is often used as a tool to help implement technology rather than to understand and improve the use of information. Thomas Davenport, while a partner and director at Ernst & Young's Center for Information Technology and Strategy, suggested that 'the primary reason for information architecture's failure . . . is that few companies have undertaken such planning with any concern for how people actually use information' (Davenport, 1994). While Melissa Cook, an expert on enterprise information architecture, has written that 'Most current technology projects get bogged down because of the lack of understanding about process and information needs, not because the technology doesn't work' (Cook, 1996).

It is vital to put the needs of information users first; technology comes second, because it is simply one of the many support tools for using information – although arguably the most important. Check assumptions about the use of information, which is seldom as rational and logical as we would like to believe because people make decisions based on intuition, hunches and lack of knowledge as much as they do by an objective analysis of 'facts'. Including details of the theories and mental models that are used to analyse information, as well as feedback on how information is actually interpreted, helps to make the architecture more user centric and less dominated by technology considerations.

Examining information value chains will show how information is actually being used. In particular, it is sensible to explore dependencies on previous decisions and analysis, because it is not uncommon for analysis flaws to pass along an information flow without ever being spotted.

> *At a retail outlet, a quick review of the use of information showed that there was plenty of information collected about the items that customers bought, but no information was kept about requests for items that were not available. Tracking unfulfilled customer requirements led to simple changes to product lines that resulted in increased sales, happier customers and a higher return per customer. These changes required no new technology, but were not apparent until we examined the types of information and how they were being used.*

To find out how information is really used we can either observe people using it or ask users to describe how they use it. For example, we might ask someone to explain how a decision was reached or why information is structured in a particular way.

When asked to provide explanations, even someone who is very closely involved will find it difficult to describe with any degree of accuracy. People and organizations do not always think in terms of well-formed, well-defined or consistent explanations, so it is always important to look below the surface. For example, explanations might be based on habit rather than logic, and exceptions may only become apparent in rare or unusual situations.

If there is a group of people involved, each one will provide different explanations of what they do and why. Each explanation is probably as valid as the next and it might be necessary for all of them to be present, since the organization may not be able to function effectively without this diversity! For instance, accounting and marketing apply different models to similar data and end up with different information. To understand really how information is being used, it is necessary to listen to all points of view, as it is only with a complete picture that one can rationalize and explain each viewpoint.

People often do not *know* why information is used in a particular way, because its design or structure was established a long time ago. All artifacts – whether they are information structures or business processes, products, manufactured goods, software applications or training courses – are the result of a complex set of factors, many of which are long forgotten. In trying to reconstruct the past we end up with explanations that may be quite different from the original, and much history is lost forever. In these situations we have to rely on observation, deduction and experience to come up with an explanation that makes sense.

Finding out how information is actually used is not an end in itself, but is a means for improving the use of information and it is important not to lose sight of this goal by forcing users to describe everything in unnecessary detail. Documenting this knowledge is only essential for information that is of critical value, or for situations that are unusual or complex and for which explanations provide a valuable contribution to the architecture.

The following questions will help to capture explanations and justifications. Even if answers are partial, the information is invaluable for understanding why things are as they are:

- Why is this information required?
- What limitations or constraints prevent you from using this information as you would like?
- Why is the information structured in this way? What would be the ideal structure? Why were certain features included and others not?
- What discussions, deliberations and negotiations have determined the shape or form of this information? How were decisions made to balance trade-offs between various factors?

While it is not possible or practical to record everything in enormous detail, it is important to document any situation where explanations are genuinely valuable and useful. Capturing details of key decisions is especially useful if changes are likely to be made or if similar decisions need to be taken and one way of doing this is to keep a history log in the form of a journal or diary. Similar projects or developments face the same type of issues and questions, and information about discussions and decisions improves the process second time around. Capturing explanations may sound like a time-consuming overhead, but providing it is used for key information items the effort is always worthwhile.

At a financial institution, no-one could explain how they calculated interest on loans. They knew how to change the interest rate and they knew that the computer program generally calculated the end result correctly, but the detailed routine was hidden in thousands of lines of COBOL code. It was not easy to re-discover and document these business rules. The programs had been developed before structured programming became the norm and there were a large number of internal variables holding data that were used somehow in the calculation. Definitions and theory were almost completely hidden in the code and the original requirements and design, which would have contained the definitions and theory, had been lost a long time previously. The financial institution at the time earned a high proportion of its income from interest-based revenue – so the calculation was based on variables that were critical competitive factors. All that was available was the interpretation of the requirements and design in their software implementation. It took 3 months painstakingly deconstructing the code to define all of the intermediate variables and discover exactly how interest was calculated. This process of working back from interpretation to theory and definition is typically a difficult, time-consuming and human-dependent task.

Michael McMaster describes the central role of theory in Chapter 2 of *The Intelligence Advantage*, The World of Theory, where he writes:

> Theory is the source of information. We interpret data 'through the lens' of our theories. Said another way, data becomes information (patterned data, meaningful data) via theory. Without a theory, we cannot interpret data, so we either become lost in chaos or look for aid by helplessly grasping old structures no longer adequate for the task (McMaster, 1996, p. 28).

Recording theory and techniques

Information architecture is generally seen as a tool for structuring and navigating information and it is assumed that by providing well-structured information and an easy to understand interface, users will be able to access and use the information they need. But architecture can, and should, also link information users with techniques that will help them use information more effectively. Although explanations of how to interpret and use information are a vital part of information architecture, theories for understanding and interpreting information are usually described in books or magazine articles, rather than with information content. A good architecture should bring together practical tips and guidelines for using a given type of information more effectively, which can also serve as a starting point for gaining insights and ideas through the creative or innovative use of information.

There are plenty of methodologies and theories that are aimed at helping people use information, including:

- **Methodologies designed to build information systems**: information engineering, object-oriented approaches, data warehouse development, event-driven programming, workflow modelling, reverse engineering, etc.
- **Models and theories to help analyse and interpret data**: strategy planning approaches, product and market analysis, performance ratios and key indicators, etc.
- **Disciplines for structuring and using specialized types of information**: accounting practice, legal practice, etc.
- **Information and knowledge management approaches**: document management, information retrieval and filtering, knowledge or rule based systems, domain analysis, etc.

Unfortunately, information users are generally not familiar with these ideas and even if they are aware of some, it can be difficult to see how one theory, model, or methodology is used in conjunction with others. Information architecture helps by showing what information is required by each technique and the format in which it is input and output, and by combining this with step-by-step guidelines and tips on how to use each type of information. Architecture builds competence in using information by encouraging a creative cross-flow of ideas from one theory to another. This is the area where architecture provides the greatest benefit to information users!

Information value chains take advantage of techniques from each methodology and theory, as appropriate, creating a 'super' or meta methodology that can 'coordinate and connect some suitable methodologies into a holistic approach' (Nilsson, 1992). The guidelines from such a super methodology can be integrated into processes to help determine the most appropriate techniques to use in a given situation.

There are many analysis and design techniques described in these diverse methodologies and much can be gained by learning to use the techniques from each of these methodologies instead of limiting our horizons by only using one or two approaches. Most organizations do not have a complete picture of all of the methodologies in use and it can be quite illuminating to find out what *is* being used and by whom. Communication barriers between business and technical staff and between strategic planners and operational staff are reinforced by the separate, stand-alone nature of methodologies. Methodologies perpetuate divisions between business functions; on a grand scale, information value chains work to unite the efforts in management, functional and technical areas. What opportunities are there for sharing techniques and ideas, and what opportunities are there to combine techniques from two or more approaches?

> *Management consultants produced a business strategy plan and the outputs were then input to information systems planning, which had traditionally been the realm of the information technologist. The outputs from each of these methodologies was then chained into the software development process, so that the valuable knowledge gained was not wasted and new software was better aligned to organizational objectives. Outputs from the strategy plans and the user guidebook for the new software were incorporated into operational procedures, making the training of staff and the transition to the new software much easier.*

It is also useful to classify techniques by the type of information that they act upon, by mapping techniques to the information categories. Techniques can be included as part of the definition of each category – either by summarizing the technique or providing a cross-reference to a detailed explanation. If there is more than one technique for a particular category, think about how to get additional benefits or value by combining them.

The informal mix-and-match between information system methodologies has been an important part of the evolution of new methods and techniques. Architecture makes this creative process more effective by actively searching for new ways to integrate different approaches and determine the rules that would be used to select the best techniques in each situation. As information infrastructures get more complex, reliance on a single approach is less likely to provide the solution. As with carpentry, many jobs require a succession of tools and the order in which they are used varies from one task to another, so instead of being tied to a particular approach, the user is free to select a different path through the options to suit each unique situation.

Marvin Minsky, one of the pioneers of artificial intelligence and cognitive psychology, defined and popularized the idea of frames (Minsky, 1975). He argued that on dealing with a situation people select a remembered framework, which is adapted, if necessary, by changing some of the details. Each frame is therefore a structure for representing information about a stereotypical situation, describing our expectations of the information required by explaining what information to look for, how to look for it and how to use it. A frame can even include how to cope with exceptions to the expected or provide default values for information items based on expectations and presumptions.

Frames form part of frame systems, creating patterns that explain how we link pieces of information together. Each piece of theory or micro-theory should have a related frame that explains the information that needs to be captured and how it is used in order to put the theory into practice. A frame system is the complete set of links that could be made between frames. We have described the idea of an information map, representing all of the information required by an organization and showing how the pieces fit together, which effectively forms a frame system. Including background theory and practice in the definition for each type of information places this knowledge where it is most valuable by embedding it in the map itself.

From the information map we can then identify the information that provides a solution to a problem in a particular context, which corresponds to architect Christopher Alexander's definition of a pattern – 'Each pattern is a three-part rule, which expresses a relation between a certain context, a problem, and a solution' (Alexander, 1979). These contexts are documented as views on the information map. Frames and patterns provide us with tools and techniques for expressing information that was previously implicit and hidden.

Using business and management theory to identify patterns in information is a very effective technique for learning about a business or organization. Some patterns are self-evident – we all know enough background theory to recognize and process address information, but whereas we all use addresses in our daily lives, fewer people are familiar with more complex business and management models, and this is where many innovations are waiting to happen in corporate information architectures.

Consider the popular business model propounded by Michael Porter in 1980 and discussed earlier in this chapter, which is based around the notion of competitive forces, describing five forces that determine profitability within an industry. Porter's five forces were rivalry among existing players or competitors, the threat of new entrants, the bargaining power of suppliers, the bargaining power of buyers and the threat of substitute products or services. The thinking behind this model still characterizes much strategic thinking and, because it is relatively easy to use and understand, it is useful to distil the key trends and dynamics in an industry. Understanding the nature of competitive forces and recognizing which ones are most important can help an organization to define effective strategies. The Competitive Forces Model suggests that there is a close bond between information about these five forces and, if relevant, this would therefore be included as part of the information map. The theory also suggests how to frame this type of information, gives default values for slots within each frame and provides guidelines for interpreting the information in different contexts. Assuming that the concept is valid, the more background knowledge available about this theory, the greater the understanding and better the use of this type of information.

The right theory is dynamite – it blows away uncertainties and reveals hidden patterns and meaning, and if your organization develops or has access to new theories that are not available to your competitors, then there is enormous potential to apply information in ways that others have not even dreamed about. Small changes in theory can have a profound impact on practice and organizations often tweak a theory to meet their specific needs.

> *An information technology hardware manufacturer had been using Michael Porter's Competitive Forces Model to analyse their business environment and develop strategies. They recognized that the competitive environment of the late 1990s was more complex and challenging than that of the late 1970s when the model was first developed and they therefore decided to consider more than the five original forces. By expanding the model to eight forces they formed radically different interpretations of business trends that directly resulted in development and marketing efforts that were successfully distinct from those of their competitors.*

Knowing what a model or theory does well and understanding its limitations are good starting points for modifying its design. In this example, the organization created a customized version of the model, by preserving the central premise and making slight changes to allow for changed circumstances. Other options include mixing strong features of two or more models, or taking the outputs from one theory and using it as input to another. The information map lies behind all of these experiments, documenting what has been tried, cataloguing successes and ensuring that we learn from failures.

The approach is iterative, with knowledge of the use of information gradually populating the information architecture. The key architectural tools for capturing this knowledge are:

- **Information categories**, which provide an index of the various types of information used by the organization. As new types of information are added, the categories are extended or modified. If information ceases to be of importance, it is generally better to record this against the relevant categories, rather than deleting those categories; in this way, there is an explicit record that certain types of information are not considered useful.
- **The information map**, which records associations and links between each type of information. In effect, the information map shows all of the possible information value chains between information items.
- **Definitions**, which explain what information is stored and how it is used. This can include tips and guidelines drawn from organizational experience and from business or management theory.
- **Views**, which show the subset of information used in specific contexts. Views are also an excellent mechanism for grouping together the information required for a business or management theory.

When are models or theories needed?

Despite the fact that business and management theories frequently add insight and knowledge to the interpretation and value of information, they are underutilized by most information architectures. We are frequently asked about when and how to incorporate theories into the architecture and the answer depends on a number of variables.

There is usually more awareness of available models when a problem is relatively frequent or familiar and when the information used to analyse it is highly structured. The information structures in use are often derived from an underlying theory, so there is a strong correlation between the model and the use of information, and the available theories tend to be problem specific. A good example would be the competitive forces model discussed earlier, which deals with the recurring need to understand the business environment and respond with appropriate strategies. The popular diagrammatic presentation of this model shows the main interdependencies between different types of information. In these circumstances, where the situation can usually be clearly described, a search of business and management theory will find several models that could be applied. Even so, it is worth merging these theories into the corporate information map to uncover opportunities for synergy and leverage between theories.

With less familiar situations, there is generally a need to explore the problem in more detail, before prescribing a particular theory or solution. In such cases, gathering more information and mapping this to the architecture will suggest information structures that are appropriate and knowing the key information categories can then lead to relevant theories. The result may not be a specific theory, but is more likely to be a mix-and-match solution drawn from several pertinent models.

In situations where you are dealing with information that is largely unstructured, a good starting point is to use knowledge of the problem to help organize and arrange the information. It is probable that this information is not already part of the information map, but that the theories will suggest new categories of information and links to existing information structures. As new information structures emerge, it will be easier to see which parts of each theory are relevant.

The greatest need for models, theory and guidance is in situations when it is not clear what the problem is and consequently it is uncertain what information is needed. In these situations it is a question of discovering appropriate models at the same time as identifying what information is needed. The information categories are a good starting point, together with any hints of relevant theories from existing definitions and keyword searches for appropriate theories.

New business models will be required to explain effective strategies in an information-driven economy, as many popular models were developed for a manufacturing or industrial economy. The ideas on which these models are based are open to challenge as companies find new ways to compete using the information resource, which will require alternative explanations, innovative strategies and a different economic understanding. Not only this, but it will be increasingly important to see the interconnections between one business theory and another, providing a more integrated and holistic picture of the possible links and dependencies between the various models that we use to make decisions and create strategies and thus knowing where insights and understanding from one theory can add valuable input to other management models.

Even when models and theories offer alternative or conflicting interpretations, there is one level on which they are all similar: they all receive and output information. Every time that we apply a business model or theory to our thinking we create more information and before we can make use of a business model we need to gather information. Information that is output from one business model can be the input to another, and so on, so information unites disparate theories. Because information is not structured in the same way and language is not always used in a consistent manner or style for all business models, the architecture and in particular the information map must be used to consolidate and integrate diverse management theories.

What are the uses of information

Architecture is a tool to help people achieve more effective use of information, so thinking about the many possible uses of information expands the opportunities for using the architecture. Information architecture can be used in any situation where information is used – which covers just about anything that we do! Think about the people who use information: do they need information to make decisions, to improve communication or to increase productivity? Different uses of information make distinct demands on the architecture.

- **Information aids decisions**. Decision-making ability is arguably the most important business skill. Some decisions require a mass of supporting information, while others can be based on intuition and experience. Faulty decision-making is very often based on poor use of information. With the right data, decision-makers are better informed and less likely to fall into decision traps.
- **Information creates value or usefulness**. Information tells you something that is *worth* knowing. This ranges from simple facts like the time and channel for a favourite television programme, to more complex suggestions such as which locations to market a new product.
- **Information allows you to gain competitive advantage**. What information does your organization have that your competitors do not have? Information about your customers, their buying patterns and behaviour, the reasons why they buy products and services from you, which products they buy, how they use them, where they buy them,

how much they are prepared to pay . . . Do you use information in ways that are significantly different from your competitors, by using types of information that your competitors do not use and interpreting information in original ways?

- **Information helps solve problems**. The first step to resolving a problem or issue is to understand it in sufficient detail, which is an information gathering exercise. Information makes a problem simpler and easier to deal with.
- **Information helps monitor and control**. Information that is used to track accomplishments and to identify and measure the extent of any deviations. Better controls lead to improvements in performance, reduced costs and minimization of risks.
- **Information improves communication**. Communication is impossible without information! A communications audit will find out what information is sent from one person to another and discover how to improve the information content of communications.
- **Information improves service**. Information helps staff to supply or deliver products and services on time, while information about development and distribution processes helps to maintain product quality.
- **Information increases flexibility**. Good information structures make it much easier to make changes. How easy is it to introduce a new product or to introduce new job grades and titles? Having the right information makes it easier to introduce new products or combine products that meet new customer expectations; having the right information structures makes it easier to record changes.
- **Information creates knowledge**. Information has surprise value when it tells you something that you did not already know. Data mining trawls through vast quantities of information to discover buying habits and trends. Combining information in different ways unearths unexpected patterns and new theories provide fresh interpretations to familiar data.
- **Information increases productivity**. Staff can handle queries more quickly and give better responses when the required information is near at hand. With the right information, resources and scheduling can adapt quickly to changes in supply and demand.
- **Information increases revenue**. Marketing information is used to increase sales, information about processes and resources is used to cut costs and selling information – as part of a product or service – generates revenue directly.
- **Information reduces costs**. Information can be used to coordinate effort and reduce redundant efforts, reduce cycle time and improve administrative efficiency. Knowing what the costs are is the first step in reducing them.
- **Information provides metrics and measurements**. Measurements make it much easier to tell whether progress is being made or to spot deviation from a standard.

- **Information integrates and coordinates resources**. Sharing information – about projects, departments, products, customers, in fact, about almost anything – is a great way for creating synergy. Sharing customer information between departments uncovers cross-selling opportunities and sharing information about processes to learn about best practices helps reduce costs.
- **Information makes things explicit**. Information provides explanations and gives the rationale behind a decision or action, helping others to improve their skill in using information. Converting personal knowledge into explicit corporate information creates an invaluable resource that is easily shared and reused.
- **Information reduces uncertainty**. To be information, data must tell the recipient something not already known. Reducing uncertainty is particularly relevant in planning and decision making.
- **Information supplements memory**. Just like human memory, organizational memory is not always accurate. Keeping historical information about performance, transactions, past actions and decisions helps sustain organizational knowledge.

Whatever else they do, processes always require information, but the information value chain is frequently very different from a process supply chain. Raising awareness of, and increasing, information value is a core goal of architecting information and this list of the uses of information is one tool to help identify the value of information in each process. The diagnostic questionnaire, 'Diagnostic: do you see information as a distinct resource?', in Appendix A is another tool for asking key people to think about the importance and value of information. But the most effective ways of demonstrating an 'intelligence advantage' (McMaster, 1996) are to make information value chains explicit and to maximize reuse of the most valuable information.

Maximizing information value chains

It takes a lot of time and effort to create really useful information. For example, to find out the potential for a new product in different market segments requires a great deal of research into, among other things, the characteristics of existing products within those markets, customer requirements, the appeal and market presence of competitors and expected market trends. It is ironic then, that having created such information, most organizations only use it once – for its initial purpose. The main reason is that information is usually embalmed as a self-contained unit, often in a document or report and it is difficult or even impossible, to unpackage information so that it could be used in a different context. In effect, when we publish information we create a tangled web that is similar to the dreaded spaghetti code of unstructured software applications, whereas an architected approach structures information so that we can maximize its reuse.

Discrete groupings of information, which encapsulate the most important and valuable information, should be more like ravioli than spaghetti, thus making it easier to extract reusable chunks. These information groups should be loosely coupled, so that they can be combined and re-combined in many different contexts. Architecture provides the essential tools for describing how information is structured and grouped, listing the potential relationships between information groups and providing the mechanisms for combining them.

The information map is used to identify the core information – information that is critical for the survival of the organization or the information that adds most value to its products or services. Core information is that which adds most to the organization's fundamental business propositions. At its most basic a manufacturing process takes inputs such as raw ingredients or component parts and turns them into commodities that can be sold; the difference in value between the inputs and outputs determines profit or loss. Certain steps in the process add more value than others and it makes sound commercial sense to improve the value adding tasks while simultaneously striving to reduce costs. It is not always so obvious that information is created by inputting raw data, information or knowledge and that some actions or decisions increase the value of these inputs.

In many cases, users are not aware that the information they have produced could be reused in a different context and this is a matter of educating them in the potential and value of reusing information. One way of doing this is to define information value chains that show not only where information could be reused, but also where it produces a compound value. In other words, information that has a value of $10 when used in its initial context is then reused in a different context that increases its value to $100, and again in a third context, which compounds the original value to $1000.

The simplest way to put a value on information is to give each category a rating between 1 and 10, where '1' indicates little or no value and '10' demonstrates high value. There are other, more thorough ways to assess information value, but this simple rating system is quite adequate for the initial identification of the key information value chains. The rating can be applied at any level within the hierarchy of categories, but it is often useful to analyse categories that represent key clusters of information required by the organization. For example, give a rating to *customers* or *transactions*, rather than the broader categories of 'people, groups and roles' or 'events and processes', by asking, 'how important is information about transactions'.

The next step is to look at the most important information on the information map and to identify the main flows between these key items. For example, if we assume that customer and transaction information are both rated as important, the information map might show an association between these two types of information that suggests the link is used to identify the set of transactions for a particular customer or to help adapt products and services better to meet customer needs. While either of these uses might apply, the real test is whether there is any additional value in making these connections, for example in using the associated information to study buying patterns resulting in greater product sales or to identify late payments, reducing the administrative overheads for collecting them.

Each information value chain can be recorded as a view of items on the information map, with an evaluation of the value that it creates. Identifying the set of transactions for a customer may not have any inherent value until it is used in its own right to create an intelligence advantage. All value chains should be analysed to identify:

- **Information that grows in value**, which is information that lies at the core of the organization's success.
- **Redundant chains**, which duplicate other chains by providing two sources for same information, or chains that do not add any useful value.
- **Short cuts that can be introduced**, by providing quicker ways to create the same information or finding points where decisions can be made earlier.
- **Additional information that could be added** to a process to make it more productive.

Choosing the right categories at the outset results in the efficient and effective use of information. A multinational information technology company recognized that each division had a different mission and responsibilities, performed distinct activities and therefore had unique skill requirements and performance problems. At the same time, senior executives wanted a holistic, systems-based approach that could be used across all geographic areas and business units and that would develop organizational competencies that would be difficult for competitors to copy. The selected categories were all types of organizational or management information – Measurements and key indicators, Organization and management structures, People, groups and roles, Skills and competence, and Strategy and purpose.

Team leaders carefully identified what information they needed to complete the project successfully, making sure that one piece of information led to the next, adding value at each step until there was a clear action plan that would meet the objectives. The categories were sequenced into a process that made complete use of the gathered information:

- *Understand the mission, goals and objectives of each organization unit*
- *Identify the critical success factors for reaching those targets*
- *Identify the key jobs and roles supporting them*
- *Understand which skills are needed by those jobs*
- *Develop competence profiles for each of them*
- *Develop an inventory of existing skills in those jobs*
- *Measure competence gaps of individuals in those jobs*
- *Identify areas where management action was needed to improve receptivity and consensus on target performance*
- *Recommend training solutions to address competence gaps*
- *Recommend other (non-training) actions that were necessary to ensure performance.*

The three levels of understanding

Broadly speaking, we understand the information we receive in three ways:

- **By recognizing words and language and the meaning they convey**. This is the *deconstruction level*, because we break information into its constituent elements by analysing the definition and meaning of each separate information item. Deconstructing a word or phrase means literally breaking it down until you discover the constructs or constituent components.
- **By applying mental models and theories to create and explain links between one piece of information and another**. This is the *explanation level* – where we create hypotheses or theory that explain why we have grouped certain information items together.
- **By interpreting information based on our knowledge and experience**. This is the *interpretation level*, where we reflect on how we actually use information items and information clusters in practical real life situations.

The three levels of understanding are inter-related – as we interpret information we identify new theories and modify our definitions of terms, changing definitions gives new material to put into theories, and learning about theories gives a context for definitions and provides new techniques to interpret information.

The nature of our understanding and the way that we deal with information, changes at each level. We need a balance between each type of understanding to explore meaning and interpret information effectively. Not only do the levels complement one another, but the value of information accumulates through the levels: we need to know the meaning of the words before we can understand their use in a theory and we draw upon our knowledge of theories to interpret information. Ultimately, the true meaning of both definitions and theories is revealed by how we interpret and use them – it is not what we say or think, but what we do, that matters. For example, there are plenty of contemporary theories that put the customer first and emphasize the importance of the customer relationship, but this theory may be far removed from how it is interpreted in practice, which is reflected in the customer's actual experiences. Learning about information and understanding its use depends on feedback from users, so that definitions, theories and interpretations are constantly updated to reflect current needs.

Organizational knowledge is captured and dispersed through the information architecture by making links between the information categories, knowledge of mental models and understanding, by documenting value chains between information categories using the information map, and by choosing optimal ways of presenting this knowledge about information. The information map is the hub of this activity, by using key parts of the map and focusing on improving their use. As David Snowden has described this, an information map is an advanced form of data model with a knowledge wrapper (Private conversation, 2000).

Key points

Information appreciates in value the more it is used. By identifying the most valuable information and maximizing its use, information architecture dramatically increases its worth as an organizational treasure.

Information is not the same for everyone; architecting information helps people to find and use the information that they regard as useful and relevant.

Much time and effort is wasted processing data and creating confusion, confirmation, frustration or delusion, instead of helping users recognize the value of information, inspiration and innovation.

Information architecture is the business of helping people to understand and find meaning. Too often it is seen as something that is of benefit to technology rather than making it easier for people to work with information.

A unique organizational architecture emerges and evolves organically by observing patterns and finding out how information is actually used. The rules of business, the rationale for a design and theories behind practice are often not documented. Capturing explanations for key decision processes and information structures helps others to understand what has happened or why something has one design rather than another.

Document techniques and theories that will help users get the most out of information. This is probably the most obvious, but most overlooked, component of information architecture.

Thinking about the many possible uses for information expands the opportunities for using the architecture.

Information value chains, which can be easily examined using the information map, are usually very different from a process supply chain. Making information value chains explicit is key to maximizing information value.

The value of information accumulates through the three levels of understanding – deconstruction, explanation and interpretation. Adding higher levels of understanding to an information map increases its intelligence and sophistication.

The eight factors

In this chapter the essential factors used were:

- **Categories – knowledge – understanding**: used to identify the degree to which relevant data are available and compare them with the degree to which those data provide or provoke ideas or answers. The interpretation of information is a combination of understanding, categories and knowledge.
- **Understanding**: used to help users find the right information and to help them find meaning, develop theories, interpret data and innovate with information.
- **Categories – representation – knowledge**: a subset of the information resource, identified as views of the information categories and represented as an information map, is manipulated, analysed and interpreted using knowledge of mental models and theories.
- **Categories – understanding**: used to make the use of information more efficient, effective and innovative.
- **Understanding – representation**: used to decide the most effective means for making understanding available to users.
- **Categories – process**: used to identify and analyse the different uses of information and to document information value chains.

8

Improving the architecture and keeping it current

Failure is only the opportunity to begin again more intelligently.
Henry Ford

Everything is vague to a degree you do not realize till you have tried to make it precise.
Bertrand Russell

Like most things, basic maintenance is necessary to keep the information architecture and knowledge current and up-to-date, because without this effort it gradually deteriorates and becomes useless. As with geographic maps, dictionaries, encyclopaedias and other intellectual tools, much of the architecture and the information map is quite stable, but this is perceived as unreliable if the more volatile sections are not updated. Technology and process re-engineering are often the main cause of change to the architecture, followed by new organization structures, particularly from mergers or acquisitions and new industry and commercial trends. In his influential book on *The Seven Habits Of Highly Effective People*, Stephen Covey (1992) refers to this essential principle of renewal as sharpening the saw. He starts the chapter on this habit with the story of someone who cannot see the contradiction in trying to saw down a tree with a blunt saw – 'I don't have time to sharpen the saw – I'm too busy sawing' and yet this is one of the most common failings in architecting information – the toolkit is simply not updated.

More than 80% of time and money is spent on maintenance, enhancement, re-engineering and replacement of existing information structures, but despite this, most architecture approaches are geared towards the development of new software applications and information systems.

Many architectural practices therefore consume most of their energy on creating and establishing the architecture, when this should only take around 20% of the total architecture effort. This situation has occurred partly because information architectures emerged in parallel with the growth of information systems. Early methodologies described the development of transaction-oriented and procedure-based systems and the first information architectures emerged from a need to control the development of more sophisticated information systems.

Today, architecture must also come to grips with maintenance of information structures and address a wider range of information processing needs, such as supporting decision-making, predictions and forecasting, developing information-based products and services, and underpinning innovation and creativity. The architecture should explicitly address the maintenance, enhancement, re-engineering and replacement, as well as development, of information structures, thus covering all stages in the architectural cycle. Feedback should also involve business and management information users as well as technologists.

The action plan, developed in Chapter 3, is one of the main tools for tracking change, because it documents all of the planned modifications and, as these alterations are made, the architecture should be updated accordingly. As explained earlier, each step in the plan is a view, or a set of views, of the corporate information resource, so at the conclusion of each step it is easy to compare the planned view against the changes that have actually been made. This is a good time to review and update all of the steps in the action plan. Completed steps provide a history of both successes and failures, thus adding both knowledge about the use of information and greater understanding of the change process to the architecture. Changes that have not completed successfully are usually a consequence of insufficient resources, a poor understanding of information structures or attempts to do too much at a time and this knowledge will help make future planning more realistic. Completed changes should be compared against expected benefits to check that results match expectations, using any discrepancies to improve understanding of the change process and trumpeting successes to further the architecting cause. Updating views and steps makes each iteration of the action plan more practical and realistic.

Meta data are used, among other things, to keep control of the change process by recording such things as the currency of data, details of when the information was last updated and its version, the source of the information and an indication of its accuracy or reliability. Meta data can be used to schedule updates and reviews – for example, it might be policy to review all information categories on a 6-monthly basis, with meta data documenting the date when each item was last inspected.

Gathering feedback

We assume that people use information in a logical and rational manner – that everyone knows the relevant background theories and is in a position to put them into practice. In reality, we are often blissfully unaware of how we 'should' be using information and even when we know of a suitable theory we often do not apply it in practice. To make matters worse, there are often constraints and limitations built into information systems and organization structures that prevent us from using information as we might like. Constraints are imposed by the availability of people, time, budget, skills, technology and knowledge, not to mention the forces of politics, strategy, culture or nature.

There are also many situations when theories do not work, because they do not take into account all of the available information or they do not offer a satisfactory explanation of the data. We do not all have the time to study business or management theory and when we do not know of any theories that apply we have to rely on our own judgment and make our own interpretation of the information. The more unusual and unfamiliar the situation, the more we need to improvise and it is when we are under pressure with deadlines to meet that we are least likely to have the time to modify a spreadsheet or remember something that we heard during an MBA course or training seminar. In extreme pressure, theories and methodologies go out the door and it is time to roll up the shirtsleeves and get our hands dirty.

It is through interpretation – the mixture of putting theories into practice, drawing upon our personal experiences, hunches and ideas and making it up as we go along – that we discover the most exciting and innovative new ways for understanding and using information. It can rightly be said that if beauty is in the eye of the beholder, then information is in the interpretation of the user because information only has value in the meaning that someone assigns to it.

Feedback shows what is useful, what is not, what is up-to-date, what needs to be added to the information architecture and much of this comes from learning about how users interpret information. It is therefore vital to gather feedback from use and users and keep a finger on the information pulse to be aware of changing needs and emerging trends. How often should you gather feedback depends on how much you are using information, how critical it is, the degree of change and what your competitors are doing, among other things. It is better to have a routine for gathering feedback, otherwise it tends to be forgotten and we would suggest that this takes place on a 3- or 6-monthly basis for the most critical information and as part of a more general annual audit for other information. It is important to have a workable way of gathering feedback from people and two simple options are using a suggestion scheme and running periodic focus group meetings.

Here are some questions that help to find out how information really works in practice:

- **Knowledge and experience:** How do you interpret this information? What personal knowledge or experience helps you to interpret information? What insights and revelations have you discovered in this information?
- **Practice and alternatives:** How are people actually using this information? What workarounds do people apply when using information? What workarounds do people use to get their work done? What options are available for implementing alternative information designs and theories? What alternatives are there to any of the established business or management theories and models? What arguments are there against using the established theories?
- **Constraints:** What is making it difficult for you to use this information as you would like to use it? What information do you really need that is not available? What limitations are imposed by physical things (for example, a software program that does not allow you to input certain types of information or a call centre that is in a remote location that makes sharing information difficult)?

Find out how information is actually being used. Architecture that ignores how people really use information overlooks the factors that are most likely to cause information misuse and misunderstanding. These range from the deliberate misinterpretation of information for political purposes through to the accidental use of the wrong figures in a spreadsheet calculation. Find out more about the environment or context in which information is used.

Too often use of information in practice remains tacit – hidden in conversation, discussions, internal communications or the folklore of the organization. We can learn a lot from the interpretations that are put on information. It is also critical to know the limitations and constraints that are placed on information by the physical environment that is used to interpret information. Anything that we learn about the use of information in practice should be added to definitions of information items.

Spring cleaning – conducting a periodic review

Architecting organizational changes is a learning process, which necessitates a periodic review and update. The review is the information equivalent of spring-cleaning, when cupboards are tidied and anything unwanted is thrown out. As with a spring clean, it is good practice to conduct an annual review or audit of both the architecting process and the artifacts that it creates. In some respects it is similar to an annual budget review, revisiting last year's plans and making provisions for the future. Kierkegaard has said that 'life is lived forward, but understood backward' and the annual review provides the time needed to ponder and think about what has happened in the previous 12 months! Conducting a routine review is more purposeful and produces better learning than irregular appraisals.

For organizations that have previously developed or used information architectures, an appraisal of what has already been achieved is a useful way of aligning earlier work with current efforts and ensuring that everything belongs as part of the big picture. An evaluation of progress is just as important if you are starting with architecture products supplied by a vendor, as there are no guarantees that a commercial source will be an exact fit to your needs.

The success of an architecture programme depends largely on a serious commitment to managing information as a resource. At the beginning of this book we introduced a diagnostic that used ten statements about information as a corporate resource (Chapter 1, Appendix A). It is worth going back over the ten discussion points as part of this review, asking yourself whether your architecture initiatives would have been more or less successful if each factor were true. Here is a quick reminder of the ten statements:

- There is a clear and distinct vision of information as a corporate resource
- There is an organization unit responsible for information and knowledge that is distinct from the information technology function
- There is a well-defined strategy and action plan for improving the effectiveness of information use across the organization
- Information that is vital and necessary to make key decisions is always readily and easily available
- All information is available in a consistent and integrated format
- Management believes that there is considerable value to be gained from the organization's use of information
- Information management is seen as the responsibility of business people as well as the information technology functions
- Information has a key role in all business processes
- Financial approval is readily available for investment in the information infrastructure of the organization (as opposed to technology investments)
- Information is used to support innovation and creativity in product and service development, business processes and customer support.

What has been done before?

Learning from the past is difficult at the best of times: few organizations allow time for reflection, it can be difficult to uncover true links between cause and effect and there is a danger of punishing the guilty. Finding out what an organization has already done with information architecture is not always easy because initiatives include architectural tasks even though they may not be called architecture projects. For example, a project to re-engineer business processes will also need to specify the information used by each activity and the flow of information through each workflow, so inevitably it will affect the architecture itself. Architecture programmes are not always enterprise-wide, so working in the retail division of a bank there may already be some highly relevant work that has been done in the corporate division. There will always be some analysis of requirements of the business and its information processing needs before making investments in information technology – possibly in the form of data and process models or more recently object models – and this is an excellent source for defining information categories or developing the information map.

Many architectural processes and methodologies have evolved in a haphazard way in parallel with the growing volume of information and software – just like the unstructured spaghetti code of legacy systems. John Maynard Keynes once said that the real difficulty in changing the course of an enterprise lies not in developing new ideas but in escaping from the old ones and by examining previous architecture-related projects we can learn from the past and identify critical success factors for the future. Breaking free from outdated assumptions results in dramatic advancements to the architecture, with consequent benefits in productivity from, and quality in, information.

People do not always remember what has already been done, especially from projects that happened some time in the past. There could be documents and diagrams that are useful and longer-serving staff at the company may recall whether there have been any similar projects. Architectural investment is not always a steady, consistent effort and in fact it is frequently cyclical, with a burst of investment, then a period of little activity, followed by more intense efforts and so on.

A bank initiated a sophisticated, architecture-based project to redevelop not only its core banking systems but its whole approach to software development. Although the project delivered some of the key elements for its new infrastructure, cutbacks at the bank following problems with bad debts caused development to be cancelled before completion. Most of the staff involved in the project left the bank and despite the high-profile of the project, few people were aware of the deliverables it produced. Years later, the bank's systems required further updating and as part of the requirements definition process purchased a generic enterprise-wide data and process model. It was only following an information management audit by an external company specializing in architecture that the bank realized that it already had far more comprehensive models from the earlier project.

Great buildings attract writers who research and record their architectural history and information architects could learn from this. With a very few exceptions, noteworthy information-related projects are not well-documented and knowledge about them tends towards hearsay and gossip – not a trustworthy foundation for learning from the past. Listing projects and initiatives that have already taken place or are taking place and gathering together any architectural artifacts that they have already produced helps identify what has worked and what did not work in the past. It may also provide you with useful materials that you can reuse. People who were involved in these projects (assuming that they are still working there) are also an excellent source of architectural knowledge.

Was it successful?

If I start a 100-metre race but do not cross the finishing line, then I fail on the grounds that I did not run the full distance, but architecture is not a set-distance race. With information architecture it is necessary to measure its *relative* success. You will find that because information systems (both human and computer based) are remarkably resilient, even an unplanned information architecture *may* hold together, but do not expect it to work anywhere near as well as one that is designed for the task. In an organizational context, architecture that is explicitly defined and managed always outperforms one that is random, spontaneous, impulsive and unintentional!

Although projects of all types fail, failure does not necessarily mean that the architecture it produced was wrong. If a project does not deliver what was planned, runs over budget or gets cancelled, then it means that the commitment or planning was not right – it is important to separate the degree to which information architecture is effective from the project that created it. In the 1980s I worked on an ambitious information architecture project that was cancelled before it was due to end and, because of this, the project was widely regarded as a failure. However, the architecture that was created remained the foundation of its information systems, products and services and organization structure for more than 15 years, so the architecture itself was successful.

The effectiveness of information structures is often not measured. Some structures are better than others because they provide top-quality support for actions or decisions, while some are more efficient and others are more likely to lead to insight and revelation. In what ways did a project change or alter the architecture and were these changes for the better or for worse? Measures of effectiveness must link back to architectural goals and objectives – otherwise it is impossible to tell whether they achieved the desired aims.

Unless there is a detailed plan or blueprint for each relevant factor of the architecture, then the architecture is not being managed, but is being left to chance. The best way to manage architectural changes is to define explicitly all of the relevant factors, which then serve as checklists or reminders of everything that needs to be taken into account. These checklists can also be used to judge how well each factor is being *explicitly* managed.

Analysing earlier architecture efforts

Much can be learnt by studying past successes and failures, so if there is time, budget and commitment it is worth conducting a *formal* review of the architectural efforts to date through interviews and discussions with participants and sponsors. The findings can be published as a document that will highlight methodological, managerial or organizational improvements that could be adopted in future efforts.

Various types of analysis can be conducted, depending on the level of responsibility. For example, individual people in each role can be interviewed to identify critical skills or personal insights, at the project level, post-action reviews help to identify successes and learn from failures, at the level of a business function or product, writing up case studies demonstrates benefits and results, while the enterprise level is where universal principles, standards and guidelines should be documented.

Some of the key questions to ask include:

- **Objectives:** Were any architectural objectives defined? To what extent were they achieved?
- **Methodology:** What methodology or approach was followed? How could it be improved? How could it be made more effective or easier to understand and apply? What were the limitations and drawbacks of the approach? What did participants find difficult to understand or difficult to do?
- **Results:** What were the successes and benefits of the approach? What business or organizational advantages are attributable to the architectural efforts? What evidence is there for value or benefit?
- **Deliverables:** What deliverables or architectural artifacts were created? In what ways were they useful? How could they be improved?
- **Organizational culture:** How well did architectural initiatives fit in with other projects and everyday business operations? To what extent is there agreement on the benefits and value of the exercise? How significant were these initiatives to your organization?
- **Responsibilities:** Who was responsible for the funding, management and results of the projects? What additional responsibilities need to be allocated in future?
- **Skills:** In what ways could skills and expertise be improved? What skills were missing? What skills were not fully utilized? What training, skill transfer or explanations should be provided in future?
- **Information architecture:** In what ways did these projects improve or enhance the use of information? What suggestions would you offer for

improving the use of architecture, from a technical, business or managerial perspective? What advice would you give for future architectural projects? What ideas do you have for exploiting information architecture?

Many organizations start their first architectural projects by using a pre-defined framework, such as the Zachman Enterprise Architecture or IBM's Information FrameWork. If this is the case, there are some additional questions:

- In what ways did having a pre-defined architecture give you a head start?
- Was the architecture easy to understand and use?
- Did you follow an associated methodology? In what ways was this supportive?
- In what ways was a pre-defined architecture limiting or restricting?
- Which parts of the architecture, if any, were confusing or difficult to use?
- How would you improve or change the architecture?

Getting a balanced architecture

As we discussed earlier, there are three types of information that are inter-related. *Organizational information* is necessary to make decisions and guide the direction that the business takes – this would include the information required to manage a particular organization such as the ABC Banking Corporation. *Business information* is necessary to analyse how customers are using products, to find out which products are generating a profit and to develop new products or services – the ABC Banking Corporation might operate one or more inter-related businesses and therefore need to keep information about retail banking services, corporate banking services, insurance services, financial advice and estate agency services. *Information about supporting technology* is necessary to provide adequate support for both running the business and taking management decisions and for creating the best mix of technical components – ABC Banking Corporation would need information about the transaction processing systems, the ATM network, its data warehouse, the customer relationship system and the branch network.

The information architecture must support all three types of information, which are mutually interdependent. Changes to the organization itself, such as reducing the number of staff, will affect the ways in which it carries out its business and may require additional support from technology. The introduction of new technology provides business opportunities and may require training of staff in new skills.

Organizations are so large and their information systems so complex that we naturally tend to break this complexity down into something more manageable, which is why many information systems components are still developed as standalone units with a single system orientation, while coexistence, migration or integration is regarded as something that is necessary to link one component to another. Architecture often corresponds to the boundaries of these standalone systems, with separate architectures for the corporate and retail departments in a bank, or for a customer relationship application and a data warehouse.

Architecture that works in a particular context nearly always needs to be extended to fit a broader range of situations, which is one reason why it is better to start from first principles with the eight factors and develop an architecture rather than start with a preconceived one. Every component within an information system is always a part of something bigger; the standalone software applications of the 1960s became part of an enterprise architecture, which became part of cross-enterprise architectures and ultimately part of a global web.

To help determine architectural strengths and weaknesses and to develop a balanced architecture, consider:

- What is **driving** investment in information-related projects – organizational needs, business requirements or technology demands?
- What are the main **strengths** for information management – through leveraging organizational structure and competence, business products and processes or technical superiority?
- What are the main **limitations** in the use of information – inappropriate organization structures, cumbersome business processes or outdated technologies?

To help decide what is driving information-based change, ask whether investments are driven by:

- **Organizational drivers**: for example, the need to support strategy, changes in the organizational structure or the need to acquire new capabilities or skills.
- **Business drivers**: for example, the need to simplify or improve business processes, changes to business reports or the need for new business data, or changes to existing products or services or the introduction of new ones.
- **Technology drivers**: for example, the limitations of legacy software and databases, changes to telecommunications networks or the introduction of new information technology.

To help decide the major strengths for achieving information-based change, ask whether investments are achieved through:

- **Organizational strengths**: such as strong leadership and direction, a culture that recognizes the value and contribution of information to its success, or unique skills or capability in information architecture, information modelling or information management.

- **Business strengths**: such as flexible and adaptable business processes, the quality of business intelligence and data or market leading products and services.
- **Technology strengths**: such as well-integrated software systems, sophisticated communications facilities or innovative use of technology.

Finally, to help decide what is being left out or forgotten by information-based change, ask about the weaknesses or any negative consequences or results of investments:

- **Organizational limitations**: for example, little contribution to strategic direction, lack of support for organization structure or organizational culture, or little improvement to organizational competence and skills.
- **Business limitations**: for example, business processes that are difficult to change or limit business opportunities, information structures or sources that are incompatible, or products and services that only offer features and facilities that are standard or expected in your industry sector.
- **Technology limitations**: for example, standalone software systems, lack of needed communications technology or information technology platforms that are unresponsive to change.

The ideal situation would be drivers and strengths addressing the limitations in each of the three areas, to achieve a balance that meets organizational, business and technology needs. In practice, most of the organizations that we work with have an imbalance and it is not always where you might expect it to be! What this exercise does is to identify which pattern your organization falls into so that you can redress the balance. Here are some of the patterns that we have observed:

- *An organization in which business participants were fully involved in a strategic information architecture project.* There was full commitment to the use of information as a strategic resource (organization or management driven), with a strong business infrastructure that could use information to advantage (business or operational strength). Technology needed to be better aligned with business and management needs for this architecture to be fully successful (technical limitation).
- *An organization with a vision of transforming from a high street into an e-commerce company.* There was commitment (management driver) to the development of information technology, resulting in a strong technical infrastructure (technical strength) that did not achieve the full business potential. A better understanding of opportunities to

improve business information will result in a better return from information (business limitation).

- *A project to re-engineer business processes to take advantage of unique organizational skills and competence.* Those involved in operation of the business were well aware of what they could achieve using information (business driver) and the organization had the capability and motivation to make it happen (organizational strength). The power of information technology needed to be harnessed to give potential for even more effective change (technical limitation).
- *An organization provided a large budget to introduce data warehouse and data mining technology.* There was a strong awareness of the potential for using new technology (technical driver), which was recognized by senior management (management strength). Although the organization had the necessary skills and capability (organizational strength), inflexible business processes and lack of critical data (business limitation) limited the full potential to exploit the technology.
- *A business needed to consolidate information from separate divisions into a large corporate intranet.* Technology has the capability to support a major business need (technical strength). Although the opportunity was clearly defined (business driver), the lack of skill, funds and internal politics hampered its success (organizational limitation).
- *An organization wanted to encapsulate business rules into parameterized object-oriented components supporting a wide range of products.* This strategy was driven by the adoption of new technology (technical driver) to take advantage of a mixture of unique business products and processes (business strength). Unfortunately, without sponsorship and executive support it was difficult to gain budget and resources (management limitation).

Here is an example of a data warehousing project, based on a review of a client implementation, which demonstrates a lack of balance across each of the three broad categories. The project was driven by the opportunities offered by data warehousing technology to leverage strength in business data. The limitations were mainly organizational: with 78% of respondents rating 'provide good strategic support' as poor or adequate and 83% of responses saying that support for using the warehouse was poor or adequate. Although training ranked better, with 35% of respondents marking training as good or excellent, it still received a high number of poor and adequate ratings, while 10% of respondents did not receive any training at all. In this case, a project driven by technical considerations to take advantage of business strengths, did not achieve its maximum potential because of organizational limitations that could easily have been corrected with a more proactive approach.

Analysis of projects varies widely from organization to organization – for example, some companies embark on data warehousing as a strategic directive, others do not have the right business data to make the investment worthwhile, while some lack the appropriate technical infrastructure.

Extending the information categories

The set of information categories described in this book and listed in Appendix B covers more than 80% of the information resource in the majority of companies. It may be necessary to extend these generic categories by developing one or more specialized categories, the most common being specialization of Products, goods and services to cover information about the specific products your organization provides. It may also be necessary to add further categories to a section that becomes very detailed or is highly specialized. For example, Measurements and key indicators is a broad category that covers information about monitoring and evaluating the activities, processes, actions and strategies of an organization, which could be extended with a new subcategory specifically covering Financial indicators.

Suggestions for extending the information categories mainly come from using the categories and finding that something is missing, or instigating specialized information support for a particular project or business function. Whether defining new categories or extending existing ones, there are some general rules or guidelines that will ensure they conform to good architectural practice.

A large international financial institution extended the generic information categories based on a detailed analysis of key indicators used by senior managers. Analysis started using an information model with detailed definitions of the most common indicators, such as the profitability or revenue of a company, the effectiveness of a process or measurements for financial markets and trends. These were already classified into subcategories such as Demographic indicators, Customer indicators, Operational indicators and Product or service indicators.

The first step was to find out what indicators were being used, who was using them and how they were being used. We also found out how each indicator was calculated, what source information was input to this calculation and where that source information came from. At this point there was a clear picture of the indicators that were regarded as important and patterns were starting to emerge. Many of the 'important' decision-making indicators were based on financial figures and performance and we were gathering a lot of information that was specific to financial indicators but did not apply to indicators in other categories, such as human resource or organization change. So we created a new information category called Financial indicators and created a detailed information map of specialized indicators such as the Return on shareholder equity (ROSE) and Value added profit (VAP).

Each of these specialized indicators was a subtype of key indicator – in other words, it had all the characteristics of key indicators in general, but with additional knowledge and behaviour that was unique to financial indicators. The detailed financial indicator map was used to explore how key decision-makers applied this information and helped identify how to improve its use. It was quickly apparent that several sources provided the 'same' information and that some indicators were calculated in different ways, so not surprisingly, figures from different sources did not always match up. People did not realize that their colleagues were spending time and effort gathering together identical information. There was information that never really got used at all and some information that could have been used if people had realized it was available.

Creating a more detailed information category allowed us to analyse financial indicators in more detail, resulting in reduced information processing costs and more effective decision-making.

Getting the right categories

How do you know that you have the right categories? Here are some techniques to ensure that each category is sufficiently distinct from the others and that there is a 'complete' set of categories.

Comparing and contrasting categories at the same level in the hierarchy ensures that each is sufficiently distinctive. In our suggested information categories we make the distinction between 'Organizational or management information', 'Business or operational information' and 'Information about supporting technologies'. Does this separation make sense? Is there sufficient difference between these types of information to be able to distinguish them? Some categories obviously deal with things that are conceptually distinct – 'People, groups and roles' versus 'Property and equipment' for example, while others have a closer resemblance to each other, such as 'Strategy and purpose' and 'Measurements and key indicators'. Categories should make it *easier* to use information, rather than becoming a bureaucratic overhead.

The true test for the categories is to use them, by mapping typical scenarios against them to find the information that is used in a particular situation. For example the information used to develop new products might include information about existing products, sales figures, market segments and customer requirements. If this information does not slot into place in the categories, then they need to be extended or modified.

There is a training exercise that we developed to help explain the information categories. Two teams of students are given a set of envelopes; each envelope has the name of one of the high-level information categories on it. They are then given cards with the names of 50 different information items and the objective of the exercise is to place each card in the envelope that seems most appropriate. There is no perfect or right answer, because at the end of the day categorizing information is only useful if it works. The most valuable part of this exercise is listening carefully when the students compare their results and discuss why they chose to place 'customer' in 'marketing and sales' instead of 'people, groups and roles'. We deliberately include some ambiguous items, along with the more obvious, to provoke these discussions because it is the rationale or explanations that provide a real *understanding* of how people use information.

There may be some information items that appear to belong in more than one category and it makes the architecture easier to use if this information is placed in *all* relevant categories. Some people might argue that items should only appear in one place in the architecture, with a particular type of information included only within a single category and some software implementation methodologies insist on using a single category or classification. However, there will always be people who have alternative opinions or viewpoints and our opinion is that information architecture should be flexible enough to accommodate these differences and putting an information item in two (or more) categories simply increases the chance that users will find the information they need. It also makes it quite clear that there are alternative interpretations and these complementary *views* can be recorded to highlight the categories that are required in different contexts.

Listing detailed information categories

Developing a comprehensive list of categories is a good way to verify that they are correct and complete. It is also a key task in populating the information map. Making the list of information categories as complete as possible at an early stage makes it easier to deliver an architecture that is consistent and well integrated and this should be based on feedback from the initial projects. Categories do not need a detailed definition until they feature as a key part of an action plan, when definitions become important for understanding and using it. Creating a comprehensive list of categories before architecting major organizational changes helps to verify that the information categories are correct and provides a firm structure for future developments.

If you have a background in data or object modelling you may be tempted to think about normalization, inheritance or other ways of rationalizing the categories as you list them. These techniques are important, but not now. The objective now is to list the types of information from the perspective of the information *users*. If someone says that they work with *customer* information, then *customer* is a valid information category and if another person says that *customer* information is information about a *person* or an *organization*, then *person* and *organization* are also valid categories. It may be necessary, later on, to cross-reference and map these two different perspectives of what is possibly the same information, to see where and how they differ or overlap, but this is done using *views*. It is also better to work out what information is important without worrying about relationships between different types of information.

Labelling categories

Of all the architectural tasks, identifying and labelling the information categories is one of the most important. Some labels or names are better than others, so here are some cautionary notes to be aware of potential traps. The following labels are not necessarily wrong – in fact they are all drawn from information architectures that have been or are still in use – but using these labels could trip you up if you do not know how to handle them.

The special case of customer

Structuring and using customer information causes no end of problems – witness the large number of vendors who are providing solutions to help manage customer relationships or to mine customer information. There are multiple sources for customer information, storage formats vary widely and it is difficult to keep customer information up-to-date.

There are three alternative ways of dealing with customer information. The first is to treat 'customer' as a category in its own right. However, this can lead to some complications because while a person is always a person, he or she is not always a customer. Whether someone is a customer or not depends on additional information, which defines the context for being a customer and this contextual information can be interpreted as a *role* or as a *relationship*. Here is a brief description of each option, together with the pros and cons of each approach.

Customer is an established and recognized business concept and users are comfortable talking about customer information and intuitively 'know' what they mean by customer – so the simplest approach is to treat it as a distinct and separate category called *customer*. This approach is easy to understand because much customer information is stored in this way, but there is a high risk of duplicating information and it does not produce a very flexible information structure. It does not make it clear whether a customer is a person or organization and it is difficult to analyse relationships with other parties. It is also makes it difficult to analyse the commercial value of a customer.

The logic for treating customer as a role is that a person takes on different roles in different situations, so customer is one of the many roles that can be taken on by a person or organization. If I go into a clothes shop and actively look for a new shirt, I take on the role of prospective customer or *prospect*; if I make the purchase I become a *customer*. If I wear the shirt twice and it starts falling to pieces I may take on the role of *dissatisfied customer* – which is something quite different from the role of the *satisfied customer* and so on. In this sense, *role*, *person* and *organization* are separate information categories, while *customer* is one possible type of role. This is the best structure for exploring different types of behaviour, through examining different roles and it is easier to spot relationships with other parties than storing the information in a 'customer' structure. It could still be difficult to analyse the commercial value and relationships are still not necessarily explicit.

The final approach is to treat customer as a relationship between a person or an organization and another type of information such as product. The justification for this approach argues that someone is only a customer because of a relationship that explains the nature of the link. I am a customer because I *buy* or *use* a product – I am a customer because I *bought* the shirt or when I *wear* the shirt. I am a customer of a bank because I *deal with* the staff at my local branch or because someone *is* my financial adviser at their head office. Using this interpretation, *person* and *organization* are separate information categories, while *customer* is implied through the relationships with a product or with a product provider. This is best for exploring relationships with other parties or information categories, making it easier to analyse the commercial value of a relationship. The structure is easily extended and modified and it is simple to record information about the start and end of a relationship and changes to the status of a relationship. However, initially it is more complicated to set up.

The most flexible architectures combine all three options, making *person* and *organization* the two main categories, creating a *customer* category to present information in a way that is familiar to users, providing a set of *relationships* to other relevant categories such as product, address, agreement and other people or organizations and using *role* to explore behaviour in different situations. It is a useful exercise to find out how many different definitions of 'customer' are being used in an organization; there are usually as many as ten to thirty distinct definitions in a typical corporation.

Involved party, participant, party, actor and agent

Because customer is a confusing label that can refer both to individuals and organizations, there have been several attempts to come up with a neutral label that can be used to refer to both. 'Involved party' is a phrase first coined by Robert Peake when he was responsible for data resource management at Westpac and the phrase was later used for one of the nine data concepts in IBM's Financial Services Data Model (FSDM). Other information architectures have abbreviated this to 'party' or replaced it by 'participant', while another common equivalent is 'third party'. 'Actor' and 'agent' are two terms that are popular with object-oriented methodologies.

Unfortunately, each of these labels (involved party, participant, party, actor or agent) can be confusing and possibly irritating, to anyone not used to dealing with abstract modelling language and the terms should therefore be avoided unless it really is the language in common use. If there is an explicit need to refer to a person or organization without making the distinction, the phrase 'person or organization' can be used. Abstract concepts should only be used when they add a great deal of benefit. Many of the relationships for an organization are also true for a person, so from a modelling sense, an abstract concept, such as 'involved party', can be used to show information and relationships that are common to both an individual and an organization. Information architects must be bilingual, translating *modelling* language into *everyday* language when dealing with users and being careful not to overuse modelling language with anyone that regards it as jargon.

The term 'involved party' implies a party that is actively involved in a situation, such as a signatory to an agreement and to avoid confusion it is important that such abstract concepts are clearly defined and used. For example, is a prospective customer, who may not know that they are about to become part of a sales campaign, involved?

Why 'data' and 'object' do not work as categories

'Data' masquerades as an information category in many first- and second-generation architectures. It reflects the growing use of database technology and the widespread adoption of data modelling methodologies at that time and is a legacy of describing information from a technology perspective. I included data as one of the ten columns of the Information FrameWork (IFW) in the 1990s, because the Financial Service Data Model was a major component of that architecture, but in hindsight this column is incongruent with the other nine.

In popular usage 'data' refers to information that is factual, attributive and stored in a computer system. It is usually taken to mean facts, figures and symbols that are precisely defined and structured, such as information that is structured using entity relationship models or stored in the columns and rows of database tables. The word data is also used to distinguish that which is input to an interpretation process from the information that is output. It is not an information category in the same way that we would refer to *information about* a person or *information about* a location. Data is a format to represent or structure knowledge that is easily codified or that is a source material for creating information. Functions, locations, people, goals and events are all things that are important to the business and data about them could be represented as an entity relationship diagram or stored in a database table. There could be data for any of the information categories.

Putting the phrase 'information about' in front of any category is a quick check to see if it is a good label for a type of information and should be used as a simple rule to test potential information categories. A business data model describes information about products or information about locations; it does not provide 'information about data' unless it is a meta-model.

On the other hand, conceptual categories in a data model are often good information categories. An industry data model included various data concepts, including product, location, arrangement, condition and event. Each of these concepts indicates a type of information that in a data model happen to be presented as an entity relationship diagram, although each could be described or shown in many different ways. Data models are good at representing a type of knowledge that is explicit, formal and relatively simple to structure. Such high-level categories or concepts in existing data models should be used as information categories in the architecture.

As with data, an object is a formal style or presentation for modelling information, which is used to specify, visualize, construct and document information systems. It is generally regarded as a composite that describes an information structure in terms of its attributes and the set of behaviours that operate on those attributes. Again object-modelling techniques can be used to model any type of information. Information from any category could be represented as an object model or a data model.

Resource and asset

Using the suggested categories that we have provided (Appendix B), resource and asset, without additional words to qualify them, are very broad terms, spanning several different information categories. Information about *financial resources* is included in the 'Accounts and finances' category, information about *human resources* is covered by 'Skills and competence', *physical resources* are part of 'Property and equipment', *intellectual assets* are within 'Intellectual assets and knowledge' and *technical resources,* such as computer programs, are under 'Software applications and interfaces'. The information included within each category should be conceptually similar, whereas the many types of resource and asset cover a wide range of items across a number of other information categories that are conceptually diverse.

The important point here is that the set of information categories in an architecture should form a logical and congruent set. Resource and asset do not work as a high-level category in the category hierarchy that we have been using in this book, because there are different types of resource or asset that we have defined in other categories. It is possible to define a different set of categories and an alternative approach could therefore make 'resources and assets' into a high-level category and then subdivide it into financial resources, human resources, etc. However, this would result in a totally different structure to the one that we have shown in Appendix B.

It is possible to include additional high-level 'categories' from both approaches within a single information architecture by using the concept of views introduced in Chapter 4 and defining a view to link items from several different categories. For example, we could define a view called 'resources and assets' connecting together the different types of resources.

Function and process

Function and process are both words that have a wide variety of meanings, which can result in a great deal of confusion. On one architecture project, an inordinate amount of time was wasted debating the meanings of these two words, instead of using different labels to make each distinct meaning clear. For example, function and process can mean:

- A closely related set of ongoing activities generally performed within the boundaries of an organization; a set of people, processes and activities that are related and are identifiable within an organization, such as accounting, manufacturing, or sales. An alternative label for this might be 'Areas of responsibility'.
- In the context of functional flow modelling, an activity that has defined inputs and outputs. Consider using the word 'activity'.
- A discrete unit of work performed by a software application for the software user; most applications perform multiple functions. Consider using 'software application'.

There are plenty of other labels that can have alternative meanings and it often pays to find a distinctive label for use as the category and using any confusing terms as synonyms. This can become a particularly vexing problem when there are a wide variety of similar words – such as process, task, procedure, routine, business activity and workflow.

Using the eight factors

Many architectural frameworks are too simplistic and while no one wants to make architecture unnecessarily complicated, it must be sufficiently comprehensive to be useful! This does not mean that it has to cover all eight factors right at the outset, but it should be possible to extend it easily, as organizational needs become greater. Appendix K can be used to assess the extent to which each factor is being used and to suggest other aspects of each factor that could be useful.

Some of the most common early failings include:

- **Coverage of a limited range of information types**, such as a data architecture that is limited to business or operational information of a factual or attributive nature. Architecture should not be limited to a predetermined set of information categories and should be easily extended to cover all types of information.
- **Creating a number of subject area architectures rather than a single architecture**. A building has a single architecture, although this may be subdivided into architectural plans for a particular stage in its construction, or into component specifications. In a similar way there should be a single information architecture, which can be subdivided if necessary into areas such as business architecture, organization architecture or data architecture. All types of information are interrelated and subject area architectures should therefore be seen as views or subsections of a larger, comprehensive information architecture. Keeping each as a separate architecture is more likely to create inconsistencies and make it harder to achieve integration.
- **Providing limited understanding about information items**: for example, only providing technical definitions or failing to provide guidelines on how to use and interpret information.
- **Providing limited guidance on the use of alternative representations**: architectures normally leave style and representation of information to the whim of users.
- **Providing limited support for the evolution of the architecture over time**: architecture too often presents a static picture of how information is structured at a given point in time.
- **Tendency to focus only on explicit, codified information**: which only represents a small proportion of the total organizational information needs.
- **Defining a limited set of responsibilities**: such as focusing mainly on ownership issues.

It is better to define a broad overall scope for an architecture. Although it is unlikely that all aspects of the architecture will be required at once, they will inevitably be required at some point in time (otherwise the organization is storing information that is not serving any purpose or adding any value). It is therefore better to start by defining a broad scope and then work on views or subscopes, thus ensuring that these are consistent with and integrated to the full architecture.

Work with information users to find out what would help them to use information more effectively and then include this in the architecture. This might range from business definitions and examples to explain how information is used, describing variations of use in different situations, providing details of useful theories or models and guidelines on how to interpret the information. Provide guidelines and training on publishing and representing information, publish style sheets and document templates and give users the opportunity to present the same information in alternative ways.

Provide mechanisms to ensure that the architecture evolves in a positive way over time and introduce training and skill transfer to build competencies in using information more effectively. Gradually extend the architecture to cover more uncertain, fuzzier or implicit information and knowledge. Use the architecture to deal with ignorance and misinformation. Extend the architecture to cover responsibilities such as the liability for quality, integrity, consistency, control and stewardship, by assigning these responsibilities at appropriate levels within the organization and develop the architecture explicitly to include all aspects of the relevant architectural factors.

Guard against the assumption that architecture is only long-range in its outlook and that it therefore takes a long time before there are results from an architecture program. Certainly architecture provides a foundation or infrastructure and if you were to build this from scratch it would inevitably take a long time before it was established but, as we have stated earlier, there must be some form of architecture in place, even if it is accidental and unplanned, for information to exist. If you accept this, then it is easy to plan small, iterative changes to the architecture, each of which delivers value or benefit to the organization; every change should result in additional value or benefit.

Plan projects that deliver results quickly by defining the overall direction and long-term goals of the architecture and identifying major problems and issues that urgently need to be addressed. These determine the vectors that are driving architectural change and should be used to decide what can be done over the coming 12 months to address the problems and move a stage closer to the long-term objectives. To achieve a steady and gradual evolution requires a comprehensive framework to ensure that each change is part of a consistent architectural approach. There are constant changes in the use of information and information structures – most of them are beneficial – and the trick is to make sure that all changes conform to the overall architectural direction.

If you do not already have one, acquire a comprehensive, generic information map. Good models of the problem domain make it much easier to identify business needs, analyse requirements, communicate and explain those requirements and focus agreement on key issues and projects. The information map is used to compare requirements across and between projects or business units, quickly to identify overlaps and opportunities for synergy. Understanding requirements can be done much faster, with less time wasted in debating things that are already defined in a generic information map.

Publish your results and let everybody know your achievements through internal publicity and marketing. Too many architecture projects do not trumpet their victories, only to find that they have lost support from business and management sponsors who did not know what had been done. Architects should not be too shy and retiring and must learn the skills of self-promotion.

Key points

Basic maintenance is necessary to keep the information architecture and knowledge contemporary, so gathering feedback and finding out how information really works in practice are vital maintenance tasks.

We assume that people use information in a logical and rational manner. Information is in the interpretation of the user – the mixture of putting theories into practice, drawing upon personal experiences, hunches and ideas and making it up as we go along – this is where we discover the most exciting and innovative new ways for understanding and using information.

Architecting organizational changes is a learning process, so a periodic review and spring-cleaning of the architecture is mandatory for understanding what worked and what did not. The architecture is only as strong as its weakest link and architectural plans must take into account true organizational capabilities.

The basic architectural principles are common to all organizations but their application varies widely. Develop architecture drivers and strengths in organization, business and technology areas and improve on things that were done well. Address any weaknesses and limitations by finding different approaches for things that did not go so well.

Extend the information categories to take into account more detailed and specialized domains. The generic set of categories provided in this book will meet 80% of situations, but will need to be extended to cover the 20% more specific or unique requirements. Avoid labels that are confusing or ambiguous by basing categories and labels on language that people in your organization commonly use.

The eight factors that are essential for effective information management allow for the gradual but steady development of an enterprise architecture. The checklist in Appendix K can be used to assess the extent to which each factor is used.

The eight factors

In this chapter the essential factors used were:

- **Meta levels – categories**: used to keep control of the change process and schedule reviews of each type of information.
- **Knowledge**: used to find out how information is actually used.
- **Evolution**: used to schedule periodic reviews of the architecture, categories, responsibilities, processes and other factors.
- **Categories**: used to extend the architecture to take into account more detailed or specialized domains.
- **All eight factors**: used to ensure that the architecture matches the needs of the organization.

Conclusion: case study

9

Begin mechanically, step-by-step, until you know what it feels like
and can act intuitively.   John Chris Jones

Every time we say 'Let there be!' in any form, something happens.
                                                        Stella Terrill Mann

To change and change for the better are two different things.
                                                           German proverb

Following a spate of acquisitions, BAIS (a European bank that provides
global financial services) embarked on a massive exercise to rationalize
operations, cut costs and increase revenue per employee. Many functions
were duplicated in different locations and management systems, processes,
software and technology were often incompatible with each other. Senior
management recognized that, in parallel with cost cutting, they needed
to introduce a consistent infrastructure based around information as the
key corporate resource. Consequently, the bank instigated an enterprise-
wide initiative to architect information.

The business case for architecting information

Although senior managers were convinced that an information-based
strategy was critical in the financial services industry, they asked for a
business case to show how architecting information would reduce costs
and improve profitability. They also asked for a proposed action plan for
the next 5 years.

   Of the various approaches for creating a business case, BAIS chose the quickest and most convincing, which identifies and evaluates the inefficient use of information. By focusing on existing issues, the problems and opportunities became more obvious and it was easier to determine costs. Analysis of existing information structures found that certain issues cropped up again and again. For example, business managers could not determine the cost or profitability for an individual customer, a particular product or the operations of a branch – making it difficult or impossible to make fundamental business decisions. Information about customers was stored separately for each product or service, so the only way to get a complete picture of the bank's dealings with one person was to gather all of this information together in one place – a process that was difficult and time-consuming and, therefore, costly. Similarly to analyse the profitability or costs for a branch meant taking information that was stored by product and filtering out the information for a particular location. For each information-related problem, its costs were calculated based on the additional time that it took to extract, combine or compare the information. The newly-formed architecture team also studied the business impact using measures such as increased risk, lost opportunities or customer dissatisfaction. It did not take very long to show that information inefficiency alone was costing the bank more than 20 times per annum the one-off cost of improving the information architecture!

With a clear business case, the I-team – as the architecture team had become known – worked with external advisers to complete a rapid 5-day information audit, which:

- Identified the information categories that were critical to operations and decision-making.
- Identified the main information-based problems and their business impact.
- Identified the strengths and weaknesses in the ability of the bank to manage and use information.
- Developed a detailed plan of short-term improvements to information – its content, structure, processing or uses.
- Defined measurements and indicators that would prove whether any changes were effective or not.

The I-team now had a business case and a high-level action plan, which they presented to senior executives. Based on this presentation, the board was convinced that, whereas many financial institutions were investing heavily in technology such as data warehousing to address similar problems, BAIS should put an equal amount of effort into improving the structure and content of the information itself. Furthermore, to be successful it was important to develop new skills and competence in information architectures, information modelling and information management. Finally, the senior management team made it clear that any changes had to produce business benefits that were measurable in a timeframe of less than 6 months and, at the same time, short-term changes had to contribute to the longer-term goals of reducing information complexity, increasing information management capability and ensuring that the bank built a unique competitive position from its use of information and knowledge.

Significantly, the meeting with the board voted that architecting information was a separate group-wide discipline within the bank, with overall responsibility for managing the information resource. It would have representatives from senior management, each business function and the information technology department. As such it received its own budget allowance that was totally independent from the budget allocated to technology and reported directly to the board of directors. The focus was to be on 'information first, technology second' – referred to as 'I1T2'.

The action plan

The information audit identified 14 high-level information categories that were essential to the bank's information needs, together with an outline of the major changes in each category that the bank would need to make over the next 5 years.

Earlier attempts at creating an enterprise-wide data model convinced BAIS that developing its own information map was out of the question and instead they decided to purchase a generic map, which had originally been produced for the financial services sector. It took BAIS less than a month to train the I-team to use the information map and to customize it to their needs.

Now the I-team had to produce a more detailed plan to show how information would evolve over the next 2 years and it was the first activity to benefit from using the information map. A major organizational goal was to increase customer retention and the I-team realized that this would require some serious changes in four related information categories – People, groups and roles; Measurements and key indicators; Processes and events; and Products, goods and services. They started by listing the challenges they were facing and the ideal solution that they hoped to reach for each high-level category. The problems and ideals were then recorded in a table (see Table 9.1), with an 'as is' column describing the current situation and a 'to be' column listing how things would be if there were no constraints or limitations at all.

Comparing the 'as is' with the 'to be' gave a very quick overview of the key changes that had to be made to achieve fully the defined objectives. (We have simplified the example by showing only a single objective and a fairly narrow information scope; in most cases the situation is more complex than this, but the approach is exactly the same.) Completing the initial analysis against the information categories kept the analysis at a high-level, while providing enough detail to define and prioritize action plans. Then they divided the 2-year plan into eight stages, each of 3-

Table 9.1 Case study action plan

Information category	As is	To be
People, groups and roles	Why do customers leave? How can we retain customers? No single customer database; customer information held in several different places	Fully integrated database for all customer information
Measurements and key indicators	What are the best measurements for customer retention?	Key customer retention indicators easily available via a Customer Retention Scorecard. Each measurement can be analysed from multiple perspectives
Processes and events	Customer-facing processes not well defined. Processes different for each product. What are the triggering events that cause customers to leave?	Key processes fully defined in a format that makes it easy to make improvements and changes to the actual processes
Products, goods and services	Information about products is poorly structured. Difficult to get a complete picture of the set of products used by a single customer, or by a household	Products grouped into 'families'. Product features and rules isolated so that it is easy to match them to customer requirements

months' duration, and defined tasks that would create genuine business benefits in each stage, as well as making the architecture more adaptable and flexible so that it would be better able to cope with future needs. Using the information map and the hierarchy of categories they could easily drill down into greater detail for each change. The map was also used to plot information value chains in detail and calculate the business benefits for each alternative new design. Table 9.2 offers a summary of the changes that were required and how long they were expected to take.

Table 9.2 Case study timeline

Information categories	Timeline		
	+ 3 months	*+ 6 months*	*+ 9 months*
People, groups and roles	Find out why customers leave Start rationalizing customer databases	Define steps for retaining customers Continue rationalizing customer databases	Continue rationalizing customer databases
Measurements and key indicators		Establish measurements based on knowledge of why customers leave and steps for retaining them	
Processes and events	Start defining customer-facing processes	Start rationalizing processes Identify triggering events based on knowledge of why customers leave	Continue rationalizing processes Build measurements into all key processes
Products, goods and services	Identify what information about products is critical for customer retention	Build links between systems to make it possible to get a complete product view for each customer	Continue building links between products

The chart makes it easy to show dependencies between tasks – for example, it is necessary to find out more about the reasons for customers leaving before deciding on appropriate measurements. Blank cells indicate that no changes were planned during that period of time. It was clear that a lot of work had to be done in each information category before BAIS could manage customer retention effectively. Even after 9 months, the 'to be' situation would not be reached and some of the ideals – especially in Products, goods and services – would not even have started. Initially the

I-team were criticized because the *final* objective was taking a long time to achieve, but using this chart they were able to demonstrate that an incremental approach was necessary and that each step delivered a tangible and useful business benefit. At least with this approach, sponsors saw that their objectives were being steadily met, whereas the past had been characterized more by inertia and inaction.

The next step was to determine the changes required at the next level of detail. Of the four information categories, People, groups and roles required changes to information about customer, groups of people, households, person, role and team. The 'as is' situation was similar to that for the higher-level category, but described more specific issues. Every change is a step towards achieving the overall objective to increase customer retention.

Table 9.3 shows the first few cells of the action plan, to show what this next step looked like.

To make sure that BAIS had the required skills and resources to complete the proposed changes, the team summarized each step by the type of change required to achieve it, thus providing a high-level picture of the effort that was required to make the changes and the likely benefits that would accrue. In the first 3 months a new records structure for customer as a group of people was a creation (see section on assessing the degree of change pp. 70–1) – adding information that was not available before, whereas extending a customer file to distinguish between a person and a group of people is an augmentation of an existing structure. The analysis showed that significantly more change was expected in the +9 months column than in earlier periods; three augmentations and a transformation required more effort than two augmentations and an optimization in the +6 month column and much more effort than a creation and an augmentation in the +3 month column.

So to keep the planned changes on track required more resources and greater skills – giving BAIS 6 months to find external help. The team completed another simple test by comparing their level of capability against the information categories to help them decide where they needed most support. BAIS wanted to augment Group of people information and transform Household information and yet the capability for both of these types of information was only at the entry level; it therefore decided to bring in support from external specialists who had greater skills with these information categories.

The architecture team now had a very clear picture of what needed to change and how and when. Although there was a separate budget allocation for architecting information, the team was expected to recoup their costs from the business and management functions that they helped, so before they could start they had to establish internal agreements with these information users to fund the work. First of all the information map was used to create a big picture showing the information that would be changed over the next 2 years; this step was simply a case of selecting the appropriate information categories into a project 'view' and printing the results as a

Table 9.3   Case study detailed action plan and timeline

Information category	Timeline		
	As is	*+ 3 months*	*+ 6 months*
Customer	No single customer database; customer information held in several different places. Cannot easily distinguish between a person and a group of people in the customer name field; this has to be done by searching for keywords such as 'company'		Start to rationalize customer information by transferring records to the master file and explicitly record- ing whether each customer is a person or a group of people
Group of people	No existing information structures explicitly recognize that a group of people might be a customer	Create a new record structure for customer as a group of people, as opposed to individuals	Improve links between market- ing needs and the supply of information from customer files
Household	Although marketing uses the concept of household, it is impossible to extract household information from existing structures		
Person	Difficult to distinguish customers who are individuals from a group of people, such as an organization	Decide which customer file is the master record. Extend this to cover and distinguish between a person and a group of people	

big picture diagram. The next step was to identify the key stakeholders – business departments, senior executives, project managers, group functions, product developers or operational managers – anyone who had any responsibility for information governance, stewardship, infrastructure or usage, to identify who was accountable for each type of information. Deciding the contribution for each stakeholder was not easy at first because this was a very different way of funding these changes, but it was a great improvement on previous attempts that had tried to establish information 'ownership'. As the principle of shared responsibility was understood and costs were linked to measurable benefits, there was a general recognition that this approach eliminated many of the territorial battles that had hindered earlier efforts. Using the information map and making information value chains explicit also helped to support the proposed changes, especially when information users realized that the I-team would provide training in the use and interpretation of the information resource.

The first 3 months

With the action plan approved and responsibilities assigned for its implementation, the I-team embarked on the first 3-month period of architectural evolution. The information map served both as a meta model of the information structures that were being changed and a source for neighbourhood diagrams and other documentation that provided a blueprint of the changes that were required. Not all participants received the same documentation – the views that had been defined on the information map were used to highlight the information that was pertinent to each participant, instead of burdening them with details that were irrelevant to their needs. As the team worked on the changes they updated definitions to reflect their understanding of how the information was used. The updates included examples of use, details of business models that were used to interpret the information and any other comments or questions that users provided. This material not only helped complete the changes on time, it also built a wealth of new organizational knowledge.

As the I-team worked with information users, new views were added to the information map, reflecting personal opinions, variations from the previously defined views and new perspectives. By comparing and contrasting different viewpoints, the team was able to build a consensus view of how the information was being used and also to identify many suggestions on how it could be improved. In particular, the team found that there were many opinions and ideas on why customers left the bank, which proved invaluable in later months. They also found that the information map was an excellent tool for analysing customer-facing processes and identifying the information about products that might help customer retention. Information users frequently commented on how the big picture and neighbourhood diagrams were at just the right level of detail and used language with which they were familiar.

The architecture group also kept their promise to publish their knowledge about information structures and transfer skills in theories and interpretation to users. Much of this was achieved through publishing big picture and neighbourhood diagrams and by making definitions, theories and personal comments available on the intranet. Users appreciated the effort that was made to publish material in ways that were meaningful and useful to them, while the I-team found that having a single source for this knowledge in the information map made it easy to extract independent views.

When the first 3 months were nearly over, the team reviewed progress against the action plan. They had added some new categories to allow for factors that had not seemed important before and had to extend time scales to allow for plans that had been too optimistic – in particular, gathering information about customer-facing processes was taking longer because there were more variations than they expected. Updating the action plan took hardly any effort at all, because the factors affecting the plan had been documented as they occurred using the architectural management tools such as the information map, the checklists based on the eight factors and the views. The unanimous feeling, both within the architecture group and from everyone who had been involved in the first 3 months, was that architecting information and changes was a very positive innovation at the BAIS. The action plan kept the bank on track by relating all changes to the single, comprehensive information architecture. It also kept the team focused on the next set of business deliverables, maintained a history of the improvements and achievements, and attuned the bank's vision of strategic advantage through information and knowledge.

Once the modifications had been made to the action plan, information map, views, checklists and value chains, the relevant extracts from the architecture were updated and published on the intranet and to those who would be involved during the next 3 months.

On the intranet, the architecture team published a list of the deliverables that were being created as part of the bank's architectural initiative, because they wanted everyone to know what was available and the benefits each tool provided:

- A **framework or master plan** that shows how all of the pieces fit together (the eight factors on which the architecture was based).
- A **catalogue or inventory** that lists information components.
- **Definitions** and descriptions of individual pieces of information.
- **Guidelines** for creating and using the architecture.
- **Blueprints or designs** for structuring, grouping, and organizing information. These form the basis for developing *information structures*, whether those are supported by technology or not.
- **An information map or model**, which charts the information resource, showing the organization, arrangement and relationships between *information structures*.
- **Standards and protocols** to ensure conformance to the architecture.
- **Templates and patterns** to make it easier to understand and use information. These were to be published in the form of neighbourhood diagrams.
- A **methodology** and techniques for architecting information and organizational changes.

- **Charts, diagrams and schedules** for implementing the architecture. These included the action plan, which would be updated on a 3-monthly basis.
- Descriptions of the **requirements** of information users, including lists of the information that they need and explanations of how it is used. These would be documented as views of the information categories and the information map.

They made sure that the list of artifacts was made available to all information users and not just to the IT departments. They also pointed out that there were two main groups of deliverables – materials used in the management of information as a resource, which they referred to collectively as the *Information architecture management toolkit*, or simply the *Management toolkit* and materials that provided a complete overview of the information resource and helped people make better use of it, which was referred to as the *Information map*.

Two years to 5 years

In the first couple of years some parts of the action plan had been hopelessly unrealistic, but with experience and growth of the architecture, forecasts became increasingly accurate and down-to-earth. The 3-monthly review was a great incentive to keep everything on track and ensure that there were regular deliverables with business benefit, while reporting directly to the board maintained the high-profile that was necessary to establish information as a corporate resource. At the end of each year, the detailed action plan was extended to show the next 2-year horizon; so at the end of year 1, the action plan was extended to show year 3 as well as year 2. The extension of the action plan was part of an annual review, similar to the budgetary reviews for finance, which included an information audit and ensured that all actions were related to the overall strategies of the bank. The annual review took place in June so that it did not clash with reviews of financial and human resources and so that it followed the bank's strategic review and publication of the annual report.

During the second year, the I-team introduced new measures, such as Return from information (RFI), the Ratio of investment between Information content and Information technology (IC/IT) and Information complexity, to monitor work in progress and prove that the bank was making significantly greater use of its information resource. These measures were published in the bank's annual reports and used as key indicators during information strategy planning.

At the end of the third year, the annual information audit showed that business managers were able to access more information but did not feel overloaded with it and there had been steady improvements in both communications and productivity. Customers had voted the bank into number one position on the basis of the flexible reports and graphs that provided the information they wanted to manage their own finances.

In year four, the chief information officer (CIO) gave a keynote speech at an information management conference. She described the whirlwind of activity that followed purchase of the information map, referring to it as an 'advanced data model with a knowledge wrapper' and to architecting information as 'modelling at the speed of design'. The presentation explained the importance in combining information architecture and knowledge management as the foundation of their approach, showed how BAIS had customized the information categories and the map in less than a month, described how these had been used to develop the action plan and implement changes. The CIO then demonstrated how the simplicity of assigning responsibilities and publishing the action plan gained the organizational commitment to transform the bank in less than 4 years. The following question-and-answer session clearly proved that the talk was both illuminating and inspiring.

Going public and exposing so much about their system was part of the BAIS plan for the next 5 years. The bank had customized and extended the information map so that it contained a vast repository of business rules and knowledge that distinguished BAIS from its competitors. It was estimated that any competitor would take 4 years to catch up with BAIS, by which time the 'intelligence advantage' would have been developed still further. Although the architecture and the information map were key to the BAIS information strategy, any competitor could purchase a generic information map and the techniques they had used were becoming more commonplace. Talking about their success in public did not give the game away, it merely served to raise the public profile and achievements of the bank. The real knowledge of the bank had been captured in the views of the information, by documenting information value chains and by understanding of how information was used and interpreted, and these intellectual assets were securely protected. Just as important were the organizational skills, experience and capability, which would be impossible for competitors to duplicate because they took time to evolve.

During the next 5 years the bank was planning to integrate more of its media resources into their information map, extending it from text-based knowledge with new media such as audio, video, graphs, charts and presentations. BAIS were also going to explore opportunities in forming alliances with other companies to extend their information value chains and make it even harder for competitors to break into their market space, based on the principles that 'information is more valuable the more it is used', and that 'the most valuable information chains are those that extend organizational reach and influence'.

Work would also proceed with the development of a specialized map of key management performance indicators, further integration of information from the 14 core categories and structuring of products into 'family hierarchies' to make it easier to develop new and customized services. 'Information first, technology second' was an established doctrine at the bank and the maxim for the next 5 years was to continue to evolve the 'just-in-time infrastructure'.

Key to planning the strategy for the next 5 years was to create a big picture of the information that might form the basis for synergy with other companies. Using the information map, the I-team searched for information that had the most potential to add value in an extended information chain, using the map to guide and arrange thoughts in a process called 'structured brainstorming'. Work already completed, showed that high-net-worth customers brought a large volume of the more profitable business to the bank and the I-team was asked to identify the information about these customers that could be leveraged to create a powerful new value chain. After selecting the most promising information categories, the group explored innovative ways to use information and searched for information patterns. A big picture emerged that included information about the high-net-worth customers themselves, the companies that they owned or worked for, the profitable deals and agreements that they developed and the international economy within which they operated. From these categories, the group explored possible value chains, deciding on two chains to examine in greater detail during the next 3 months. The first one was aimed at the high-net-worth individuals; because they were usually involved in international meetings requiring a lot of travel, the proposed value chain was to form an alliance with travel companies so that people could conduct their banking business while travelling and gain easier access to banking facilities in overseas locations. Such an alliance had potential links between the airlines, hotels, travel agents, conference and business centres and a host of other services. The second value chain, aimed at international companies, was to simplify the use of banking services in many countries and time zones by providing a centralized, consolidated account structure that could be customized to meet the specific needs of the client. Before the information architecture was available, discussions like this would have taken several months and even then it would have been difficult to justify and explain decisions. With the information map, defining two innovative new information-based services took less than a day.

Looking at the responsibilities involved and capabilities required for these extended value chains showed that there was still much planning work to be done before these proposals could proceed and while BAIS were keen to leverage the information resource, the bank was well aware of the potential difficulties. Senior executives from each partner company would need to meet regularly to oversee the evolution of any alliance and there would be many challenges involved in crossing organization boundaries, improving information exchange, learning from the experiences of partners, sharing their architecture and developing greater skills and knowledge. If the sum was to be greater than the parts then there had to be a culture that encouraged sharing and collaboration as well as an infrastructure that allowed partners to network their services, products and skills. The geographic spread of an alliance made it attractive to BAIS, while the same diversity would increase the complexity of the information architecture.

The I-team worked regularly with an independent advisory group to provide mentoring and skill transfer as they increased their architecting capability and someone from this group always sat in on the 3-monthly review meetings. A suggestion from this group was that an additional level of information responsibility was required, transcending the boundaries of each member of the alliance and independent from the individual companies, while serving their mutual interests. This information network would act as a broker – supplying architectural information, knowledge, expertise, experience and skills as required to the partners of the alliance. Each of the partners could contribute intellectual capital to the new organization; each partner could also draw upon the intellectual assets as required. This repository of knowledge and information would be managed by the new entity on behalf of the members of the alliance, allowing the bank and its partners to focus on their core business and allowing the new organization to focus on information and knowledge management. Alliances of this type were emerging in several industry sectors, mostly driven by technology departments. Based on the success of the architecture in the first 5 years, the opportunities were very exciting, although BAIS still needed to review the additional demands that this new venture would put on their architecture resources before they could proceed.

In only 5 years BAIS had used the discipline of information architecture and the power of knowledge management to turn their under-utilized information resource into a powerful competitive weapon. In the next 5 years they would consolidate their position by leveraging the information resource still further – through alliances and extended value chains. BAIS recognized that as more information was architected, the potential to increase its value increased exponentially, through opportunities to reuse information and extend information value chains.

Key points

Information is a key corporate resource. Its potential can be unleashed by combining the discipline of information architecture with the power or knowledge management to drive organizational changes.

Information is the most under-valued and under-utilized resource. The on-going costs of information inefficiency far exceed the one-off cost of improving the information architecture.

An information audit identifies information that is critical, information-related problems and their business impact, evaluates the capability of an organization for architecting information, develops a plan of short-term improvements to information and identifies how changes will be measured.

An action plan documents information-related problems and the actions that will solve them. Information categories and regular timeframes break a complex problem into discrete chunks that deliver measurable business benefits. The architectural factors make it easy to see the big picture or to zoom into greater detail.

The levels and types of responsibilities, degrees of change and levels of capability ensure that there are sufficient resources and commitment to carry out the action plan.

The information map, views and information value chains are used to understand information requirements and ensure that changes produce measurable business value.

Regular reviews and updates of the action plan ensure the steady evolution of the architecture and improvements to the information resource.

Architectural deliverables are used as tools for architecting information and change and to help users gain more efficient, effective and innovative use of information.

As more information is architected, the potential to increase its value exponentially increases, through opportunities to reuse information and extend information value chains.

Further reading

Details of each book follow in the bibliography. We make no excuses for including books that were published in the last century – information architecture will take some time to absorb the theory and practice from diverse disciplines and sources. Here we have provided brief notes on books that have had a particular influence on our thoughts about architecting information.

Chapter 1: Architecting organizational changes

General discussions about the nature of information abound in most textbooks on information systems, management information and similar topics. The writings of Michael McMaster, Don Marchand, Jeremy Campbell and Richard Saul Wurman provide a more thorough discussion of the contemporary role of information and contribute to an understanding of what we mean by information.

The Intelligence Advantage by Michael McMaster is a book about organizational design, based on the hypothesis that intelligence is the source of an organization's capacity for survival. McMaster presents an original theory of organization in this highly readable and accessible book, describing the transformation from machine-based to information-based organization. In the introduction McMaster says that 'the shift we are making is made possible by computers and includes increasingly extensive (and effective) use of information technology, but *the shift is not really about computers. It is about information itself* and includes communication technology, display and public access, graphics, algorithms, organizing our work practices, *organizing information, accessing information and generating information*' (our italics).

In *Competing with Information*, Don Marchand describes how information can be used as a competitive tool throughout the company. It focuses on how information management creates business value in four ways: minimizing risk, reducing costs, delighting customers and creating a 'new reality'.

Grammatical Man by Jeremy Campbell relates the fascinating story of information theory. He writes: 'Information is easier to remember when it is in an orderly state, rich in pattern and structure, highly interconnected, containing a good deal of redundancy' (p. 214).

John McKean argues that to achieve the full potential of customer relationship initiatives requires a broad and deep information competency, and explains how this is accomplished by balancing technology with investments in people, skills, organization structure, culture, leadership and information itself (*Information Masters*).

Jay Galbraith suggested that as the amount of uncertainty facing an organization increases, coordination mechanisms (such as goal-setting, the organizational hierarchy, and rules) must usually be supplemented by design action either to reduce the need for information or to increase the capacity to process information – both roles of the information architecture (*Organization Design: An Information Processing View*).

Stephan Haeckel, in his definitive work, *Adaptive Enterprise*, explains the predicament of creating organizations that are able to sense and respond to an unpredictable future, with many examples throughout the book of flexible and adaptive information structures.

Leveraging the New Infrastructure by Peter Weill and Marianne Broadbent is based on research with over 100 businesses in 75 firms in nine countries and although it describes information technology there is a wealth of material that can easily be adapted for planning information architecture.

There are plenty of books that give practical tips and guidance for project management, change management and persuading people to give their support and commitment. We have listed a few in the bibliography.

Joseph O'Connor and Ian McDermott explain how to use systems thinking to see beyond isolated events to deeper patterns and connections in *The Art of Systems Thinking*.

George Lakoff and Mark Johnson's *Metaphors We Live By* is a detailed discussion of how metaphors and analogies are deeply embedded in our language, culture and the way we think. The metaphors we choose therefore affect how we experience and interact with the world and other people.

Chapter 2: The essential eight factors

D. W. McDavid's paper, *A standard for business architecture description*, describes a high-level semantic framework of standard business concepts – abstracted from experience, enterprise business models, the organization of business terminology and the various generic industry reference models. There is an excellent discussion on what constitutes business architecture and the nature and use of information categories, although concepts such as product and agreement seem to be missing.

John Zachman's *A framework for information systems architecture* is the seminal work that first introduced the Zachman Framework to a wider audience. Although written at a time when the emphasis was on mainframe technology and standalone systems, Zachman's analogies and description of information architecture continue to have a strong influence on contemporary practice.

The Information FrameWork was a brain dump of my thoughts on information architecture, based on 5 years experience of using the Information FrameWork which I developed for IBM. The article is heavy going and the ideas have evolved into the eight factors described in this book, but this is a good historical summary of second generation architectures.

Peter Stecher provides a good overview of the Retail Application Architecture, a contemporary of the Information FrameWork in *Building business and application systems with the Retail Application Architecture.*

Our article *Third generation information architecture* provides a more detailed discussion of the evolution of architecture and explains the differences between the three generations of information architecture.

Chapter 3: What and why, and when and how

Levels of capability and degrees of change are based on similar techniques that are used in other disciplines that we have adapted for information architecture.

W. H. Davidson, *Beyond Re-Engineering* describes three phases of business transformation – optimize, enhance and redesign – which formed the basis for our ideas on three types of change within the information architecture.

The Software Capability Model (see the Software Engineering Institute (SEI), Pittsburgh, USA) is a popular model for analysing the capability of an organization to develop software. If you are familiar with this model, then many of the ideas can be adapted to analyse any type of capability, such as that required for information architecture.

Chapter 4: Who's responsible for what: assigning responsibility for changes

Paul Strassmann describes seven levels or layers of an 'Information Constitution', which is based on the management of information as a 'multi-layered federation'. Strassmann's seven layers are Level 1: Global; Level 2: Enterprise; Level 3: Functional processes; Level 4: Business; Level 5: Application; Level 6: Local; Level 7: Personal (*The Politics of Information Management*, Chapter 6, Federation, and pp 120–121).

Chapter 5: Developing an information map: how to navigate the information resource

Defining information items is central to information architecture, yet there are surprisingly few guidelines for writing good definitions, even in books devoted to information modelling techniques. An information map is at a meta level above the models created by information engineering or object-oriented methodologies, however, books covering these approaches have guidelines that can be adapted to the idea of creating an information map.

Tony Buzan has written several books on mind mapping and *Mapping Strategic Thought*, edited by Anne Sigismund Huff, collects together articles covering research and mapping methods. If you bear in mind that an information map is midway between information technology models and conceptual mapping or mind maps, then you will find plenty of suggestions that are useful in all of these books.

Chapter 6: Making it available: adding exponential value

Nonaka and Takeuchi's *The Knowledge-Creating Company* has plenty of case studies that illustrate the effective use of information, as well as describing their theory about the creation of organizational knowledge. The book is a salutary reminder of the delicate balance between tacit and explicit knowledge and of the varied uses of information.

Steven Spewack's book on *Enterprise Architecture Planning* contains detailed step-by-step guidelines for many information architecture tasks. Written in 1992, it is based quite heavily on best practice of that time – with a strong leaning towards techniques drawn from Information Engineering and use of the Zachman framework. The book provides an approach for developing information systems and is accordingly limited to developing blueprints for data, applications and technology.

Melissa Cook's *Building Enterprise Information Architecture* covers similar ground to the book by Spewak, however, it is aimed more at a business than a technical audience. It also assumes use of the Zachman framework, an information system as the end-result and an approach that is loosely based on Information Engineering, and is therefore insufficient for all contemporary needs. However, written for a non-technical audience, the book is useful as a source of ideas for explaining information architecture to information users.

Bernard Boar's *Constructing Blueprints for Enterprise IT Architectures* states a preference for the Index model of architecture, defining a rigorous approach for creating a detailed specification or blueprint for technology architectures. Although Boar includes discussion of several information architectures, the strength of the book is in providing a vocabulary and diagram standards for recording *information about* technology components.

Chapter 7: Using it: making the best use of corporate information

Russo and Schoemaker's *Decision Traps* is divided into four parts (decision-framing, information-gathering and intelligence, coming to conclusions and learning from experience), describing the errors that most decision-makers commit and explaining how to avoid them. It provides practical guidelines for effectively using information for decision-making.

Design Methods, by John Chris Jones, has been described as the seminal work on design methodology, describing methods to assist designers and planners become more sensitive to user needs.

Information Architecture for the World Wide Web by Louis Rosenfeld and Peter Morville is representative of a recent use of the phrase information architecture to refer to the structure and design of a web site. There are plenty of techniques that apply to a broader use of information architecture, although the step-by-step guidelines are aimed at web site construction.

Jeremy Campbell states that ' . . . it is an observation worth repeating that the whole point of any theory, whether in linguistics or in physics, is that it does not merely account for the limited number of facts already known, but predicts the existence of additional facts which are still unknown. In short, a theory generates new information. It makes a lot of knowledge out of a little data' (*Grammatical Man*, p. 166).

In *Information Anxiety 2*, Richard Saul Wurman provides a range of tools and techniques for finding meaning in data.

Chapter 8: Improving the architecture and keeping it current

The reason for assessing what has been done before is to learn from the past and to improve upon what has gone before. *The Learning Company*, by Pedler, Burgoyne and Boydell has plenty of examples and ideas that will help make an organization capable of adapting, learning and developing.

Stewart Brand's *How Buildings Learn* is a wonderfully illustrated and well-written argument that buildings are not permanent edifices, but are constantly adapting and changing, and there are many parallels with the evolution of information.

Bibliography

Ackoff R. L. *Creating the Corporate Future*, John Wiley & Sons, New York, 1981

Alexander, C. *The Timeless Way of Building*, Oxford University Press, 1979

Beckhard R. and Pritchard W. *Changing the Essence: The Art of Creating and Leading Fundamental Change in Organizations*, Jossey-Bass, San Francisco, 1992

Boar, B. H. *Constructing Blueprints for Enterprise IT Architectures*, John Wiley & Sons, 1999

Boisot M. H. *Knowledge Assets: Securing Competitive Advantage in the Information Economy*, Oxford University Press, 1998

Boynton A. C., Victor B. and Pine II B. J. New competitive strategies: Challenges to organizations and information technology, *IBM Systems Journal*, **32**, (1), 40–64 1993. Describes the notion of Mass Customization, bringing the notion of 'custom' back into customer, with examples from the banking industry

Brancheau J. C. and Wetherbe J. C. Information Architectures: Methods and Practice, *Information Processing and Management*, **22**, (6), December 1986, 453–463

Brancheau J. C., Schuster L. and March, T. Building and Implementing an Information Architecture, *Data Base*, **20**, (2), July 1989, 9–17

Buzan T. *The Mind Map® Book*, BBC Books, 1993

Brand S. *How Buildings Learn: what happens after they're built*, Phoenix Illustrated, 1997

Campbell J. *Grammatical Man: Information, Entropy, Language and Life*, Penguin Books, 1982

Carnall C. *Managing Change in Organizations*, Prentice Hall, 1995

Cook M. A. *Building Enterprise Information Architecture – Reengineering Information Systems*, Prentice Hall, 1996

Covey S. R. *The Seven Habits of Highly Effective People – Powerful Lessons in Personal Change*, Simon & Schuster Ltd., 1992

Curtis B., Krasner H. and Iscoe N. A Field Study of the Software Design Process for Large Systems, *Communications of the ACM*, **31**, (11), 1989

Davenport T. H., Hammer M. and Metsisto T. J. How Executives Can Shape Their Company's Information Systems, *Harvard Business Review*, March/April 1989, 130–134

Davenport T. H. Saving IT's Soul: Human-Centered Information Management, *Harvard Business Review*, March/April 1994

Davidson W. H. Beyond Re-Engineering: The Three Phases of Business Transformation, *IBM* Systems *Journal* **32**, (1), 65–79 1993

Dearlove D. *Key Management Decisions: Tools and techniques of the executive decision-maker*, FT Pitman Publishing, 1998

Devlin B. *Data Warehouse: from Architecture to Implementation*, Addison Wesley Longman, 1997

Drucker P. Planning for Uncertainty, *The Wall Street Journal*, 22 July, 1992

Egan G. *Change-Agent Skills A: Assessing & Designing Excellence*, University Associates, 1988a

Egan G. *Change-Agent Skills B: Managing Innovation & Change*, University Associates, 1988b

Eriksson H.-E. and Penker M. *Business Modeling with UML: Business Patterns at Work*, John Wiley & Sons, 2000

Evernden R. New Financial Service Models of the 1990s – Why Banks Need Industry-wide Models to Manage and Control Information, *Euromoney's Financial Technology Review*, April, 1994, p. 10

Evernden R. The Information FrameWork, *IBM Systems Journal*, **35**, (1), 1996

Evernden R. and Evernden E. 3rd generation information architecture, *Communications of the ACM*, March, 2003

Finkelstein C. *An Introduction to Information Engineering: From Strategic Planning to Information Systems*, Addison-Wesley Publishing Company, 1989

Freeman P. (ed.) *Software Reusability*, IEEE Computer Society Press, 1986

Galbraith J. R. Organization Design: An Information Processing View, *Interfaces* **4**, 28–36 1974

Galbraith J. R. *Organization Design*. Addison-Wesley, 1977.

Garvin D. A. Competing on the Eight Dimensions of Quality, *Harvard Business Review*, November/December, 101–109 1987

Gelernter D. *Mirror Worlds: Or, the Day Software Puts the Universe in a Shoebox . . . How it will Happen and What it will Mean*, Oxford University Press, 1991

Glazer R. Marketing in an Information-Intensive Environment, *Journal of Marketing*, **55**, October, 1991

Goldberg B. and Sifonis, J.G. *Dynamic Planning: The Art of Managing Beyond Tomorrow*, Oxford University Press, 1994

Haeckel S. H. and Nolan R. L. Managing By Wire, *Harvard Business Review*, Sept/Oct, 122–132, 1993

Haeckel S. H. *Adaptive Enterprise: Creating and Leading Sense-and-Respond Organizations*, Harvard Business School Press, 1999

Huff A. S. (ed.) *Mapping Strategic Thought*, John Wiley & Sons, 1990 – reprinted 1994.

Ing D. and Simmons I. Envisioning Businesses – Metaphors, Purposeful Systems & Understanding, ACM OOPSLA '97 Workshop on System Envisioning, in Atlanta, October, 1997

Jones J. C. *Design Methods*, Van Nostrand Reinhold, 1992

Kay J. *Why Firms Succeed – Choosing Markets and Challenging Competitors to Add Value*, Oxford University Press, 1995

Kosko B. *Fuzzy Thinking: The New Science of Fuzzy Logic*, Flamingo, 1994

Leonard D. *Wellsprings of Knowledge: Building and Sustaining the Sources of Innovation*, Harvard Business School Press, 1995

Lévy P. *Collective Intelligence: Mankind's Emerging World in Cyberspace*, Plenum Trade, 1997

McMaster M. *The Intelligence Advantage – Organizing for Complexity*, Butterworth-Heinemann, 1996

McMaster M. *The Praxis Equation: Design Principles for Intelligent Organization*, Knowledge Based Development Co Ltd. 1997

Minsky M. A framework for representing knowledge In *The Psychology of Computer Vision* (P. Winston ed.), McGraw-Hill, 1975.

Neef D. *The Knowledge Economy*, Butterworth-Heinemann, 1998

Nilsson A. G. Business Modeling as a Base for Information Systems Development, Paper presented at *The Third International Conference on Information Systems Developers Workbench – Methodologies, Techniques, Tools & Procedures* Gdansk, Poland, 22–24, September, 1992

Nolan R. L. and Mulryan D. W. Undertaking an Architecture Program, *Stage by Stage*, **7**, 1987

Nonaka I. and Takeuchi H. *The Knowledge-Creating Company – How Japanese Companies Create the Dynamics of Innovation*, Oxford University Press, 1995.

Pedler M., Burgoyne J. and Boydell T. *The Learning Company: A Strategy for Sustainable Development*, McGraw-Hill, 1991

Pine B. J., Victor B. and Boynton A. C. Making Mass Customization Work, *Harvard Business Review*, Sept/Oct, 1993, 108–119

Pinker S. *The Language Instinct: How the Mind Creates Language*, HarperCollins, 1994

Podolsky J. ThinkWrap, Parks, not Buildings, *Datamation*, October 15, 1994, **90**

Porter M. E. and Millar V. E. How Information Gives You Competitive Advantage, *Harvard Business Review*, July/August, 1985

Porter M. *Competitive Strategy*, Free Press, 1980

Prieto-Díaz, R. and Arango, G. (eds) *Domain Analysis and Software Systems Modeling*, IEEE Computer Society Press, 1991

Robbins H. and Finley M. *Why Change Doesn't Work – Why Initiatives Go Wrong and How to Try Again – and Succeed*, Orion Business Books, 1997.

Rosenfeld L. and Morville P. *Information Architecture for the World Wide Web*, O'Reilly, 1998.

Ruggles III, R. L. *Knowledge Management Tools*, Butterworth-Heinemann, 1997

Russo J. E. and Schoemaker P. J. H. *Decision Traps – The Ten Barriers to Brilliant Decision-Making and How to Overcome Them*, Simon & Schuster Inc., 1989

Savage C. *5th Generation Management: Co-creating Through Virtual Enterprising, Dynamic Teaming, and Knowledge Networking*, Butterworth-Heinemann, 1996

Schrage M. *No More Teams! Mastering the Dynamics of Creative Collaboration*, Currency Doubleday, 1989

Schwartz P. *The Art of the Long View: Scenario Planning – Protecting Your Company Against an Uncertain World*, Doubleday, 1991

Senge P. M. *The Fifth Discipline*, Century Business, London, 1990

Shannon C. E. A Mathematical Theory of Information, *Bell System Technical Journal*, **27**, 379–423, 623–656, 1948

Sherman H. and Schultz R. *Open Boundaries – Creating Business Innovation Through Complexity*, Perseus Books, 1998

Smith M. and Taffler R. Improving the Communication of Accounting Information Through Cartoon Graphics, *Accounting, Auditing and Accountability Journal*, **9** (2), 68–85, 1996

Sowa J. F. and Zachman J. A. Extending and formalizing the framework for information systems architecture, *IBM Systems Journal*, **31**, (3), 590–616, 1992

Spewak S. H. *Enterprise Architecture Planning – Developing a Blueprint for Data, Applications and Technology*, John Wiley & Sons, 1992

Stecher P. Building business and application systems with the Retail Application Architecture, *IBM Systems Journal*, **32**, (2), 1993

Strassmann P. *The Politics of Information Management: Policy Guidelines*, The Information Economics Press, pp 45–49, 1995

Tapscott D. *The Digital Economy: Promise and Peril in the Age of Networked Intelligence*, McGraw-Hill, 1996

Tracz W. (ed.) *Software Reuse: Emerging Technology*, IEEE Computer Society Press, 1990

Tufte, E. R. *Envisioning Information*, Graphics Press, 1990

Tufte E. R. *The Visual Display of Quantitative Information*, Graphics Press, 2001

Vitalari N. P. Creating New Architectures for Anywhere, Anytime Information, PEP Paper 30, CSC Research and Advisory Services, London, May, 1995

Von Halle B. *Business Rules Applied: Building Better Systems Using the Business Rules Approach*, John Wiley & Sons, 2002

Weill P. and Broadbent M. *Leveraging the New Infrastructure: How Market Leaders Capitalize on Information Technology*, Harvard Business School Press, 1998

Winograd T. (ed.) *Bringing Design to Software,* Addison-Wesley Publishing Company, 1996

Winograd T. and Flores F. *Understanding Computers and Cognition: A New Foundation for Design*, Addison-Wesley Publishing Company, 1986

Winslow C. D. and Bramer W. L. *FutureWork: Putting Knowledge to Work in the Knowledge Economy*, The Free Press, 1994

Wurman R. S. *Information Anxiety 2*, Que, 2001

Zachman J. A. A framework for information systems architecture, *IBM Systems Journal*, **26**, (3), 276–292, 1987

Zuboff S. *In the Age of the Smart Machine: The Future of Work and Power*, HarperCollins, 1988

Appendices

A: Diagnostic – do you see information as a distinct resource?

Table A1 is a diagnostic designed to provoke discussion about the use of information as a corporate resource. We have used this in training and seminars, but also to initiate discussion with senior executives, gaining recognition that information architecture requires full management commitment and support.

It is a quick and easy way to assess your organization's use of information as a distinct resource and to analyse the potential benefits of information architecture. Some of the things you can do with it are:

- **Use this diagnostic at all levels within the organization**. We have used it at the board level to get executive sponsorship for architecture and with members of individual business units to discover how to make a big impact with information initiatives.
- **Get a number of different participants to provide their responses**. The more people who participate, the better you will know whether there is a consensus of opinion across the organization.
- **Use the diagnostic statements as the basis for a workshop**. The statements will stimulate discussion and expose areas that could be improved. Use it to structure the results of the discussion and come up with suggested areas for action.
- **Identify areas of strength and highlight weaknesses**. Find out if there are any patterns in the strong and weak points.

There are ten statements, each requiring a response ranging from 5 if you agree with the statement, to 1 if you disagree. An answer of 3 indicates

Table A1   Diagnostic – do you see information as a distinct resource?

		Score
1	There is a clear and distinct vision of information as a corporate resource	
2	There is an organization unit responsible for information and knowledge that is distinct from the information technology function	
3	There is a well-defined strategy and action plan for improving the effectiveness of information use across the organization	
4	Information that is vital and necessary to make key decisions is always readily and easily available	
5	All information is available in a consistent and integrated format	
6	Management believes that there is considerable value to be gained from the organization's use of information	
7	Information management is seen as the responsibility of business people as well as the information technology functions	
8	Information has a key role in all business processes	
9	Financial approval is readily available for investment in the information infrastructure of the organization (as opposed to technology investments)	
10	Information is used to support innovation and creativity in product and service development, business processes, and customer support	
	Total Score	

that you do not have a strong opinion either for or against the statement, while 2 and 4 are somewhere between.

What your score reveals

Once the diagnostic has been completed, calculate the total or, if there is more than one participant, calculate the average result. Alternatively you can use all of the individual responses to compare differences of opinion.

There are no 'perfect' answers, as it is intended to promote discussion and help to demonstrate the need for information architecture. It is actually most instructive when there are differences of opinion as this often brings the most important changes to the fore. The questions do provide a reliable indication of whether there is a need for urgent action, as well as providing a focus for discussions around this theme.

Based on your score, here is a brief indication of the urgency to change.

A score greater than 40 indicates that information is already regarded as a key resource, that processes to manage information are well defined and effective and that there is a good information infrastructure in place. The techniques in this book will provide you with greater mastery of the information resource and even better returns from information.

A score between 30 and 40 suggests that there is some recognition of information as a resource, but that there are still several areas that need attention. Efforts to use information could be better coordinated, as there are opportunities to introduce a more formal information management approach and introduce techniques that will enhance work that has already been done.

A score between 20 and 30 shows that there is a need to establish information as a resource, guidelines for managing information need to be defined and the information architecture is in need of development. The lack of information architecture poses a threat to the survival and success of your company and the techniques described in this book will enable you to bring this situation under control.

A score between 10 and 20 means that information as a resource needs urgent attention and that there is little or no information infrastructure in place. You need to take immediate action to get the information resource under control because currently there are many information-related costs with few of the benefits that result from using information effectively. Apply the practical ideas and techniques in this book to give your company a better return from information.

Chapter 1 provides a detailed discussion of the ten statements in this diagnostic.

B: Checklist – example information categories

Organizational or management information

- **Business environment and competition** – includes information about: The business environment, Competitive forces, The economy, The weather and elements, External influences, Internal constraints, Political forces, Social factors, Technological factors
- **Community and culture** – includes information about: Assumptions, Cultural carriers, Culture, Government, Norms, Reward structures, The socio-infrastructure, systems [in the systems thinking sense]
- **Intellectual assets and knowledge** – includes information about: Information, Intellectual assets, Knowledge, Organizational knowledge, The work space
- **Measurements and key indicators** – includes information about: Accounting periods, Benefits, Costs, Key indicators, Measurements, Points in time, Time periods, Timesheets, Value
- **Organization and management structures** – includes information about: Areas of responsibility, Companies, Controls, Departments, Employers, Employment positions, Industries, Legal structures, Organizations, Organization boundaries, Organization design, Organization structures, Organization units, Political structures, Tasks, Work structures
- **People, groups and roles** – includes information about: Competitors, Customers, Employees, Family, Groups of people, Households, Identification, Individuals, Roles, Stakeholders, Teams

- **Skills and competence** – includes information about: Characteristics, Competencies, Experience, Learning, Personality, Skills, Stages of growth, Techniques, Training
- **Strategy and purpose** – includes information about: Action plans, Critical success factors, Goals, Mission statements, Opportunities, Principles, Problems, Purpose, Quality, Requirements, Strategic alignment, Strategic responses, Strategies, Strengths, Sustainable advantage, Targets, Threats, Vision, Weaknesses

Business or operational information

- **Accounts and finances** – includes information about: Accounts, Account categories, Account entries, Account structures, Budgets, Deposits, Depreciation, Estimates, Invoices, Tax status
- **Agreements and contracts** – includes information about: Agreements, Collateral, Conditions, Contracts, Parameters
- **Marketing and sales** – includes information about: Markets, Market position, Segments, Segmentation
- **Places and locations** – includes information about: Addresses, Administrative areas, Cities, Continents, Countries, Electronic addresses, File locations, Locations, Map references, Telephone, Time zones, Towns, Villages
- **Processes and events** – includes information about: Activities, Agents, Calculations, the calendar, Change, Communications, Contacts, Events, Exercises, Payments, Projects, Results, Schedules, Transactions, Triggering events, Value chains, Visits, Workflows
- **Products, goods and services** – includes information about: Channels, Credit cards, Customer experiences, Deliverables, Fees, Interest rates, Loans, Products, Work orders
- **Property and equipment** – includes information about: Books, Buildings, Documents, Equipments, Furniture, Inventories, Property, Resources, Rooms, Vehicles

Information about supporting technologies

- **Software applications and interfaces** – includes information about: Application architecture, Application components, Program structures, Software applications, Software interfaces, Technologies, User interfaces
- **System platforms** – includes information about: Hardware, System platforms, System software
- **Communication networks** – includes information about: Authorization profiles, Devices, Networks, Network architecture, Network component

Example architecture scopes

Here are some of the more common architectures, with an indication of the information categories each includes in its scope. Each is open to interpretation and you may come across slight variations in the use of a term, but this outline will provide some indication of the scope of each. Note that none of these labels covers the complete set of information categories listed in the appendix above.

- **Business architecture** – covers the key components that are necessary to define and operate a business. This is typically based around information about *processes and events*, including the information needed by each process, information about the *people, groups or roles* that carry out processes. It may also include information about the *places and locations* where processes are performed and the *organization and management structures* responsible for processes.
- **Technology architecture** – also known as Enterprise IT Architecture (Boar, 1999), covers the information technology components that support the operations of the business and management of the organization. This typically covers information about *system platforms* and *communication networks*. If application architecture is not regarded as a distinct architecture, then it will also cover *software applications and interfaces*. It may cover, or provide strong links to, the data architecture.
- **Application architecture** – covers information about *software applications and interfaces* that support the operations of the business and management of the organization. Some application architectures are purely technical, specifying how application components are constructed and designed. Others may also describe the functionality by providing information about the *processes and events* that each application supports.
- **Enterprise architecture** – is the term popularized by John Zachman and originally referred to as Information systems architecture. Enterprise architecture is used to refer to a number of subarchitectures within the same framework. Most commonly it refers to a data architecture, applications architecture and technology architecture – these being the first three columns of the Zachman framework (Spewak, 1992). Less commonly it is used to refer to all six columns in the Zachman framework. It has also been referred to as Enterprise information architecture (Cook, 1996). Note that use of the word 'Enterprise' implies that the architecture has been defined and is used across the whole of an enterprise or organization.
- **Data architecture** – covers attributive information that is stored in databases and manipulated by software applications. The term was originally popular with the early development of computer systems at a time when information management was little more than data management. The term therefore tells you more about the nature of the information that is being described (attributive information that is precisely defined and manipulated using information technology) rather than explaining the scope of the architecture.

C: Checklist – example levels of responsibility

- **Global level** – global information is generally recognized as not belonging to any particular industry or enterprise group. This is information that is often in the public domain and therefore not owned by any particular group or individual, or information that is the responsibility of international standards organizations as a global standard.
- **Cross-industry level** – responsibility for information that is common for different industry sectors. It should be a separate level if there is some commonly perceived value between the separate industry groups in doing so. For example, with deregulation in the banking industry there is a merging of industry barriers between banking, insurance, building society and estate agency, which might require the definition of common data elements or processes at this level.
- **Industry level** – responsibility for information that is common to all or most organizations conducting business in a particular industry sector. It is difficult to say that such information is the responsibility of a particular enterprise and there are often groups that define and maintain standards for this type of information – such as standards organizations, regulatory bodies, government departments or communities of organizations who work together for a common interest. For example, the industry level would include information that is common to all organizations operating in the banking, finance and securities industries.
- **Enterprise level** – responsibility for information that is common across all or most departments or lines of business within an organization. For example, when an enterprise sees value in maintaining common definitions of data, processes, strategies, roles and other information categories. The advantage of enterprise level responsibility is that there are substantial economies in building a consistent foundation that can help coordinate effort across business units and projects, manage duplication of effort and improve communication and understanding. For example, an organization may develop enterprise-wide models for data and processes.
- **Geography level** – geographic information is characterized by factors such as cultural variations in information and knowledge, translation of terminology into various local or national languages and inclusion of information specific to a geographic area, such as unique regulatory or legal types.
- **Local level** – responsibility for information localized to a particular part of an organization, including responsibilities for information at the project, product, location, line of business or organization unit levels. It is not possible to manage everything at the enterprise-wide level because there is a need for local variations and extensions. These extensions can be managed from a central, enterprise-wide responsibility or they may be managed at the local level.

- **Personal level** – responsibility at the personal level includes all information that is important or relevant to an individual and which may not warrant control and management at other levels. Such views may be beneficial to the organization, but are not necessarily managed by the organization. Information at this level might include personal addresses, a personal calendar or a filing cabinet of news cuttings that have been collected by an individual.

D: Checklist – example types of responsibility

Table A2   Checklist – example types of responsibility

Type of responsibility	Example verbs used	Example activities
Governance responsibilities – controlling and directing the use of information	Fund, support, plan, control, resource (and if you must use it – own)	Fund information systems Plan information development Support information architecture
Stewardship responsibilities – looking after information	Create, update, distribute, archive, delete, enhance, source, generalize, transform, optimize, specialize, normalize, gather	Create information Update information Distribute information Gather information
Infrastructure responsibilities – creating the environment for using information	Define, design, structure	Define information items Design information structures
Usage responsibilities – using information efficiently, effectively and productively	Use, analyse, decide, evaluate, validate, verify, assess	Use information Analyse information Requesting changes

E: Checklist – suggested time frames

Table A3 gives some suggestions on the time period that should be represented by each column of an action plan, which varies depending on the overall duration of the project.

Using a diagram with a longer time period helps to explain why some changes are simply not possible in a shorter timeframe. People often expect changes within an unrealistic time frame, but using a simple time chart demonstrates why this is impossible. If there is an expectation for unrealistic changes in a 2-year timeframe, additional columns in the diagram can show the time that is actually required to meet the objectives.

Table A3   Checklist – suggested time frames

Duration of change		Suggested time frames to be used				
Short	As is	+ 3 months	+ 6 months	+ 9 months	+ 12 months	To be
Medium	As is	+ 6 months	+ 12 months	+ 18 months	+ 2 years	To be
Medium-long	As is	+ 6 months	+ 12 months	2 years	4 years	To be
Long	As is	+ 6 months	+ 12 months	5 years	10 years	To be

F: Checklist – suggested degrees of change

Optimization: takes existing structures to make them more efficient or more effective. It improves the quality of things that are already in place.

- This is the most common type of change – although not necessarily the most appropriate because it may perpetuate fundamental problems.
- Often relatively small changes.
- Good for incremental and iterative improvement.
- Requires least effort, but also delivers fewer benefits.

Augmentation: goes beyond simply optimizing existing structures. It extends them to provide additional value or allows them to be used in different ways.

- There is a danger that augmentations are bolted on to existing structures without sufficient thought as to how the new design will function. This is especially true if a lot of augmentations are made to the same structure.
- Apparently simple additions may have a knock-on effect, requiring changes to related structures.
- Can be good for meeting short-term needs.

Transformation: throws out the existing structures to replace them with a totally new design.

- This requires serious commitment and a degree of creative and innovative thought.
- Change to one structure usually has a broad impact requiring changes in many other structures.
- Often what is required, but the difficulty of making radical changes prevents it happening.
- Requires most effort, but delivers greater benefits and advantages.

Creation: introduces new information structures that did not previously exist.

- In some cases new structures can be created without major impact to the architecture.
- To integrate new structures fully into the architecture can require a lot of effort.
- There is often an informal, tacit structure in place.

G: Checklist – suggested levels of capability

Suggestions for levels of capability are outlined below. The descriptions here could apply to an organization or an individual.

Introductory or entry level: little or no knowledge about information architecture. Understanding is elementary, from common knowledge, conversation, conferences or popular works on the subject. Any education is informal or introductory, such as reading a book on the subject, rather than through formal training programmes. There is no direct, relevant experience of information architecture, although there is awareness of some of the concepts and ideas. The organization is developing capability while learning to use information architecture. Practices, procedures and plans start to emerge for managing information architecture.

Someone at this level would be able to assist others on a limited basis and perform work with some assistance.

Basic or competent level: some formal knowledge about information architecture. There is understanding of the main features, but this understanding is general and lacks detail. Education is formal, covering satisfactory completion of basic offerings. Experience in using architecture is limited and lacks breadth.

An organization at this level is able to execute or perform tasks with some assistance and support.

Intermediate or proficient level: knowledge of information architecture has been practically applied in several situations or projects. This level requires a combination of formal training with a variety of experiences. Education is advanced, with satisfactory completion of an assortment of offerings. The practitioner has gained practical experience by using information architecture for some time.

An organization at this level is able to act or perform work without assistance.

Advanced or specialist level: considerable knowledge and experience in using information architecture. This level requires a complete working knowledge of the subject, with practical experience of specialized areas, as well as a broad understanding. Most training in the subject is available and has been completed by staff. Someone at this level is able to pass their skills and experience on to others.

An organization at this level has a highly successful and effective information architecture.

H: Checklist – example criteria used to decide presentation

Presentation issues include:

- **How information is organized or sorted**: Richard Saul Wurman has said that information can only be organized by location, alphabet, time, category, or hierarchy – to which he gives the acronym LATCH (Wurman, 2001). However, this list shows how much we focus on visual information; imagine e-mails that were sorted depending on the emotion of the messages or voicemails that were arranged by the relative pitch of the speaker!
- **The level of detail**: for example, whether the information is aggregated, summarized or abstracted.
- **Which sense or senses are being used to access the information**: sight, smell, sound, taste or touch. Each of these could be further classified, for example:
  - **Sight**: colour, pattern, shape
  - **Sound**: pitch, tone, duration
  - **Touch**: sense of pressure, sense of temperature, sense of contact, sense of pain or pleasure, etc.
  - **Taste**: sweet, sour, spicy
- **Visual representation type**: diagram, document, list, picture, sign or symbol. Diagrams might be further classified into node-and-link diagrams, grid or table diagrams, etc. Signs and symbols might be classified into ideograms, phonograms, numerals, text, etc.

I: Checklist – activities that use information architecture

Here is a checklist of the main activities in using information architecture. The list is not exhaustive – so you may want to extend it. Expanding the ways in which information architecture is used will deliver better value from your investment.

Analyse and understand organizational use of information

- Analyse the organization structure, strategy and skills
- Define goals and objectives, critical success factors and constraints
- Identify organization structure changes
- Identify organization strategy changes

- Identify skill requirements
- Review organization impact of business or technical requirements

Analyse and understand business use of information

- Identify required functions
- Identify required data
- Analyse business activities and critical business processes
- Identify required activities
- Map functions to data
- Map functions to activities
- Map activities to data
- Review business impact of organization or technical requirements

Analyse and understand use of information about technology

- Identify technical requirements
- Define application architecture
- Define network architecture
- Define system platforms
- Review technical impact of organization or business requirements

Plan or design how information will be used in a particular context

- Design workflows
- Design information structures
- Specify data storage and data access
- Specify application functionality
- Specify technical support
- Design organization structures
- Specify required skills, experience and training
- Review business requirements and designs
- Review technical requirements and blueprints
- Review organization requirements and designs
- Examine organization, business and technical benefits and costs
- Priorities solutions
- Plan implementation

Implement changes in the use of information

- Develop information structures
- Develop data storage, databases, object bases
- Develop software components and code
- Develop test environment
- Develop interfaces to existing systems

- Re-engineer processes
- Develop training and support materials
- Implement operational solutions

Use information effectively

- Analyse strategies, competitive environment, skills and competence, organization design, and management structures
- Analyse processes and workflows, functions, data and information use
- Analyse existing application, network and system architecture
- Analyse existing databases, applications and systems
- Review organization impact, business requirements and technical architectures
- Priorities redevelopment needs

J: Checklist – example meta levels

The precise number of levels and their descriptions depend on the needs of each organization. They will vary depending on the sophistication of the information architecture, the complexity of the organization itself, the complexity of the information resource, the modelling methodology employed, and the use of software support. If there is any doubt on this subject – contact an information specialist to explain this in more detail!

Each higher meta level describes the meta level directly below it. Or to put this the other way, every element at a lower meta level is an instance of an element at the next meta level up. For example, Roger and Elaine are each the name of a person – Roger and Elaine at level 1 are instances of 'person name' which is at level 2.

For example, 'Fred Bloggs' and 'Sue Mansfield' are the names of two people who are customers at the organization and their names are stored in documents, files and databases that form the corporate *information resource* (level 1). Fred and Sue are both people and these two names are examples or instances of 'individual' or 'customer', which are labels, describing types of information used by the organization, which form part of the *information map* (level 2). Individual and customer are examples or instances of 'information categories', which is one of the constructs used in the *design of the information map* (level 3). The information map is stored in a software application, which happens to store information categories as 'entities' (a different piece of software might store them as 'objects'); entity and object are both *constructs in a software tool that are used to store an information map* (level 4). Entity and object are examples or instances of 'object type', which is one of the basic building blocks used to construct an information-modelling tool (level 5).

Table A4 Checklist – example meta levels

Meta level	Suggested label	What it describes	What it includes
5	Software Tool Developer level	Describes the methodology that is supported by software tools, such as a repository	A blueprint or design for developing a CASE tool or repository – methodological constructs for developing a tool
4	Software Tool (e.g. Repository or CASE tool) level	Describes how the constructs in a software tool are used to store an information map or information model	A model of the constructs that are available in a software tool
3	Information Map Developer level	Describes the design of the information map	A model of the constructs used when developing an information map
2	Information Map or Information Model level	Describes the corporate information resource	A map or model of the corporate information resource – used to understand and analyse the organization, its business and supporting technologies
1	Information User Level	Corporate information	The information resource itself

Variations on the suggested levels include:

- *Repository meta model (level 4),* which is a model of the *Information model (level 3),* which is a model of the *Business model (level 2),* which is a model of the *Corporate data (level 1).*
- The *meta-metamodel layer (level 4),* which is used to derive the *meta model layer (level 3),* which is used to derive the *model layer (level 2),* which is used to develop the *user objects layer (level 1)*

In knowledge management a distinction is often made between intellectual capital, property and assets. It could be argued that these form three separate meta levels:

- Intellectual capital: knowledge with potential for value, e.g. ideas
- Intellectual property: articulated knowledge with defined ownership, e.g. patents
- Intellectual asset: knowledge having value, e.g. licensed patents.

K: To what extent are you using the essential eight factors?

There are eight factors that form the basis of all information architectures. Use Table A5 to assess the extent to which each factor is being used. This analysis will not only show which factors are already in use, but will also suggest other aspects of each factor that could be useful.

Table A5 Diagnostic – to what extent are you using the essential eight factors?

Factor	Minor use	Moderate use	Major use
Categories	Focus largely on operational information, e.g. customer transactions, accounting data. Focus mainly on computerized data	Good coverage of business and operational information, with some coverage of management and technical information. Not purely focused on computer manipulation of information	Covers business and operational information, organizational and management information and information about supporting technologies. Includes both computer and manually processed information
Understanding	Definitions exist only for most critical data items. Language is technical rather than business. No descriptions of underlying theories	Descriptions exist for the main business and management theories that are in use. Definitions are quite comprehensive and in business language	Covers detailed descriptions of most business and management theories, as well as providing feedback loops to learn from their use. Detailed definitions of all information items and information clusters
Presentation	Some thought goes into deciding the best way to present information. There is a basic understanding of the different representations that are available. Representations decided by non-users	Information is available in a variety of different formats. Information users are trained in using and interpreting different types of representation	The same information is readily available in more than one representation. A team of information architects, users and designers work on the best representations. Information is presented and used in innovative and creative ways
Evolution	There is some recognition	There is an active effort to	There is a comprehensive

(Contd)

Table A5 (Contd)

Factor	Minor use	Moderate use	Major use
	that information structures and the capability to process information change over time. Development plans anticipate changes in structure and capability over the next 12 months	improve the effective use of information. Development plans anticipate changes in the use of information over the next 3 years. Future use of information is based on analysing possible scenarios	programme in place to ensure the effective and innovative use of information. Information structures are designed for flexibility and adaptability, in order to respond to futures that cannot be anticipated
Knowledge	Focus is mainly on explicit and codified knowledge. Most problems are addressed through the application of information technology	Some aspects of knowledge management are used in conjunction with information management. There is recognition that information management requires a balance between use of technology and the individual or organizational capability to use information	There is widespread recognition that the effective use of information requires an understanding of factors such as uncertainty, ignorance, politics, culture and other forms of tacit knowledge. The balance between technology and knowledge is well established
Responsibility	Responsibilities are largely delegated to an information technology department • Responsibility is mainly based on ownership	There is a more formal process for defining and allocating responsibilities. Business users take on greater responsibility	Responsibilities are shared horizontally across organizational boundaries and vertically within a domain of knowledge. • Responsibilities are defined across most of the other information dimensions

Table A5 (Contd)

Factor	Minor use	Moderate use	Major use
Process	There are some initial attempts to analyse and understand the use of information. Key processes and their use of information are documented	There is greater distinction between the main types of process. Guidelines are provided to improve information processing. Information users are aware of the benefit of information value chains	There is a strong distinction between the governance, stewardship, organization and use of information. Information value chains are well defined. Feedback loops are used to enhance and redesign information processes
Meta levels	Meta models are used to define technology support for information storage and manipulation	There are active efforts to create an integrated meta model. All types of information users are becoming aware of the benefits of meta models	Meta modelling is well coordinated and integrated. Business users as well as technology providers actively use meta models. Meta models are integrated with information access technologies

Index